AD Non Fiction
346.0168 B143*

Badgett, M. V
gay people get married : what happens
9001012745

W9-CBZ-673

When Gay People Get Married

M. V. Lee Badgett

When Gay People Get Married

What Happens When Societies
Legalize Same-Sex Marriage

New York University Press • *New York and London*

NEW YORK UNIVERSITY PRESS
New York and London
www.nyupress.org

© 2009 by New York University
All rights reserved

Library of Congress Cataloging-in-Publication Data
Badgett, M. V. Lee (Mary Virginia Lee)
When gay people get married : what happens when societies
legalize same-sex marriage / M. V. Lee Badgett.
p. cm.
Includes bibliographical references and index.
ISBN-13: 978–0–8147–9114–1 (cl : alk. paper)
ISBN-10: 0–8147–9114–X (cl : alk. paper)
1. Same-sex marriage—Law and legislation.
2. Gay couples—Legal status, laws, etc.
I. Title.
K699.B33   2009
346.01'68—dc22   2009003251

New York University Press books are printed on acid-free paper, and their binding materials
are chosen for strength and durability. We strive to use environmentally responsible suppliers
and materials to the greatest extent possible in publishing our books.

Manufactured in the United States of America
10 9 8 7 6 5 4 3 2 1

9001012745

This book is dedicated with love to my late parents, Bill and Betty Badgett, whose marriage was the first one I studied, and to my wife, Elizabeth Silver, who helps me put theory into practice.

Contents

Acknowledgments

Teachers rarely know what will stick in students' minds, and sometimes it takes a long time to find out. This book had its origin two decades ago, when Professor Lloyd Ulman told me that I should do an international comparative study if I really wanted to understand institutions in the United States. I tucked that idea away and came back to it when I found the right one to study, so I owe him belated thanks for that sage advice, in addition to my gratitude for his support and guidance over the years.

I also learned about marriage from my friends and colleagues Leslie Whittington and Rhonda Williams, both of whom we lost too early. Their ideas and our conversations have inevitably worked their way into this book.

I owe an enormous debt of gratitude to many friends and colleagues over the years for their willingness to engage, correct, and improve my thinking and writing about marriage: Randy Albelda, Janis Bohan, Mary Bonauto, J. B. Collier, Mattias Duyves, Bill Eskridge, Nancy Folbre, Gary Gates, Gert Hekma, Mary King, Marieka Klawitter, Zak Kramer, Liz Kukura, Holning Lau, Toni Lester, Joya Misra, Lisa Moore, Torie Osborn, Jenny Pizer, Ingrid Robeyns, Adam Romero, Glenda Russell, Brad Sears, Evan Wolfson, and Doreena Wong.

In particular, I thank Todd Brower, Ellen Lewin, Jonathan Rauch, Elizabeth Silver, and the anonymous referees for their careful reading and feedback on chapter drafts. Their generous and insightful comments made this a better book.

I also thank several people who provided excellent assistance with the many research tasks needed to finish this project: Liz Kukura, Gail Wise, Amy Ferrer, Darcy Pottle, Naomi Goldberg, Chris Ramos, and Mandi Dove. Thanks to Martin Tulic for an excellent index.

I have been fortunate to work within three institutions that have made it possible to complete this project. I offer sincere thanks to the staff of the Williams Institute on Sexual Orientation Law and Public Policy at UCLA School of Law. I also thank the funders of the Williams Institute, particularly the Gill Foundation and the Evelyn and Walter Haas, Jr., Fund. For two years I had the time and resources I needed for my book research and, better yet, access to the best brains in the field of sexual orientation research. I am grateful to the economics department and to the Center for Public Policy and Administration at the University of Massachusetts Amherst for sabbatical and research support for this project. I also thank the participants in the lively yearlong seminar "Marriage and Its Alternatives," which was part of the Interdisciplinary Seminar in the Humanities and Fine Arts at the University of Massachusetts Amherst. I appreciate the hospitality and support of the Amsterdam School for Social Science Research at the University of Amsterdam.

This book also benefited enormously from feedback I received at presentations and seminars in many contexts: the University of Linz, Stockholm University, the University of Amsterdam, the American Political Science Association, the International Association for Feminist Economics, Yale University, Yale Law School, the Center for Public Policy and Administration at UMass, The New School, the Association for Public Policy Analysis and Management, UCLA Law School, the UCLA Sociology Department, the University of Connecticut, the Tulsa Gay and Lesbian History Project, the National Council on Family Relations, and the American Psychological Association.

This book would not have been possible without the help of two groups of people: the Dutch couples who agreed to be interviewed and the people who helped me locate those couples. I am very grateful to Ingrid Robeyns, Gert Hekma, Mattias Duyves, Willem DeBlaauw, Yo DeBoer, Martha and Lin McDevitt-Pugh, and Gloria Wekker for their help with recruiting couples for this project. The couples in the study were remarkably generous to share their thoughts and experiences with me. I learned enormous amounts from them and hope that I did their stories justice in this book.

Finally, I would not have started or finished this book without the love and support of Elizabeth Silver, my wife in Massachusetts, Connecticut, the Netherlands, and everywhere else.

Permissions

Portions of chapters 4 and 9 appeared in an earlier form in two articles:

"Will Providing Marriage Rights to Same-Sex Couples Undermine Heterosexual Marriage?" *Sexuality Research and Social Policy: Journal of NSRC,* Vol. 1, No. 3, Sept. 2004, pp. 1-10.

"Predicting Partnership Rights: Applying the European Experience to the United States," *Yale Journal of Law and Feminism,* Vol. 17, No. 1, Spring 2005, 71-88.

1

Introduction

A Different Perspective

The summer of 2008 was the summer of love and commitment for same-sex couples in the United States. Thousands of gay and lesbian couples stood in line for wedding licenses all over California in the first few days after that state opened marriage to same-sex couples. On the other side of the country, Massachusetts took the last step to full equality by allowing same-sex couples from other states to marry within its borders, in the very first state to give gay couples marriage rights.

I spent that summer traveling back and forth between California and Massachusetts, amazed at the transformation of the policy landscape between landmark court decisions in Massachusetts and California. Although I think of myself as an informed optimist, I must admit that this scenario in 2008 was almost unimaginable only a few years before.

In 2003, I was eligible for my first sabbatical, the one true perk of academic life. My partner, Elizabeth, and I had decided to use this amazing opportunity to uproot our family and live in another country for a year. As we prepared for our adventure, the nature of our second-class citizenship became clearer. Living on only half of my salary, as opposed to two reasonable full-time salaries, meant that our finances would be stretched thin. When we realized how much Elizabeth's health insurance would cost while she took an unpaid leave from her job, we wondered if we could make it.

If the "Lee" in my name had marked me as a man, instead of reflecting my southern parents' decision to name their first daughter after her grandmothers ("Mary" and "Virginia Lee"), Elizabeth and I could have been married in the Commonwealth of Massachusetts, our permanent home. She would have been eligible for coverage under my health insurance benefits. We would have saved thousands of dollars. We would have saved more on our collective income tax bill. We would have even been able to fill out a single Customs form when returning to the United States.

Instead, our excitement was tempered by the occasional burst of outrage against our country's and state's unwillingness to offer even a half-way measure toward recognizing our relationship.

The contrast became starker. Our destination, the Netherlands, has allowed same-sex couples to marry since 2001, although we learned that we would not be eligible, since neither of us was a Dutch citizen or long-term resident. When we approached the intimidating "Foreign Police" for a temporary residence permit application, the forms shocked and delighted us. While only I qualified for a work and residence permit as a visiting scholar at the University of Amsterdam, Elizabeth was eligible for a residence permit as my partner. We just had to check a box and sign a statement that we had been living together as partners for five years. The official who processed our paperwork didn't bat an eye when we arrived together with our stack of forms and money.

The Dutch government became the first to legally recognize our relationship when we finally received our temporary residence permits. At the time, it felt a bit like what I thought getting married might feel like. As the (temporary) sole earner of the family, I had to promise to support Elizabeth and to share my income with her. She got to stay with me, even though she had no other official reason to be in the Netherlands, just because we were family. I wanted her there, and she wanted to be with me. The willingness of the Dutch to acknowledge and honor our relationship, compensating for the less progressive policies of our own and many other countries, showed us in a profound way that we were indeed in another country.

Once we got to Amsterdam, we met many new and interesting people. Two stories about our new friends and acquaintances stand out.

Our first foray into Dutch culture was an invitation to attend a talk by a noted Dutch lesbian feminist. At the crowded reception after the talk, I introduced myself to other people and told them of my plan to study same-sex marriage while in the Netherlands. One woman after another gave me more or less the same line, almost as if they were reading from a common script: "Oh, marriage—that's a patriarchal institution for heterosexuals. I'm a feminist and don't believe in marriage, so I'm not married."

After escaping from the throng to wait in line at the bar, I began the same conversation with another woman, a feminist academic whom I'll call Martina. Martina listened with interest to the description of my project and pointed out that I had already spoken to her partner. In fact, her partner was one of the most vehement opponents of marriage I'd met.

"She feels very strongly about it," Martina confirmed. But, she added wistfully in a soft voice, "I would like to get married."

Two other friends, Stephanie and Ingrid (also pseudonyms), told us their rather unromantic wedding story. Although as a feminist Stephanie "hates marriage"—her own words—she and Ingrid decided to marry on the advice of their accountant, since they own a business together. The first time we talked about marriage, Stephanie quickly dismissed their legal marriage as an insignificant step in their twenty-year relationship. When the topic of marriage came up again after we'd gotten to know them better, we got the rest of the story.

Stephanie and Ingrid scheduled their wedding at city hall for 9 a.m., since the early hour ensured a free wedding ceremony (apparently an incentive for frugal Dutch people to fill an unpopular time slot). They invited Stephanie's sister and a few friends to attend. After the short ceremony, the group took a little boat trip on the canals—also apparently a common feature of Dutch weddings—and celebrated with champagne and fruit.

During the boat ride, Stephanie impulsively pulled out her cell phone to call her father and tell him that she had gotten married. She was surprised when her father reacted badly to the news that he had not been invited to the wedding, and she was stunned when he began crying because he had missed this significant event in his daughter's life. At least that's how he saw it, even though Stephanie did not. Not inviting her father caused a rift in their relationship that Stephanie could not repair before her father died a few years later.

These early encounters and contrasts gave me a wide-angle view of the larger meanings of marriage in a country that had opened up marriage to same-sex couples:

As a legal institution, marriage gives the state enormous power to recognize whether a family legally exists and, in many cases, whether a family can practically persist. This power allows couples to be together in a literal sense, as immigration laws did for me and Elizabeth in the Netherlands. Or the power can determine the conditions in which couples survive, such as the granting of health care and pension benefits.

As a legal institution in flux, marriage is always being shaped and reshaped. The Dutch lesbians I met at the reception were suspicious of marriage at least partly because of its historical meaning for women. In the twentieth century alone, marriage in the United States and some European countries went from being a status that largely obliterated women's independence to being a gender-neutral set of rights and responsibilities that spouses have with regard to each other and to the state. But concern about the impact of marriage on the lives of women is understandable and continues—especially if those marrying want to avoid traditional gender roles.

As a personal decision, choosing whether to enter into a marriage involves complex and sometimes unconscious motives and barriers, as well as potentially sticky negotiations for the two individuals. For some of the lesbian feminists at the reception, being denied the right to marry for so long was itself evidence that marriage was a flawed institution. A long history of living outside the protection of family law also gave root to new and creative ways of establishing the social legitimacy of relationships without the endorsement of the state. So opening up access to marriage would not necessarily lead all same-sex couples to flock to city hall to marry, especially the Dutch feminists I met who aren't sure what they might gain and lose from marriage. But predicting how many and which couples will marry is not easy, since members of a couple may have very different views about that decision, as did Martina and her partner.

As a deeply rooted social and cultural institution, marriage is powerful in ways that we might not always appreciate and in ways that we certainly cannot control. The strong reaction by Stephanie's father illustrates the profound meaning and value that the act of marrying has for many people other than the two getting married. Far from building a wall around the two people marrying, marriage is an experience that connects the couple to other people in their social circles–whether the couple wants it or not. Ironically, at a time when many demographers take for granted the "deinstitutionalization of marriage" for heterosexual couples, that is, the fading away of the social and legal meanings of marriage that structure how married people live their lives, the experiences of gay and lesbian couples suggest that marriage has a continuing relevance and meaning.

I had traveled to the Netherlands to study same-sex marriage in Europe, so these events gave me an intense introduction to what access to marriage meant for same-sex couples two or three years after such marriage became possible. In the early days of our stay, I was constantly trying to make sense of these stories as well as the news and analyses of same-sex marriage that appeared in my daily life. The irony, of course, was that same-sex marriage arrived in the United States while I was studying it in Amsterdam. Two months into our trip, in November 2003, we got amazing news from home: the Massachusetts Supreme Judicial Court ruled that our state could not legally prevent same-sex couples from marrying. Three months later, Mayor Gavin Newsom of San Francisco allowed same-sex couples to marry in his city until a court order stopped him. In May 2004, weddings of same-sex couples began in Massachusetts just before we returned.

In between these big events, my partner and I closely followed the legal, political, and cultural debates that were raging back home. I participated in those public debates from a scholarly perspective, since I have long studied the economics of marriage as it relates to gay and lesbian people. In fact, much of this book was inspired by those public debates, which continue to the present day in the United States and other countries. As I talked to people in Europe and read about the European experience with giving rights to same-sex couples, I realized that the marriage debates in the United States and elsewhere share many common themes.

But, more important, the fact that a growing number of European countries are granting same-sex couples either the right to marry or some package of the rights and responsibilities of marriage means that Europe could be a social laboratory, in a sense, to help us predict what marriages by gay couples might mean in the United States. Gay and lesbian couples have been registering as partners in Denmark since 1989, and Dutch gay couples have been marrying since 2001. The political and cultural experiences of these and other countries may offer a crystal ball of sorts as the United States asks some of the big questions.

Outside the religious and legal arguments, the big questions in the political and cultural debate boil down to these, as I hear them:

Will gay people change marriage? The Chicken Littles argue that giving gay couples the right to marry will destroy heterosexual marriage and maybe even Western civilization as we know it:

- Tony Perkins of the Family Research Council on the 2008 debut of same-sex marriage in California: "When the clock chimes 5:01 p.m. (PST), the California ruling that threatens to undo thousands of years of natural marriage will officially take effect, triggering five months of social chaos that could wreak havoc on every state in America."[1]
- Janet Folger, founder of Faith2Action: "I'm praying and working to protect marriage in California (and the rest of the country) not only because I care about marriage, but because I care about civilization. And, if we obey God, he just may spare us from the judgment we deserve."[2]
- The writer and marriage promoter Maggie Gallagher: "Losing this [same-sex marriage] battle means losing the idea that children need

mothers and fathers. It means losing the marriage debate. It means losing limited government. It means losing American civilization. It means losing, period."[3]

On the other side of the issue, many optimistic feminists hope that gay couples will change marriage by reshaping the troubling gender dynamics still embedded in heterosexual marriage.[4] In between those two positions are many people who appear to be worried about the unknown consequences of letting gay couples marry.

Will marriage change gay people? Some hope so, arguing that gay men will be more monogamous and gay relationships more stable if same-sex couples can marry,[5] and gays and lesbians will be better assimilated into the larger culture.[6] Opponents of marriage equality believe that gay and lesbian people will not be able to gain from marriage, though.[7] Others in the gay, lesbian, and bisexual communities fear that distinctive features of gay life will be transformed in negative ways.[8]

What path should change take in the United States: immediate or gradual? Do we need alternatives to marriage? Some observers want to see a more gradual expansion of rights for same-sex couples to see what the social impact will be.[9] Others farther right on the political spectrum see the big changes in the United States—especially in Vermont, Massachusetts, and California—as further examples of undemocratic judicial activism foisted on an unwilling public. Some in the gay community argue that change is happening too fast to avoid political backlash and that creating alternatives to marriage, both for same-sex couples and for other family forms, might be a better way to go.

Frankly, the public debate has not been particularly careful or insightful with respect to these questions. Dire predictions on one side are matched by a lot of head-scratching from those who think same-sex couples should be allowed to marry. These advocates have a hard time figuring out how greater access to marriage for additional couples will somehow undermine marriage, so they sometimes resort to jokes:

- Representative Barney Frank ridiculed the implication of opponents' fears in the context of the 1996 Defense of Marriage Act: "Defense of Marriage? It's like the old V-8 commercial. As if this act didn't pass, heterosexual men all over the country would say, [smack] 'I could've married a guy?!'"[10]

- During a televised debate in the 1990s, Elizabeth Birch, then head of the Human Rights Campaign, asked the thrice-married conservative Representative Bob Barr, "You know, Representative Barr, there is some confusion. Which marriage are you defending? Your first, your second, or your third?"[11]
- A recent *New Yorker* cartoon also captures the liberal confusion about what the fuss is about. A woman is headed for the open door with two packed suitcases. She explains to her flabbergasted husband why she's leaving him: "There's nothing wrong with our marriage, but the spectre of gay marriage has hopelessly eroded the institution."[12]

With one side worried about the end of civilization and the other side cracking jokes in bewilderment, it's hard to see any room for reasoned discussion. Even in 2008, four years after Massachusetts opened marriage, the emotional force of the issue shows little evidence of cooling. To some extent, this disconnect in the debate stems from two entirely different perspectives that result in the two sides talking past each other.[13] People on the conservative end of the political spectrum tend to look at the issue from the broad cultural perspective: what does "marriage" mean and how might that meaning change? Those on the more liberal end of the spectrum take a narrower individualistic view of people's behavior: if people get married because of the unique qualities of the person they are marrying, then why would their decision to marry (or stay married) change just because a fairly small number of people are choosing to marry entirely different people who happen to be of the same sex?

Maybe there is a more productive way to bridge the gap between these positions by shifting how we think about these issues and about the evidence of change that we draw on. In my view, the debate highlights the difference between thinking about the meaning of marriage—a noun, an idea—and thinking about marriage as an act—marrying as a choice that individuals make. Marriage as a noun and marrying as a verb are closely related, of course. The broad cultural and social meaning of marriage creates social incentives and social pressure for individual people to decide to marry. These decisions to marry and the experiences of those marrying will shape the larger social and cultural meaning of marriage, and possibly the larger cultural understandings of sexual identities. But I make the distinction because it helps to understand what to look for, especially when seeking evidence in Europe for the impact of giving marriage or marriage-like rights to gay couples. We need to look both at the actual decisions made by couples and at how marriage or registered partnerships of same-sex couples might alter the cultural understanding of marriage and of what being gay or lesbian means.

To date, the arguments trying to explain these cultural and behavioral effects are, by and large, based simply on beliefs, not on facts. Few people have offered careful analyses of the actual experience of the first wave of eight countries that gave significant rights to legally registered same-sex couples between 1989 and 2000: Denmark, Sweden, Norway, Iceland, the Netherlands, Belgium, France, and Germany.[14] Those countries provide years of experience that could be tapped to understand the debate in the United States that reignited in 2008 with the state supreme court decisions in California and Connecticut to allow gay couples to marry. (As this book went to press, however, California voters took away the right to marry from gay couples, but that vote is being challenged in court.) More countries have joined that list relatively recently, including Finland, Canada, New Zealand, Spain, South Africa, Luxembourg, Switzerland, Slovenia, the Czech Republic, and the United Kingdom, but obviously we will not know much about what happened in those countries for a while. Figure 1.1 summarizes the three general kinds of legal options open to same-sex couples in these fifteen countries: full marriage rights, near-marriage rights through registered partnership, and less extensive packages of marital rights and responsibilities. In this book, I use these European experiences, along with what experience we have had in the United States so far as a social laboratory for asking the key questions about marriage and change.

The next chapter begins the discussion with the verb: why do same-sex couples choose to marry, and what can we learn from that process about the meaning of marriage? My interviews with Dutch couples suggest some similarities with as well as some differences from heterosexual couples, although the similarities are perhaps more surprising and revealing than the differences.

In chapter 3, I compare the actual rates of same-sex marriage or registered partnership across countries to see whether the low rates that people have noted are evidence of a disrespect or lack of need for marriage. However, what I find is that the vast majority of gay and heterosexual couples alike choose marriage when they have options for legal recognition.

Chapter 4 plunges more deeply into the demographic changes in these countries to ask whether same-sex couples have somehow changed

Figure 1.1

Countries With National Recognition of Same-Sex Partnerships[15]

Country (year enacted)	Marital rights and responsibilities	Examples of marital rights not included
MARRIAGE		
Netherlands (2001) Belgium (2003) Spain (2005) Canada (2005) South Africa (2006) Norway (2009)	All or almost all	Parental status for second parent of a child born to a married lesbian (NLD, BEL) Adoption rights (BEL)
REGISTERED PARTNERSHIP		
Denmark (1989) Norway (1993) Sweden (1994) Iceland (1996) Netherlands (1998) Finland (2001) New Zealand (2005) (civil unions) United Kingdom (2005) (civil partnerships) Switzerland (2005) Hungary (2009)	Almost all	Right to church wedding (DEN, NOR, SWE, ICE, FIN); joint adoption rights (DEN, NOR, ICE, FIN, HUN); access to assisted reproduction (DEN, NOR, ICE, HUN)
REGISTERED COHABITATION		
France (1999) Belgium (1999) Germany (2001) Czech Republic (2006) Slovenia (2006) Luxembourg (2004)	Liability for debts; common property; joint taxation; housing; insurance (France) Support obligation; Joint tenancy; inheritance; pension and health insurance; immigration (Germany) Mutual responsibility for debts; common residence protected except after death; obligation of support (Belgium)	Inheritance rights; child-related rights; alimony (France) State-supported financial benefits (Germany) Inheritance rights; alimony; right to damages for negligent death of partner; adoption; citizenship (Belgium)

heterosexual marriage choices. Measures of heterosexual marriage and divorce behavior turn out to suggest that nothing much changed as a result of the recognition of same-sex couples. I also show that changes in ideas about marriage—mainly a belief that marriage is an outdated institution—are also unrelated to granting legal rights to same-sex couples. Chapter 5 asks the same question from a Dutch cultural perspective, drawing on the reactions of heterosexual family, friends, and other social institutions to the marriages of Dutch couples.

Chapters 6 and 7 take the other angle: will marriage change gay people? Chapter 6 looks at the positive gains from marriage that same-sex couples experience, particularly from their new full inclusion in social and legal institutions. In chapter 7 I primarily use the Dutch couple interviews to argue that access to marriage—the crowning achievement of legal equality—might well change lesbian and gay identities over time in ways that might be stressful for lesbian and gay people.

Chapters 8 and 9 look more directly at the political angles of change in Europe and the United States. I feel the need to briefly justify drawing on the European political experience to understand American policy change. A political truism holds that policy models from other countries are not very helpful in the United States. The idea of "American exceptionalism" is the usual trump card for arguing that what happens elsewhere is neither important nor interesting for us in the United States because "we're different." And until recently European examples have not obviously played a big role in policy discussions in the United States. Although some European countries have intriguing social welfare, health care, labor market, and child care policies that have captured the imagination of academics and some political activists in the United States, their influence has been limited. The political winds of the past few years seem to be keeping Americans firmly on their own soil with regard to foreign as well as domestic policy. Many Americans' unease with the unilateralism put in place by President George W. Bush has moved the debate about our relationship with European countries from academic journals into the mainstream media.

Ironically, but not so surprisingly, gay organizations in the United States have practiced their own form of unilateralism. The progress of gay and lesbian social movements has occurred fairly separately on the two continents. While gay tourists often cross the Atlantic Ocean in both directions, GLBT political activists and activism have had much less crossover. As several researchers who study gay social movements have noted, gay organizations in Europe have worked together much more systematically than they have with organizations in the United States.[16] The global separation of the U.S. gay movement contrasts sharply with the rich connections between GLB organizations in European countries and even throughout the rest of the world.

For example, consider the Web sites of the two largest national gay political organizations in the United States, the Human Rights Campaign and the National Gay and Lesbian Task Force. Both sites have just a hand-ful of references to legal developments in other countries, and neither contains links to organizations in other countries. In contrast, the Dutch equivalent, the COC, has a button on its homepage with descriptions of its worldwide networking. Belgium is the home of the International Les-bian and Gay Association (ILGA), which works in Europe and beyond to connect gay movements in different parts of the world.

But recent developments have moved international comparisons to a more prominent role in the debate over marriage equality in the United States. The first development came in 2003 when Ontario became the first place in North America that allowed same-sex couples to marry. After three Canadian provincial courts struck down the exclusion of same-sex couples from marriage, the federal government set in motion a nationwide opening of marriage.[17] As a result, all Canadian same-sex couples have had equal marriage rights since 2005. Gay and lesbian couples from the United States regularly cross the border to tie the knot in Canada for the symbolic, although not yet practical, value of marriage.

A second globalizing nudge came from inside the United States. In July 2003, the U.S. Supreme Court struck down the so-called state sodomy laws that criminalized sexual contact between two people of the same sex in *Lawrence v. Texas*. Many lawyers were surprised at some of the reason-ing in Justice Anthony Kennedy's majority opinion, which used decisions by the European Court of Human Rights and other international actions to justify overturning sodomy laws:

> Other nations, too, have taken action consistent with an affirmation of the protected right of homosexual adults to engage in intimate, consensual conduct. . . . The right the petitioners seek in this case has been accepted as an integral part of human freedom in many other countries. There has been no showing that in this country the govern-mental interest in circumscribing personal choice is somehow more legitimate or urgent.[18]

Where might the European influence turn up next in Supreme Court de-cisions? In his dissent in the *Lawrence* case, Justice Antonin Scalia men-tions Canadian court decisions when he warns that the bar to same-sex marriage in the United States might be the next to fall.[19]

Conservative writers immediately seized on Scalia's warning. After the Massachusetts marriage decision, the writer Stanley Kurtz began spinning a link between gay marriage in Europe and the decline of marriage in two conservative publications, *The Weekly Standard* and *National Review Online*. He drew on existing academic and journalistic publications about European demography to argue that the Scandinavian and Dutch experiences foreshadow a horrible future for the United States if gay and lesbian couples are allowed to marry here: "Will same-sex marriage undermine the institution of marriage? It already has."[20] "The stakes are nothing less than the survival of marriage itself."[21] This new—and, perhaps most important, secular—argument about the harm of marriage equality began showing up in local debates, newspaper op-ed pages, court briefs, and even the Senate debate about the Federal Marriage Amendment. In the context of these legal and political developments over the last few years, the American exceptionalism argument misses the point in the marriage debate in the United States.

In chapter 8, I argue that the experience in Europe and in states like Vermont and California suggests that alternatives to marriage are useful only if they are transitional statuses on the way to full equality for same-sex couples. The experiences on both sides of the Atlantic show that new legal statuses for same-sex couples can sometimes act as barriers to future change, and they are not particularly useful for other kinds of family structures, either.

In chapter 9, I show that changes in marriage law related to same-sex couples in the United States look very similar to changes in European countries. In the United States, fifty-one separate sets of laws define access to marriage, since the federal government usually leaves laws about family matters to the states (and the District of Columbia, sometimes).[22] As I write this book, each state can still act independently to allow same-sex couples to marry or to create an alternative status for same-sex couples. So far Massachusetts, California, and Connecticut are the only states to let same-sex couples marry, although California's gay marriages ended with the election in November 2008. New York recognizes same-sex marriage from other states or countries. In Vermont, New Jersey, New Hampshire, and Connecticut, civil unions provide same-sex couples with all of the rights and responsibilities that states can give, and the domestic partnership status in California and Oregon are quite similar. Hawaii's reciprocal beneficiary status, Washington's and New Jersey's domestic partner laws, and Maine's domestic partner registry all give a more limited set of rights to same-sex couples. The variation in approach in the United States looks a lot like the variation we see across Europe. As I argue in chapter 9, the pace of change is also very similar in the United States, where the same political and social factors that predict change in Europe predict change here. Change is taking place in a sensible and unsurprising way, with more liberal states taking the lead and providing examples that other states might someday follow.

As a result of increasing attention to the useful changes in the recognition of same-sex couples on the other side of the Atlantic, a closer look by Americans at the European experience with gay marriage seems like a productive thing to do. From a scholarly perspective, the task is a bit daunting. For one thing, the big questions that I outlined cut across many bodies of social science research and theory. That breadth also means adding to the economist's usual toolbox of ways to understand what is happening in the actual world, not just the theoretical world. In the end, I collected new data, interviewing many actual same-sex couples who have thought about getting married or who actually got married. I drew on surveys of gay, lesbian, bisexual, and heterosexual people in the Netherlands and the United States. I gathered information from many different countries about marriage, families, social policy, political actors, and the gay and lesbian communities. I consulted other scholars and studied their research. And I learned some new techniques to carefully interpret and analyze all of those data to find answers to the big questions at the heart of this book and the political debates. So, while my training and experience as an economist are inevitably present in my research, I would classify this book as the product of an interdisciplinary social scientist.

Although this is a book rooted in social science research, I began this introduction with my own story. Marriage is not just an academic topic for me. When Elizabeth and I arrived in the Netherlands, we were not allowed to marry, either by Dutch law or American law. When we got home to Massachusetts, the world had changed. We were faced with the decision that thousands of other same-sex couples and millions of different-sex couples have had to make: would we marry?

Putting the author's personal story in a book based on research might seem like an odd thing to do. Whether or not I mention them here, my own experience and position will, at the very least, determine my enthusiasm for the topic, as well as the particular questions that I ask. Does that mean I am necessarily biased in some way and that my conclusions are tainted? Obviously, I do not think so. We all have primary data when it comes to families—our own lives are often our first "data point," as an economist might say. Our experiences shape how we see and interpret the world around us, and that is universal, for marriage equality opponents and proponents alike. The value of including stories of marriage in the context of real people—those of the Dutch couples I interviewed and even my own story—is to add a layer of knowledge that has been largely missing in the debate. The personal stories link the broad abstract numbers and the powerful cultural institution to the individual lives affected by the law.

Those personal perspectives are most likely to be a problem in research when we are not aware of their influence. My training and practice as an economist over the past twenty years have instilled in me values that include a willingness to question my own assumptions and to rethink and revise after putting my ideas before the careful scrutiny of other scholars. The give and take between researchers generates debate and constructive criticism, and I believe my own ideas and conclusions here are the better for having gone through that process.

To be honest, though, I did feel an effect from the other direction while working on this project. My opinions about marriage and my personal decision about marrying were greatly affected by what I heard from the people I interviewed and by the things that I read and thought about as I participated in the public debate. Listening, thinking, and debating are powerful forces for change for individual people and for societies. I invite readers to think through these important questions with me in the context of this book.

Note on terminology: The Dutch are quick to say, "There is no gay marriage here—it's just the same marriage for everybody." And it's obvious when you think about it. The legal status is the same for same-sex couples and different-sex couples, so there is no need for a separate term like "gay marriage" or "same-sex marriage". A better term for the subject of this book would be something like "equal access to marriage for same-sex couples." But, while that is clearly correct, in this book I often use the term "same-sex marriage" to avoid unwieldy sentence constructions. Also, here I mostly talk about same-sex marriage as relevant to lesbian and gay people. Although bisexual people might well marry or want to marry a same-sex partner, recent research shows that they usually marry different-sex partners.[23]

2

Why Marry?

The Value of Marriage

Picture a moonlit night on a bridge in Amsterdam, a city with canals so charming that some spots have become famous for romantic marriage proposals. On one such bridge, Liz nervously proposed to her partner, Pauline—but then immediately got cold feet and backed out.

"I think that actually the first time I asked you, you said yes and that freaked me out," Liz recalled to Pauline when I visited them in their cozy suburban home several years later. "She said yes, and then I was like, 'Oh my God, no!'" The romantic moment quickly cooled in the face of Liz's sudden reversal.

Pauline remembered the emotional roller coaster of that scene. At first, she recalled, "I was so scared to say yes, but just following my heart I said yes. But that was interesting because I was always the kind of person who never commit[s] to anything. . . . But then when I said yes, she was just begging out of it. So I was like, 'Oh you know, this is so stupid. Why did I even say yes?'"

Once Liz recovered from her shock and indecision, she later tried again to convince Pauline to marry her. The next time, though, Pauline turned her down.

Why did Pauline say no? "I think in the start I had the feeling that it was more like a practical statement [from Liz], so I didn't want it," she recalled.

"That was only because I phrased it as a tax thing," Liz acknowledged somewhat sheepishly.

"Yeah," Pauline agreed, laughing.

"That was my mistake because she wouldn't say yes for a long time after that," admitted Liz.

Pauline was looking for a romantic statement: "If I [would] marry, then of course [it's] because you love each other, but that was clear to me. I knew that was really OK . . . but still it has to be something really romantic—I mean something hopefully that you do just once!"

The third proposal was a success, but it took another year for Liz to convince Pauline that Liz was in it for the right reasons. At that point, Pauline finally said yes.

I got the sense from talking to Pauline and Liz that they were still a bit relieved that they finally got married after this initial clash of head and heart. Pauline's romantic view of marriage conflicted with her anxiety about making a commitment. Her view of marriage did not match Liz's more practical perspective, even though they had a relationship that was already on solid ground. Because they saw marriage differently, the couple had to navigate a difficult situation in their relationship, each being attentive not just to her own emotions and goals but also to the other person's.

While this story might sound familiar or even ordinary to those of us who have known heterosexual couples struggling with the same kind of uncertainty about marriage, grappling with marriage is a remarkable experience for same-sex couples that is far from mundane. The decision to marry a same-sex partner is one that, until quite recently, most lesbians and gay men never expected to have to make. But looking at why—and whether—same-sex couples decide to marry gets us quickly to weighty questions at the heart of the public debate about same-sex marriage. What is marriage in the twenty-first century? Do gay couples think about marriage and marrying in the same way that heterosexual couples do? Do same-sex couples really want and need to be able to marry?

So far we have practically no data to answer those questions with respect to same-sex couples, other than some simple numbers. More than 8,000 same-sex couples out of an estimated 53,000 same-sex couples in the Netherlands have married, and another 10% or so have registered as partners to receive almost the same rights and responsibilities.[1] Adding the two legal statuses together, we find that only about 25% of same-sex couples are in a legally recognized relationship, as opposed to 80% of Dutch heterosexual couples. Official statistical agencies in other countries also report that relatively small numbers of same-sex couples are marrying or registering as partners.[2]

After the political debates are over and same-sex couples are free to marry, we could look at personal decisions about marrying as a sort of referendum on marriage in the gay, lesbian, and bisexual (GLB) community. Some commentators have noticed that relatively few couples have married or registered as partners in the Netherlands and Scandinavia, and they have interpreted the statistics as evidence that same-sex couples are disdainful of marriage or opposed to it for ideological reasons.[3] Or maybe, they argue, same-sex couples want to marry for the "wrong" reasons: "just for the benefits." Since tangible benefits are few in the Dutch and Scandinavian contexts, we might then reasonably expect few same-sex couples to marry. A careful look at the reasons couples marry will reveal how couples view the institution of marriage and might begin to suggest how both the institution and the couples might change as they interact.

Since numbers alone cannot tell us why couples marry or not, I went directly to the source, finding Dutch same-sex couples who were willing to speak with me about marriage.[4] The couples I interviewed included some people from nonnative Dutch ethnic groups, so to some extent I will see whether gay marriage is an important issue across ethnic groups.[5] The nineteen same-sex couples I interviewed told funny, amazing, and moving stories of how their relationships evolved, from the accidents of fate that brought them together through discussions about marriage and on up to the present day. Since same-sex couples had felt like outsiders for so long, the path to a decision about marriage involved more than the usual soul-searching and negotiations that heterosexual couples experience. When a gay or lesbian couple decided to marry, the partners sometimes experienced more changes than simply a change of legal status.

As noted earlier, Dutch couples have an unusual bounty of relationship options to choose from, and the couples I spoke with reflect all of those possible choices. Four couples were registered partners, nine couples had married, one couple was planning a wedding to take place a few months after our interview, and two couples were "living apart together." Since marriage was not an option for same-sex couples until three years after registered partnerships became possible, three of the four registered partner couples probably would have married had that option been available at the time. Because of those similarities, I lump them together with the legally married couples in this chapter. In the next chapter, I explore further why couples might choose to marry instead of registering as partners. The five couples who were not married (or not yet married) saw their relationships as no less meaningful and worthy of social recognition than married relationships, however. Understanding why the two sets of couples differ in terms of their legal status is, therefore, not a simple matter. In the end, my own view of the numbers shifted considerably after I interviewed these couples, and maybe the more appropriate question is why so many same-sex couples have chosen to marry.

The Importance of Choice

To learn something from the choices same-sex couples make vis-à-vis marriage, I had to first sort out "choice" in its various meanings in relation to marriage, since so many aspects of choice emerge in the public debate and in my discussions with same-sex couples. For instance, *having a choice* means one thing; *making a choice* means something else. Opening up marriage to same-sex couples meant that they had a choice. In this chapter I focus mainly on the actual personal choices made by nineteen couples. However, in the interviews I heard the word "choice" used in so many different ways that I have decided to begin here by briefly putting the personal elements of choice in the historical and social context experienced by the Dutch couples.

Historically, the debate about same-sex marriage reflects a *political choice* on the part of the gay rights movement. Most, if not all, European and North American countries have (or had) active political efforts to win the right to marry for same-sex couples led by GLB organizations. In all of these countries, some parts of the GLB community have taken issue with a political goal of the right to marry for the movement, a subject I discuss further in chapters 7 and 9.

Anneke and Isabelle, who have not married, were part of a group of feminists in the 1980s that had a different choice in mind—what Anneke called "the division between the political and the private choice." "We were against marriage," her partner, Isabelle, said. "You can fight for gay marriage, but it's better to fight against all marriages—down with the idea of marriage." Once abolishing marriage seemed to be out of the question, though, Isabelle shifted her perspective: "It also has to be a choice for gay people who want to marry. So we didn't change our mind for ourselves, but we will fight for the right for gay people to have the option." Every person I interviewed believed that same-sex couples should have that option, even if they themselves did not want to marry and even if winning the right to marry was not their own political priority.

The result of this political choice and political victory for the GLB movement is that same-sex couples have the same *right to choose* as heterosexuals in the Netherlands. This right to choose itself can have an important effect, regardless of the personal choices made by individual couples. Jan, a gay man who was among the first to marry another man in his town, observed the larger significance of this right to choose: "Even if you do not get married, you've got the choice to get married, and that gives me the feeling that our relationship is the same as straight relationships. It's on the same level. It's got the same importance."

Another significant aspect of choice in the Dutch setting is that there are, in fact, at least four *legal options* for state recognition of either a same-sex couple or a different-sex couple. Just about the only way a couple can avoid some degree of legal recognition is to live apart. Once the couple lives together for a period of time, the government recognizes that they are a unit for certain purposes. The couple can add onto that set of default rights and responsibilities by signing wills and a *"samenlevingscontract,"* or cohabitation agreement. Even without the contract, cohabiting couples get three-quarters of the rights and responsibilities of marriage with respect to taxes, parenting, immigration, and other areas.[6] The biggest difference between cohabitation and marriage comes if the relationship ends. People in informal relationships have no automatic inheritance rights, and the division of joint property or alimony is not set out by law for unmarried couples unless the cohabitation agreement includes such matters.

"Registered partnership" was born in 1998 as a compromise position to give same-sex couples something close to marriage rights.[7] Both same-sex and different-sex couples can register as partners and get almost all of the rights and responsibilities of marriage. Registered partnerships are easier to get out of than marriages, and some citizenship and parenting rights in such relationships are different from those that attach to marriage. But the two statuses are close enough that at least one person in three out of the four registered partner couples I interviewed thinks of himself or herself as married.[8]

Finally, since April 2001, same-sex couples have had access to marriage. The only remaining difference is that a child born to a married woman in a different-sex marriage is presumed to be the legal child of the husband, while that same presumption is not made for same-sex couples. This wide range of choices for same-sex couples (and different-sex couples), as well as a default status that involves some recognition, is unique to the Netherlands and creates the context within which these nineteen couples make decisions about marriage.

The unusual number of choices also reflects the fact that, in the Netherlands and elsewhere in Europe and North America, marriage is *a matter of personal choice instead of a social obligation* to achieve adulthood, parenthood, or full citizenship. Several people I interviewed noted that the old days of getting married because "you're supposed to" are over. Couples have a choice on the cultural level as well as the legal level. Ironically, for Rachel and Marianne, two of the youngest people I interviewed, this change in social expectations and the accompanying changes in legal status actually made it psychologically easier for them to marry. Rachel explained: "There is no big difference between marrying or not marrying, and the fact that you don't need to marry makes it even more a choice you can make. Because when you were supposed to marry, I think we wouldn't have done it."

Yet another way people used the term "choice" reflected the personal and social significance of making a *choice to marry a particular person*. For Lin, having a choice and making the choice to marry Martha was the whole point:

> I want to be able to stand up, just you know, basically just like my brother, just like my sister did and say, "This is the gal." In my family it's kind of an important thing to be able to do—to stand up and say, "This is my choice." And that I had that choice, and that I was able to make that choice as freely and as possibly as my brother had done twenty years earlier and my sister had done twenty-five years earlier— this was for me perfect. It was like, this is it. This is finally the way things should be.

Declaring her choice of Martha through marriage was a way for Lin to tell her family that Martha was now one of them.

In the rest of this chapter, I focus on a somewhat different perspective than is embedded in these other meanings of "choice." Given the same politically granted right to marry, specific legal options, a particular social and cultural context, and a personal relationship with another individual, why do some couples choose to marry whereas others do not? I argue that that decision—that *individual and collective choice*—reveals important information about the meaning of marriage for the gay community and the larger society above and beyond the other kinds of "choice" experienced by these couples.

Making a Decision

I visited Rachel and Marianne in their apartment in one of the oldest parts of Amsterdam. They made me an espresso with one of their wedding gifts and told me about their wedding.

Marianne created a four-sided wedding invitation that they sent to as many friends and family members as their apartment could hold. The first side of the invitation displayed the question "Guess what?" Below, the answer in small letters was "Marianne and Rachel are getting married." The second side asked, "Guess where?" and listed the location. The third side, "Guess when?," included the time and date. The question on the fourth side, with no answer, simply invited more questions: "Guess why?"

The invitation provoked a lot of discussion about why they were marrying. "People just couldn't stop asking us," Marianne remembered. But they weren't being coy. Rachel noted, "I think you made this invitation also because we weren't really sure about why."

How can we tell why people choose to marry or not, especially when they might not be sure themselves? One obvious way is to ask them directly, which Rachel and Marianne's friends did, and I did the same thing early in each interview. The direct answers I heard were informative and probably captured a big part of couples' thinking about marriage and why they chose to marry or not. In addition to those explicit answers, I also looked at what they said about marriage—the idea or cultural construct—in other parts of the interview, since those statements confirmed, supplemented, or even contradicted what the respondents had said earlier related to their own decision about whether to marry. Finally, I also assessed the life experiences of the couples to look for conditions that might have influenced their decisions, such as having children together, being in a family that particularly valued marriage, or needing some legal protection as a couple.

The usual approach of social scientists is to filter information from interviews through a theory. Economists argue that people make a conscious rational choice to marry to improve their sense of well-being, mainly in material terms. A committed relationship, sealed by a legal marriage, lets couples divide labor in the household more efficiently to better provide the things in family life that people care about, such as meals, goods, or children. The legal status might also come with incentives, that is, rewards, for getting married that enhance the attractiveness of marriage. The predominant framing of the same-sex marriage issue in the United States is the need for equal access to a host of legal and financial benefits, suggesting that economists might not be far off the mark in arguing that financial well-being and other practical matters loom large in couples' decisions.

Aside from economists' theories, it turns out to be difficult to find a theory of why an individual couple chooses to marry or not. Some sociologists see the decision to marry as part of the "script" for a relationship that defines the stages that relationships go through. Anthropologists focus on cultural constraints and rules that shape marriage behavior. Same-sex couples might marry to tap into the social approval that married couples traditionally experience or because it's seen as the next stage of the relationship, especially if the couple plans to have children. All of these perspectives suggest plausible social or cultural pressures on couples to marry, but these perspectives do little to explain why a particular long-term, committed couple might decide not to marry in spite of those pressures.

Demographers look at the differences between couples who marry and those that live together outside marriage. Several studies show differences in certain characteristics between people in the United States who cohabit and those who marry. These studies find that people are more likely to marry than cohabit if they are religious and not politically liberal, as well as if they have strong intentions to have children, have traditional ideas about gender roles, and do not value their individual freedom highly.[9] The demographer Kathleen Kiernan concludes that the choice to cohabit may involve a conscious decision to avoid an undesirable status:

> Cohabitation may symbolise, particularly for women, the avoidance of the notion of dependency that is typically implicit in the marriage contract. Women may be anxious that the legal contract may alter the balance of power in their partnership arrangements and make the relationship less equitable. On the other hand, for some cohabitation may be a response to insecurity. For example, rising divorce rates may well have increased the perceived risks of investing in marriage and the emergence of cohabitation may have been a logical response to this uncertainty.[10]

Couples may decide to marry, then, if marriage matches their intentions about children and their beliefs about commitment and interdependence without conflicting with their beliefs about gender roles and the likely stability of their relationship.

The social science theories and studies are at least a good starting point for questions related to same-sex couples, even though they all come from studies of different-sex couples. In my conversations with same-sex couples, I observed an intricate, layered process in choosing whether to marry that involved factors from all the social sciences. Figure 2.1 presents the different pieces of that process. I would expect different-sex couples' decision-making process to be at least somewhat similar, given the overlap of my approach and that of other social scientists, but some of the factors involved here are much more relevant to gay and lesbian couples.

Figure 2.1

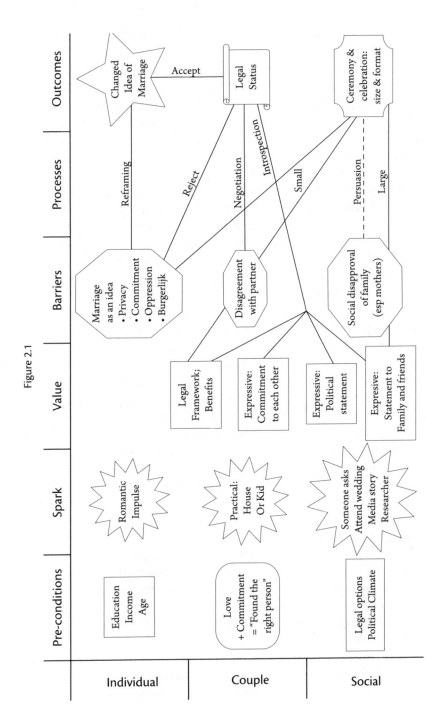

The couples I interviewed shared important *pre-conditions*, such as personal characteristics. As I discuss further later, almost all of these relationships are also committed, loving relationships of several years' or more duration. To get to the point of making an explicit choice about marriage, something has to happen. That *spark* to think through or rethink the possibility of marriage can be romantic or practical. The fact that the couples share the pre-conditions and potential motivations to marry but differ in their actual legal statuses means that other factors must influence the decision about marriage, however.

The next three parts of the decision-making process suggest why some similar-appearing couples will choose to marry and some will not. As an economist, I am tempted to portray this process as a weighing of the benefits of marriage against its costs in financial, social, and emotional terms. However, both the benefits and the costs are different from those usually considered by economists. Once motivated, couples consider the *value* that marriage might have for them, whether practical (as in legal and material benefits), emotional, expressive, or political, and the value varies from couple to couple and from person to person. Couples often face nonfinancial *barriers* to marriage, such as their own political beliefs, a disagreement with a partner about the desirability of marriage, or parental disapproval of the idea of their marriage. Those barriers are not insurmountable, though. Individuals and couples can, either consciously or unconsciously, use certain *processes* to get over those barriers: reframing, negotiating, and persuading.

Marital status is the most obvious *outcome* that I'm trying to explain. I also observed two other outcomes related to this process. Sometimes the contradiction apparent when someone who held antimarriage principles got married was resolved by the person's reframing the idea of "marriage." For couples who married, the form of the marriage—the ceremony and celebration—also reflected the value of marriage as well as the individual's or couple's ideological beliefs.

By pulling apart the pieces of a process for making choices about marriage in this way, I do not mean to imply that each piece is a distinct step that every couple goes through to make a careful, conscious decision. Some of the people I spoke with had a clear idea of why they had married or not and how they had gotten to that point; some did not. Nor does decision making happen only once. Some of the people I spoke with continue to engage in either joking or serious conversations about marriage with their partners on a regular basis. Instead, I offer this framework to organize and tell the revealing stories that I want to share. It can also highlight some interesting and important but largely unexplored dynamics that help explain how marriage and GLB people might change as the institution opens to same-sex couples.

Pre-Conditions: Finding the Right Person

Most of my couples share what I would call basic *pre-conditions* that influence their decision. They all live in the Netherlands in the same legal and political climate. The Netherlands is known for its history of tolerance for minorities, but that country is also now the site of an intense debate about the assimilation of immigrants from Muslim countries and immigrants' ability to accept Dutch values of equal treatment for women and for gay men and lesbians. The law allowing same-sex couples to marry is considered to be a particularly difficult policy for some conservative Muslims to accept.

Probably because I drew on my own social networks to find couples to interview, the couples share other relevant *pre-conditions*, too.[11] They are mostly university educated, middle class, and middle aged, as I am.[12] These characteristics might influence how and why couples make decisions. As Rob pointed out, because he was well educated and has a good income, he can sort out—or can pay someone to sort out—the complicated legal differences among cohabitation contracts, registered partnership, and marriage. More customized arrangements require the help of a lawyer, so marriage or registered partnership might be more accessible to those who want a legal relationship but have lower incomes, a group not represented in this study even though undoubtedly there are lesbians and gay men and same-sex couples with low incomes. It is possible that lower income couples would make different decisions and use a decision-making process different from the one I outline here, since they have different economic pre-conditions, but I strongly suspect that some of the same factors come into play regardless of income.[13]

Beyond these basics, before getting married was even potentially on the table, the partners had to reach a stage in their relationship that was characterized by love, some degree of commitment, and some expectation of a continuing relationship. Martha had long considered the prospect of marriage, stating, "I thought that if I found the right person that it would be something that I would do, that it would be fun." Recall that for Pauline, "[i]t has to be romantic. Love must be [there] in the first place."

All of the couples that I interviewed had been together in a romantic, intimate relationship for several years. Despite that similarity across couples, the crucial importance of finding the right person before marriage can be an option comes through in two ways.

First, there was some variation in how long the partners had been together before they married. Two couples that were not married expressed doubts about the long-term sustainability of their relationships, and that doubt clearly guided their decisions. Paul explained why he had chosen registered partnership over marriage in his relationship with Javier, who had immigrated to the Netherlands to live with Paul: "Because he is much younger, and I never thought I would be sure of the future with him. . . . I don't see it as a relation[ship] for long. I never did from the start." Because of his doubts, Paul chose registered partnership, a legal status that achieved a practical goal—giving Javier citizenship rights—without sending the social message implied by marriage.

Nancy and Joan were also finding it difficult to be together as a binational couple. Taking the step of marriage seemed premature to Joan in view of the other challenges that they faced. She still lived in the United States and had not successfully found a job in the Netherlands. Nancy was raising a child, working part-time, and still living with her ex-partner. Joan worried that marriage would not get them what they needed at this stage of their relationship, which was a practical way to be together in one place.

A second way to see the importance of the stage of relationship came from the histories of each relationship that couples gave me. Most of the couples I interviewed were living together and sharing financial responsibility for the household. Two couples were "living apart together," as demographers put it, but spent nights, meals, and much of their daily lives together. All spoke of love and a desire and expectation to continue the relationship into the foreseeable future (other than Paul). All of the married couples had reached this point before they took the plunge.

Many couples had already made a personal commitment to their relationship before marriage became an option. For Pauline, that commitment point came long before her wedding. "I think for me the big commitment was when she came over from the States, giving up her job and giving up everything . . . to live with me," she recalled. "So I think that was the moment . . . for both of us that really felt like commitment. . . . So getting married was very special, very romantic, and I'm really happy that we did it. But my real commitment was way before that."

Although reaching a stage of commitment and love appeared *necessary* for couples to marry, it is important to point out that this stage was not *sufficient* to move couples toward marriage. All of the nonmarried couples

I interviewed had also reached this point. Something more had to happen for couples to decide to marry.

The Spark

To get a couple to consider marriage, some kind of spark had to ignite a discussion and push the couple into a decision-making mode. The motivation to decide was sometimes seemingly random, sometimes not. In some cases, the push came from practical concerns, often related to another decision, such as to buy a house or to have a child together. In other cases, the spark was an impulse, usually a romantic one. For other couples, some prompting from friends or family motivated thinking about marriage.

A Practical Push

When I asked Marta and Tineke why they had decided to marry, they didn't stop to think. "Children," Marta responded quickly, and Tineke agreed. Marriage to Marta, their son Albert's birth mother, gave Tineke "parental authority" to make decisions for Albert. Eventually, Tineke would be able to legally adopt Albert and have full parental rights. Notably, all five couples who had or were planning to have children together were married or registered partners.

Similarly, Laura and Ria registered as partners for practical reasons when they bought an apartment together. According to Laura,

> It seemed like a very easy way to organize our lives legally and financially so that if anything happened to either one of us, at least it would be clear that we had had essentially a marriage, and that she would have access to any assets I had, and vice versa. . . . Everyone seemed to suggest to us that this was probably the best thing to do in terms of making our life financially one.

Practical motivations moved Laura and Ria to act twice, in fact. When I interviewed them, they had recently found out that Ria was pregnant, and they were about to convert their registered partnership into a marriage to ensure the same parental authority for Laura that Marta and Tineke had sought.[14]

The importance of the practical side of marriage comes through in the interviews with unmarried couples, too. Anna and Joke (pronounced YO-kah) just didn't see a good reason for them to marry, but they also noted that they had not experienced one of the common conditions that make marriage practical. As Anna put it when I asked her why they had not married, "Difficult question, because as long as you just live together, it is not necessary in any way—as long as you don't want children, of course, which we don't. I guess that it would really become a conscious choice the moment we buy a house together."

But a practical need is a tricky reason to propose marriage, as Pauline's resistance to Liz's practical proposal showed earlier in this chapter. A "paradox of practicality" showed up in several couples' discussions. Erik and James did not have wills or a cohabitation contract when I spoke with Erik, even though they had been discussing the need to formalize their relationship in some way for more than a year. "I don't want to get married just to arrange the financial side of my relationship, but to arrange the financial side of my relationship I consider getting married. It's a strange Catch-22," Erik astutely observed.

Pauline and Liz got around this Catch-22 by consciously moving away from a discussion of the practical implications and instead focusing on the romantic and political side of marriage. As long as marriage is not *just* to arrange the financial side but also affirms a loving and committed relationship, then practical needs can be an important motivator of marriage. This paradox suggests that same-sex marriage opponents who criticize gay couples for seeking only the practical benefits of marriage are misguided, since the practical piece exists alongside an existing emotional commitment.

A Romantic Impulse

Romantic feelings also motivate marriage, not surprisingly. The appearance of intense romantic feelings is often unexpected, though. As we sat at her sunny dining room table in Amsterdam, Ellen recalled how another sunny day had led to her impending wedding with Saskia. Ellen and a friend were on a motorcycle trip through the Dutch countryside. To her amazement, the relaxing trip generated a romantic surge from out of the blue: "And so I was sitting there in this beautiful May sun in the countryside in Friesland and I had this vision, this picture that I want . . . to ask Saskia to marry me. So this was very surprising for me," Ellen laughed in amazement.

Social Pressure

Social prompting took any number of forms for the couples I interviewed. Walking by a bridal shop, hearing a news story, or attending a wedding prompted a discussion (either serious or not so serious) about marriage for some couples. Even my request for an interview prompted some unmarried couples to revisit their decisions about marrying. We often hear about unmarried heterosexual people who get pushed to marry by their parents, friends, or other family members. What about same-sex couples? Lin joked, "There's no pressure on us to marry!" But, in fact, all of the unmarried same-sex couples reported some questions, encouragement, or even pressure to marry from friends or family.[15]

Marianne first thought that maybe it was the media discussion that had put the marriage idea in her head when I asked her why she and Rachel had gotten married. But Rachel reminded her, "Actually, your grandfather brought it up. We had dinner with your grandparents, and then her grandfather said to us, 'Why don't you get married? This is possible now, so why wouldn't you?'"

"He talked about it the whole night," Marianne continued. "He had all these questions: 'Well, you two love each other and why not? And 'It's possible now, and it's the best thing you could do!' So we got really convinced."

Making a Decision

Once the romantic, practical, or social spark motivated at least one member of the couple to consider marriage, that person had to engage in more active decision making that involved individual contemplation and negotiation with his or her partner. And sometimes this process got repeated for couples who chose not to marry at one or more points in time and ended only when the couple married.

The Value of Marriage

Identifying the value of marriage was a key part of this process for couples and individuals. Tangible material benefits generally did not play a role in couples' decisions, though, mainly because of the legal recognition granted to unmarried Dutch couples for many purposes. Strikingly, only one couple could name a material benefit that it had received as a result of marriage. Willem was employed by an airline that gave flight benefits to Gert because they were registered partners. For most couples, as noted earlier, the practical value of marriage came not from monetary benefits but from access to a legal framework that was both broader and simpler than a set of individual legal documents like a cohabitation agreement or a will. The practical value of the legal framework was most evident for couples who had or planned to have children. All of those couples were married or registered as partners. As noted earlier, marriage gave the nonbiological parent joint authority for children and perhaps eased the way for adoption. Those couples who simply want something practical have other legal options, at least in the Netherlands. A larger survey of couples found that both same-sex and different-sex couples in the Netherlands share practical motives for considering the formalization of their relationships, such as those related to having children or buying a house, although practical reasons were more important for those registering a partnership than for those marrying.[16]

Couples saw other benefits to marrying that were at least as important—and often more important—than the practical value. Couples considered the emotional and expressive value of marriage to be its most important element, because they wanted to express their commitment.[17] On one level, marriage is a statement to one's partner, as Martha pointed out: "The idea of marriage for me is that . . . you make a commitment . . . so it's like a *drempel*." "A threshold," Lin translated. Martha continued, "Like a threshold that you cross." Gert noted that marriage is a statement both to a partner and to the rest of the world: "But the thing to get [registered] is just to tell each other and the outside world that you're gonna be there for the rest of your life. You're committed to each other."

This statement of commitment to each other and to others has value to the people getting married. "It gives some extra dimension to the relationship," noted Marianne. "That it's not just you say you love each other, but you will stay together. And not just with someone but this particular person. And I think it does for me feel different than just living together and saying things just to each other. And now everybody knows. So I think for me it's a little extra."

Even the dyed-in-the-wool antimarriage feminists recognized the power of the statement. Anna has no intention of marrying, but she admits, "Well, the commitment and the public commitment, I think—there is something beautiful about it. I won't deny that."

In some ways, the state-sanctioned public statement is so powerful that some couples worried that marriage could overwhelm the relationships they had constructed before marriage was an option. Isabelle worried that marriage would diminish the value of the earlier part of their relationship. If she married Anneke after living with her for sixteen years, the marriage might be mistaken as marking the moment that a serious relationship began. "It's a little bit stupid to marry tomorrow, and then over four or five years [later] we will celebrate that we were married for five years," Isabelle protested. "No! It's not honest to the former period."

Similarly, Ria was ambivalent about the public part of marriage: "But I wouldn't mind a ritual where everybody who I love would be . . . a witness of our commitment. But it's clear—so clear—for everyone that we are committed." Ria argued that she and Laura would have to be careful to avoid invalidating that commitment. "We would come up with different reasons than getting married if we do a party. A party—our life together, celebrate our life together, and share it with friends."

I saw one vivid example of the power of marriage's social statement for one couple actively struggling with the decision-making process when I interviewed them. During my conversation with Nancy and Joan, Nancy had difficulty explaining why she had proposed to Joan, who still had not given Nancy an answer. After we finished the formal interview, Joan and I chatted about developments in San Francisco, where the mayor was then allowing same-sex couples to marry. When Joan mentioned the emotional power of those marriages, which were likely to be (and were eventually) legally annulled, Nancy suddenly spoke up with an urgency missing from her earlier statements.

"Well, maybe that emotional part," Nancy began. Joan agreed, "That's a lot of it."

Nancy went on, "If we would get married right now—I mean [it] probably wouldn't make any sense, because we're not even living in the same country, but. . . ." Joan finished for her, "But we would know."

Then Nancy alluded to her earlier discussion about her family and friends wanting her to find a girlfriend who already lived in the Netherlands. I asked her, "So what do you think it would mean in that context if you got married?"

Nancy answered, "That they would see, like, oh, so it is serious or something real. Yeah," she added emphatically. "Getting married and not even living together, I mean. You can do that." And that would make their relationship "real" to her family and friends, even while Joan lived in another country. Marriage, even without cohabitation, has the power to define a relationship that others might not understand. Couples can use marriage to express to others what their relationship means and how it should be treated.

Another kind of statement that some couples wanted to make was a political one. This statement could be about gender roles, drawing a contrast between Dutch equality and American inequality, or the state's acceptance of the equivalence of gay and straight relationships. For Liz, "It has a different impact to say you're married than to say that you have a . . . registered partnership or something, especially when you're saying it to people from the U.S. Like to say, 'No, really I'm married'—that is a real statement to it, because it means the state agreed to it. And then we have the same rights as heterosexual couples." Similarly, for Ellen's partner, Saskia, equality is the message: "And so for her she wanted this to be also a symbol for my parents that it's really the same—that we have exactly the same relationship as they have as [a] heterosexual couple."

For those making a political statement, however, context is everything. The fact that they lived in a tolerant social and legal climate dulled the political point of marriage in the Netherlands, according to some couples. But, even then, they sometimes admitted that their opinions and actions might be different if they lived in another country. Rob generally opposed the idea of marriage, but, to my surprise, he noted, "I think if I lived in the [United] States at this time I would get married maybe." He valued the right to marry, even though he did not choose to marry.

The reasons for marrying mattered in another way, as well. I saw a striking link between the size of the ceremony and the particular benefit of marriage perceived by the couple. Couples who were driven to marry by the practical value of marriage had small ceremonies, with the legally required witnesses and perhaps another bystander or two. Those couples went out for coffee or a small meal after the ceremonies and then went on about their normal daily lives.

In contrast, the couples who wanted to marry to express their commitment before the world had larger ceremonies that were sometimes quite elaborate. One couple arrived on horseback at their town hall. Two dancers married on stage before a large crowd of family and friends after performing in a piece about a wedding. One couple planned an around-the-world theme for their wedding, inviting their many guests to contribute to their honeymoon travel fund. Other couples organized large parties to celebrate the occasion. Finally, none of the couples expressed a religious reason for marrying, and none held a ceremony in a church after the legally required city hall ceremony, unlike roughly half of heterosexual Dutch couples who have married since 1950, who married with a church blessing.[18] This clear association between the value of marriage and the ceremonial trappings chosen confirms that motives matter in the choices that couples make about marriage.

For some couples, a spark in the presence of the right fuel led to a burning desire to marry. In those cases, recognition of the practical or expressive value of marriage was enough to send a couple relatively smoothly to the wedding room at city hall. Most couples had to contend with factors standing in their way, however.

Roadblocks and Detours on the Way to a Wedding

Potential roadblocks on the route to a wedding had nothing to do with financial disincentives to marry, although a few couples were vaguely aware of and mentioned some potential downsides to marrying. Instead, the barriers cut across the three layers of analysis. On an internal, personal level, concerns about making a commitment slowed or stopped individuals. Also, sometimes the prospect of marrying clashed with an individual's political principles and ways of thinking about marriage.

Other barriers were external. Sometimes one partner wanted to marry but the other did not or was uncertain. The story of Pauline and Liz shows how complicated the interactions between partners can be. Both wanted to marry, but they disagreed about why—and the "why" mattered because marriage is expressive. Another social barrier was the reaction of friends and family. Family members did not always approve of marriage involving a same-sex couple. Friends who held antimarriage views pressured some couples considering marriage.

For some couples, these barriers led to detours to marriage, as they used strategies of reframing, negotiating, and persuasion to address the barriers. In other cases, these barriers firmly blocked off the option of marriage.

Concerns About Commitment

As I noted earlier, Paul and Javier had registered as partners because Paul did not expect their relationship to last. Marriage, for Paul, would have meant a commitment that he was not willing to make. "I see marriage as something for your life, which you choose for your life, and I'm not sure with him," he explained. Paul and Javier simply did not have the essential pre-condition for marriage: a long-term commitment.

Even long-term couples sometimes did not want to make a legally sanctioned pledge of commitment to each other. Their concerns suggest that couples take the traditional lifelong promise seriously and are not willing or able to make that promise. Erik described the concerns that he and his partner, James, had: "And we both feel a little bit awkward about the supposed vow for loyalty forever, thinking, you know, we can't guarantee it. Of course, we want to and the feeling now is great and everything. But I don't know how we'll feel in five years. And why should I decide now that I can never do that again or can never change my mind?"

Erik's concerns highlight the very realistic views of modern marriage held by the same-sex couples I spoke with. In theory, the commitment is lifelong; in practice, marriages often end. Marriages in many Western countries are as likely to end in divorce as in death.[19] Ending a marriage might be more legally and emotionally complicated than ending an unmarried relationship, as several couples pointed out. Tellingly, couples with doubts about marriage were just as likely to refer to unhappy marriages as to unhappy divorces in their social and family networks. Both Erik and James had seen firsthand marriages involving apparently unhappily married couples who had stayed together. After visiting those couples, Erik recalled, "[W]e look at each other and think, 'Why are these people married?'" Thus, an interesting twist: some fear that their marriages will end in divorce despite the "til death do you part" promise, while others fear that the marriage might *not* end in divorce when it should, simply because of the promise.

But it was clear that couples distinguished between commitment and the legal promise. As we sat in the garden of their lovely home in a small northern village, Isabelle tried to explain why she did not want to make a legal commitment to Anneke, her partner of sixteen years. "And I still like the idea of not promis[ing] to any institution to stay together for the rest of your life. I can't promise, but in the meantime—in the meanwhile, I see how I'm living and how I am intending never to leave Anneke. It's theory and practice," she laughed. "In practice, I won't leave her. But I don't think it's necessary to promise it down on the paper." Intentions to stay together were enough—a promise would make no practical difference but would violate her ideals.

Political Opposition to the Idea of Marriage

Although they had concerns about pledging to stay together, Isabelle and Anneke's decision to not marry resulted mainly from their deeply rooted political objection to marriage. My stories in the first chapter demonstrate that feminist suspicion of marriage, in particular, is common in the Netherlands, as it is in many European countries and even in the United States.[20] Many feminists have argued that, as Laura put it in our discussion, "Marriage is like slavery to men." The history of marriage certainly shows that the legal institution placed women in a position subordinate to that of men in many places and times.[21] Many lesbians in the

United States and Western Europe came out in the midst of fervent feminist critiques of marriage and other sexist institutions in the 1960s and 1970s, and these lesbians often retain a critique of marriage that remains a formidable personal barrier to marriage.

Most of the women I interviewed referred to themselves as feminists or expressed feminist values. Anna strongly objected to marriage, stating forcefully, "What I hate most about marriage is the whole political and religious history of the institution. I see it as an instrument of patriarchy and capitalism and you name it. So that's one of the reasons I certainly would not want to bless it by my presence."

A similar critique of marriage by Anneke and Isabelle came from their background as active feminists. They believed that marriage can still be an oppressive institution. Anneke explained, "It's much better than it used to be. Lots of regulations that are attached to marriage are still oppressive—not to women but to individuals. I think people who live alone have a disadvantage compared to couples." They both continue to feel strongly about the need to give women, in particular, the ability to live on their own outside a marriage.

Rob had a similar ideological objection to marriage, although it was not rooted in feminism. As Rob put it, "I think it is better to organize society on an individualist point of view, where people can choose what sort of relation they have, with how many people, and with whom they want. That is a better way to organize than to put everybody in a couple."

Some people rejected marriage because it involves the state in a private or personal relationship. Privacy was important to some individuals, whether on a personal or a political level. Even some people who married or registered as partners did not like this aspect of marriage. Margriet resisted giving into the state's authority: "I don't need an official somebody who says, 'OK, you are married now, and for the rest of your life, and better or worse.' . . . [I]t's my thing to think or to do, and not for someone else to tell me to do." Similarly, Laura always saw the state's role as problematic: "It got the state involved in the regulation of personal life in a way that just seemed sort of odious to me."

Getting Around the Political Barrier

These political ideas about marriage potentially raised a major barrier for some couples. Because of their individual opposition to marriage, these couples could take advantage of other ways of organizing the practical sides of their relationship, such as cohabitation agreements, which cut down on the possibility of a conflicting push toward marriage. For others, however, a strong romantic impulse collided head on with principles.

Recall Ellen's relaxing vacation and sudden "vision" about marrying her partner, Saskia. Ellen had long opposed the idea of marriage as a patriarchal institution designed for heterosexuals, and she had even refused to participate in weddings of her friends in the past. So, after her "vision", she had a personal crisis.

"And then for me it was like—what is this? It is totally not acceptable!" Ellen remembered thinking. "So I had to convince my feminist part in me that maybe it's worth[while] to consider. It is not for nothing I had this feeling . . . this romantic feeling actually."

Ultimately, after three months of internal angst, Ellen reconciled her romantic desire to marry with her strong antimarriage beliefs and history by consciously *reframing* her marriage as a politically important act. She believed that marrying both honored the past political effort to win the right to marry and contributed to the current struggle against increasingly visible and powerful conservative forces that oppose letting same-sex couples marry. "So on the one hand it was that we are living in an historical phase where it is possible, so let's value that and use it," she concluded. "And the second thing is as a statement in these times where things are getting worse."

Others with feminist beliefs reframed marriage in a different way. Miriyam was familiar with the feminist argument against marriage, but she did not find the idea of her marrying another woman to be in conflict with feminism. Same-sex couples could help make marriage more equal for women. She argued, "Well, the way to change [marriage] is to marry us to a woman as homosexuals. . . . I don't think I would have ever married when I was with a guy. . . . It would be too traditional—but now you are breaking a tradition as well."

Couples used a similar kind of reframing to get around their view that "marriage is *burgerlijk*," as quite a few people noted in the interviews. They translated "*burgerlijk*" for me as square, old-fashioned, traditional, tacky, or bourgeois. This concern did not seem to be a major obstacle to marriage for couples (unlike the political objections), but the uncomfortable tension between wanting to marry and seeing marriage as bourgeois required some resolution.

The government official who was going to marry Rachel and Marianne helped them get over this feeling. Rachel told the official, "I think gay marriage is tacky." But the official was ready for that argument and countered,

"Well, it is just like tiger prints on your clothes. That's tacky, too, but not when I am wearing it!" We all laughed when Rachel told this story, but the official's comments showed a way out of a serious internal conflict. Making marriage a personal statement and personalizing the details—especially the choice of a same-sex partner—turns marriage for a same-sex couple into something that is not tacky or square. In the Netherlands, Rachel and Marianne were able to give traditionalism a twist, since Dutch couples commonly live together without marrying: "In these days it's even more alternative to get married than not."

Disagreement With a Partner

Making a decision was relatively easy for couples when both wanted the same thing. But sometimes one partner wanted to marry, while the other did not. After Ellen had convinced herself to marry, she had to work several more months to convince Saskia, her partner, to overcome her own objections. Since both partners have to agree—and they must literally agree to the marriage in front of a government official—one partner's disagreement is obviously enough to block the couple from marrying.

I saw enough examples of disagreement among the nineteen couples to think of them as "mixed marriages," a term used in the United States mainly for interracial or interfaith marriages but obviously used here ironically. The antimarriage partner often based his or her point of view in feminist ideology. In each couple, the difference of opinion was openly discussed, and the antimarriage partner made a point of acknowledging that the pro-marriage partner's opinion did matter. The couples' primary strategy for addressing this barrier was *negotiation*.

The bargaining over marriage, whether explicit or implicit, seemed to favor the person with more intense beliefs. For example, even though Joke did not share Anna's ideological opposition to marriage, Joke had no strong desire to marry that had pushed them to the point of needing to reconcile conflicting desires vis-à-vis marriage. But the potential for disagreement simmered near the surface. When I asked them whether they could imagine any circumstances under which they would marry, the following exchange clearly suggests a tension—although a playful one—between their beliefs:

ANNA: I can't think of something that would make me change my mind.

JOKE: No?

ANNA: No, I don't really think so.

JOKE: You would say "no"? [smiling and leaning slightly toward Anna]

ANNA: I'm just hoping that you won't ask me—because I'd have a hard time saying no.

Anna's stronger feelings seemed to keep them in the default position of being legally single at this point in their relationship. At some point in the future, a practical need arising from the purchase of a house, for instance, might get Joke to try to push Anna more forcefully toward marriage. (Recently, Anna wrote to me to tell me that they had bought a house but chose to sign a cohabitation agreement rather than marry.)

Erik had a similar story. "I think if it was only up to me, we would have gotten married a while ago. Because then it's the weird thing with my relationship with James, but I actually knew in the first week that . . . I was his completely forever, and that feeling has never changed," Erik explained. "So I think, yeah, he's more against it, or he is more reluctant towards it than I am. But at the same time I must say it's never been an issue so important that I was frustrated at all that it didn't happen."

Sometimes both partners have strong opinions. In those situations, I saw a process similar to the *reframing* process discussed earlier as a way to reconcile internal contradictions. Like Ellen and some of the other feminists I spoke with, Laura shared a dislike of marriage that influenced her decision about marrying. She explained, "I really came of age in the 1970s in the second wave of the feminist movement, and to me marriage . . . just represented the subjugation of women, and it was about property. . . . So I never in my life thought that I wanted to be married, even if it had been possible." However, Laura's partner, Ria, did not share that political analysis of marriage. "It's just not really the sort of thing I'm really bothered with," she stated simply but emphatically. Laura observed that Ria "also views [marriage] a bit more sentimentally, and more romantically. And she would love to get married and have a big party, and I have a problem with it. . . . Who knows, we may get to that point someday, but I'm not there yet."

The complexity of Laura's internal reframing process is perhaps best illustrated by the fact that she seems to be saying that she and Ria are not married. But, in fact, as I noted earlier, they had been registered partners for several years and were preparing to convert their partnership into a marriage the week after this interview. When I asked about the conversion, Laura admitted, "I don't really think it makes any difference, so I don't think I could really say why we're doing this, except I think that Ria wants to say that we're married." We all laughed. Ria shot back, "I say that already!" The registered partnership gave both what they needed, in that Ria could say they were married while Laura could think they were not.

The undeniable fact of the impending conversion to a legal marriage was harder to reconcile, though. In her reframing of the conversion's meaning, Laura focused on an aspect of traditional marriage that she could still reject—the formal, public celebration. By forgoing that public piece, they could be married in Ria's eyes while not traditionally married in Laura's eyes. This use of the celebration and ceremonial aspects of marriage also turned out to be helpful for other couples who faced resistance from friends or family, discussed next.

"What If You Get Rejected?"

Same-sex couples can legally marry in the Netherlands, but that does not mean that these marriages are always warmly received at a cultural level. In a later chapter, I look in more detail at the reactions of heterosexual family and friends to see how they view the marriages of same-sex couples. Here I am more interested in how the prospect or reality of disapproval affects the decisions of same-sex couples. Martha noted the risk for same-sex couples: "I think another reason . . . that it's hard for gays and lesbians to marry is what if you get rejected? You know, what if the people in your life say, 'No, I don't think this is appropriate,' or you know, 'I'm against [it]'?"

Most of the couples reported no reaction or a positive reaction from friends and family, but some individuals faced active opposition. A child's relationship and marriage plans sometimes conflicted with parents' own ideas about marriage. Mothers, in particular, seemed to have a difficult time hearing that their son or daughter was planning to legally marry a same-sex partner.

Ellen's mother reacted negatively to Ellen and Saskia's plans. "She said, 'How can you imagine that you can get married, since marriage is for starting a family and you are not going to start a family?' So that was her thinking: it is not the same thing. She had difficulties in that she accepts Saskia absolutely as my partner, as my lover, but then the step to make an official thing of the relationship—that is difficult."

Ellen's mother's objections were not the end of the story, though. Ellen reported her mother's eventual change of heart related to the upcoming wedding once she got used to the idea: "She is coming, and she is contributing financially, and she is excited and asking questions." Strategies of *persuasion* like Ellen's might involve direct discussions or even the strategic use of time to give parents the space they need to adjust to the idea.

Other situations were not resolved so happily, though. Willem's mother hurt him by objecting to his marriage to Gert, even though she had attended a same-sex wedding of a relative earlier. He described the conflict: "And she also asked [a] couple months in advance, 'Why do you get married? Is it necessary?' I thought, why are you asking? Why are you asking? I am not a kid anymore, and I was really surprised. I was really surprised by that. That she couldn't be happy for me." Because of her reaction, Willem did not invite her to the wedding and had not had any contact with her for three years.

No one cited parental disapproval as a reason for not marrying. But negative parental reactions did affect the couple's choices about the size and format of the ceremony and celebration. Earlier I mentioned that couples reframed marriage and the role of the celebration as a way to reconcile conflicting feelings about whether to marry. Similarly, couples often made up guest lists that responded to the barrier of social disapproval. Willem refused to invite his mother because of her opposition. In the same way, other couples left out parents or other relatives who might have expressed opposition or discomfort that would have interfered with the ceremony or the planning of the couple.

Have These Same-Sex Couples Changed Marriage?

As same-sex couples maneuver around the barriers or even stop once they bump up against an insurmountable barrier, the legal end points take on a simple shape: some couples get married, some register as partners, and others remain legally unmarried. But while they appear to end up at the same place as some other couples, the routes to that point vary across couples. Whether and how they get to be married depends on the complex interplay of life conditions, their views on the value of marriage, barriers to marriage, and the processes of accepting or avoiding those barriers.

For those who marry, their reasoning sounds familiar, and it parallels the reasoning we hear from heterosexual couples. Same-sex couples in my study chose *to marry* (the verb) because they had a child, because they had some practical needs, or because they wanted to affirm and express their commitment to each other and to the world. Although they had the option to register as partners and gain most of the same legal benefits of marriage, all but one of the couples who had a choice rejected registration and instead chose to marry. Likewise, these gay and lesbian couples' Dutch heterosexual peers have similar views of marriage, as Anna Korteweg's research on unmarried Dutch people shows.[22] Heterosexual couples aren't always sure marriage will make a difference in their lives, but they see some practical circumstances that favor marriage (especially when having children). Most importantly, Korteweg's research suggests that marriage serves as an emotional barometer, with discussions about marriage revealing how committed partners are to a relationship.

The 2006 survey of Dutch married and registered partner couples by Boele-Woelki and colleagues also finds that same-sex couples are motivated in similar ways as different-sex couples.[23] Roughly 60% of gay and heterosexual married couples report primarily emotional reasons for choosing marriage, and about 40% of each group also report that practical reasons encouraged them to consider formalizing their relationships. Similarly, gay and heterosexual couples who choose to register as partners report the same main reasons for choosing registered partnerships: practical reasons for formalization but concerns about marriage as an institution.

The same-sex couples I interviewed who have not married also sound like their heterosexual counterparts. A growing number of Dutch different-sex couples choose not to marry. Roughly a third of all 30-39-year-old Dutch people live with an unmarried partner, and almost half of them do not expect to marry their partners.[24] Overall, demographers estimate that a third of Dutch people will never marry, although most of that third will live with a partner.[25] Dutch same-sex couples and different-sex couples give very similar reasons for not wanting or expecting to marry. A survey of cohabiting heterosexual couples who do not expect to marry found that three-quarters reject marriage because it "would not add anything to their relationship," suggesting that they do not need the practical, emotional, or cultural benefits of marriage.[26] Smaller numbers of those heterosexual couples gave other reasons that also sound familiar from my interviews (fewer than 20% for each reason): they oppose marriage; their partners do not want to marry; they do not want to make the commitment; or they do not plan to have children.

My interviews with Dutch same-sex couples uncover some internal personal tinkering with marriage, though, and I suspect that these adjustments may be more common for gay couples. In particular, the couple's legal status was not the only thing that changed in the process of making a choice—their own ideas about marriage sometimes changed, too. The changes that I observed were primarily reframings of the political meaning of marriage.

The lesbians and gay men I spoke with were intensely aware of the political nature of marriage, especially as it related to women or to gay men and lesbians. These couples had lived through the political efforts to open up marriage to same-sex couples in Holland and elsewhere in the world, and now they see the issue of same-sex marriage caught up in Dutch political debates about the assimilation of immigrants from Islamic countries.

Furthermore, feminists often objected to entering an institution so historically associated with the loss of rights for women. But feminists sometimes had to reconcile these ideological beliefs with conflicting feelings and needs related to marriage, especially when a partner did not share those political beliefs. The political context allowed some feminists to reframe the act of marrying as a progressive political statement and to view the idea of marriage as a feminist one. In these reframings, marriages of two women or two men undermined old-fashioned gendered roles for husbands and wives.

The idea that marriage is "*burgerlijk,*" or old-fashioned and square, was an idea that same-sex couples seemed to have absorbed from their heterosexual siblings and friends. This idea stood in the way of their choosing marriage, but many same-sex couples found their own ways around it. An individual marriage, conducted in an authentic and personal way, seemed to be the antidote to this concern. Marriage might be tacky for a younger, hip (and heterosexual) cohort, as Rachel once believed, but in the Dutch context her own choice to marry was "even more alternative."

Finally, same-sex couples sometimes adjusted the cultural trappings of marriage, mainly the wedding ceremony and celebration, to reconcile differing views of marriage within the couple or to respond to social disapproval, perhaps hinting at some other potential changes to marriage as a cultural institution. However, the variation in ceremonies of same-sex couples mostly mirrored the diversity of Dutch heterosexual weddings. The same-sex couples' weddings had three potential differences, however. First, none of the nine married couples I interviewed were married with a church blessing. Second, some lesbian couples used their ceremonies to express feminist political principles related to marriage. Third, same-sex couples were perhaps more selective in whom they invited; bad reactions of family members sometimes led to their exclusion from weddings. But that strategy was adopted to ensure a happy and relatively stress-free wedding day for the couple.

Overall, the similarities between the process that same-sex couples engage in as they decide whether to marry and actually marry and the process followed by different-sex couples are more striking than the differences. In chapter 4 I return to the question of how the idea or meaning of marriage might have changed in the larger culture as a result of same-sex marriage.

Relevance for the U.S. Debate

At this point, it seems reasonable to ask what the experiences of these Dutch couples can tell us about the debate over same-sex marriage in the United States. One obvious reason they are likely to apply to the American experience is that six of the thirty-four people I spoke with were from the United States. Gay and lesbian binational couples are particularly vulnerable in many countries because a same-sex partner does not qualify for the more favorable immigration status that foreign spouses get in the United States, leading some same-sex couples into "love exile" in places like the Netherlands, as some of the couples I interviewed termed it.

More important, over the years several scholars have studied same-sex commitment ceremonies in the United States, and one recent study examines same-sex couples who have married in Massachusetts. While most of the commitment ceremonies had no legal meaning until recently, these studies have found that U.S. couples had similar motives and faced similar barriers as same-sex couples in other countries, and some of the same factors appear to be important in other countries, too. Same-sex couples held commitment ceremonies to express their sense of commitment to each other and to express the seriousness of their relationships to friends and families.[27]

The legal and material benefits of marriage play an important role in the decision to marry in Massachusetts and in couples' stated desire to marry when marriage is not a legal option.[28] Highlighting the importance of material benefits sets American couples off a bit from the Dutch couples, who gain much less financially, if anything at all, by marrying. As I observed in the Netherlands and as others have seen in Denmark, Norway, and Sweden, the practical value of benefits such as immigration rights appear to play a role for some couples.[29] The other legal benefits, which I would interpret as the legal framework for organizing a couple's life together, as the Dutch put it, appear to be attractions of marriage in both countries. Political factors other than feminism appear to be relatively unimportant in most American couples' decisions to marry, although studies by Gretchen Stiers and Ellen Lewin reveal the complicated process by which political messages and political resistance emerge in American commitment ceremonies. As with Dutch couples, the choice to marry did not necessarily mean a capitulation to conformity or tradition in the United States or in other countries with partner registration.[30]

Some similar barriers stop same-sex couples from marrying or from wanting to marry in the United States and other countries, mainly the feminist argument that marriage is a patriarchal institution. Schecter and her colleagues report that some Massachusetts couples chose not to marry for that reason, and Eskridge and Spedale heard similar arguments in Denmark.[31] Furthermore, U.S. couples do not always agree in their ideas about marriage and its trappings, which could stand in the way of deciding to marry.[32] For those couples that have been together and have made emotional and other "investments" in their relationships, as most who held commitment ceremonies in the United States have done, marriage can seem socially or economically unnecessary.[33]

Dutch and American couples have faced some similar challenges despite having somewhat different choices to make. My study addresses more directly than other studies how couples in the Netherlands found their way around barriers at the individual level and at the couple level in the context of an actual legal option to marry. At least at a general level, couples understood the legal rights and obligations that come with marriage, distinguishing marrying from simply living together or holding a commitment ceremony. But the similarities across countries in the decision to marry or to hold a commitment ceremony add to the sense emerging from other studies that ceremonies are significant markers of commitment and meaning, even when they do not come with legal recognition.

Overall, while these nineteen couples represent only some of the thousands of same-sex couples who have married in the Netherlands and who will or would marry in the United States, the range of experiences provides a starting point for understanding the kinds of factors that might be important for couples, even though I cannot use the interviews to say how *common* those factors are among same-sex couples. However, many of my findings track closely a larger survey of Dutch couples, and the close-up view provided by my interviews provides guidance for future research designed to better understand the decision-making process at work.[34]

3

Forsaking All Other Options

The complexity of couples' stories and decisions as related in the preceding chapter provides a context for interpreting the numbers that describe gay couples' choices to marry. Fairly soon after countries started offering legal recognition to same-sex couples, European scholars noticed that the number of couples registering as partners seemed surprisingly low. For instance, after sixteen years, 2,641 Danish couples had registered; 1,808 couples registered in Norway from 1993 to 2004; Sweden saw just over 4,000 couples register in ten years.[1] Almost 10,700 Dutch same-sex couples had married as of 2007;[2] if we add in the couples that have registered as partners, we find that at least 22% of Dutch couples have formalized their relationships as of 2005.[3] After thirteen months, 18,000 couples in the United Kingdom had entered civil partnerships by the end of 2006, or also about 22% of roughly 80,000 same-sex couples.[4]

Maggie Gallagher, an American gay marriage opponent, and Joshua Baker tallied up the numbers of same-sex couples that married and compared their findings to estimates of the number of lesbians and gay men in each country (or state, for Massachusetts). Gallagher and Baker pronounced the marriage rates, which ranged from 1% to 17% of the gay population, "small," although they professed to draw no other conclusions from those low rates.[5] Other commentators, however, seized on their report to interpret the low rates as evidence that gay people don't really want or need the right to marry.[6]

Not surprisingly, not everyone agrees that the rates measured by Gallagher and others are unusually low. Expecting gay people to go from zero to 54 (the percentage of Americans over 18 who were currently married in 2006) right out of the marriage gate is probably unrealistic.[7] The pent-up demand for marriage among gay couples might take several years to resolve, and in the first few years the couples that do marry are likely to be committed couples of long standing, so year-to-year changes in rates are not typical of later annual rates of marriage.

My colleague Gary Gates argues that the annual rate of marriages among unmarried heterosexuals is also quite low each year and that the rates for gay couples do not look low from that perspective. He assumes that the numbers of same-sex marriages will not drop off too sharply after the pent-up demand has been exhausted, however. Over time, as couples marry, the pool of single gay people will shrink, so the percentage of unmarried gay people marrying each year will increase. This controversy suggests that some caution is in order when comparing rates of gay marriage to common markers of heterosexual marriage.

Nevertheless, the rates are important data in the policy debate over same-sex marriage, since they seem to reflect gay couples' opinions of marriage. However, it is just as likely that different marriage rates across countries reflect some other considerations. Looking at the rates in context can tell us more about why couples marry or not, so in the first part of this chapter I compare rates across several countries to various measures of the potential reasons for marrying. These comparisons suggest that the rates across different countries, whether high *or* low, are difficult to explain with current theories about why people might marry, so they don't provide a very useful referendum on beliefs about marriage.

In the second half of the chapter, I suggest that we focus on a different angle that will tell us more about the meaning and position of marriage by how often couples choose either marriage or registered partnership. In the Netherlands, same-sex and different-sex couples alike choose between these two different legal statuses, so the choice of one or the other reflects the relative perceived social, cultural, or personal value of marriage. As both the numbers and the comments of the Dutch same-sex couples show, marriage comes out on top every time in the emerging menu of relationship options for same-sex and different-sex couples.

Why Don't More Same-Sex Couples Marry?

The close-up perspective on individual decisions in chapter 2 gives us some new potential answers to the questions raised by the numbers. My interviews with Dutch couples as described in that chapter suggest that the reasons for the low rates of marriage are complex and probably interrelated:

- Couples that have been together a long time have created alternatives through legal documents and social support that reduce the practical value of marriage.

- Cohabiting same-sex couples get some of the rights and responsibilities of marriage in the Netherlands (and in many other European countries), and the state picks up some of the social insurance functions that marriage might otherwise provide, again reducing the practical value of marriage.
- Same-sex couples are probably less likely to have children than different-sex couples, reducing demand for marriage for that reason.
- Couples have worked hard to achieve informal recognition by friends and family of their relationship, and marriage might debase the meaning of that prior work and the value of the premarriage relationship years.
- Some lesbians and gay men have political objections to the concept of marriage related to their historic exclusion and to other ideological beliefs about the institution of marriage.

The (apparently) low marriage rates are likely a result of a combination of these forces, some of which are specific to or stronger for lesbian and gay couples than for heterosexual couples. Although different-sex couples might face some of the same pressures, for same-sex couples the newness of the right to marry and many years of creating their own relationships on their own may have amplified the effects.

Beyond the ingredients that go into making a decision, the actual process of decision making is one that can take a while, even for existing committed couples. As my interviews demonstrate, two sets of complicated motivations and ideas go into any one couple's decision about marriage, so the existence of even a small proportion of marriage skeptics could delay or block many weddings. After conducting these interviews, I could easily conclude that the rates of marriage and partnership are actually *higher* than I might expect given the context and barriers that lesbian and gay couples face.

The early numbers have generated enormous speculation, though. Our understanding of the reasons behind the statistics should improve over time, but I find some of the reasons suggested by others to be unsatisfying. Several writers, including Dale Carpenter, Paul Varnell, William Eskridge, and Darren Spedale, have all argued that gay men and lesbians might be less likely than heterosexuals to form committed couples at this point in history given the lack of legal and institutional support for gay relationships.[8] We do not have good data on the coupling rates for gay people in European countries, but in the United States most recent studies suggest that 25% to 50% of lesbians and gay men are in committed relationships.[9] Even if this pattern is also true for the Netherlands and other European countries, it does not explain low rates of registration and marriage among *actual* same-sex couples. In the Netherlands, 22% of same-sex couples have married or registered, as have 80% of heterosexual couples.

Some of these writers have argued that the low rates reflect the novelty of marriage as an aspect of gay relationships.[10] While that argument seems plausible, it does not completely take into account the childhood visions and expectations of marriage that many gay men and lesbians I spoke with recalled. Those trying to explain the low rates point to the higher uptake of marriage among same-sex couples in Massachusetts as evidence that a country's "marriage culture" matters, since the marriage culture is stronger in the United States than in Europe.[11] But rates of marriage and registration in the United States among same-sex couples are still lower than those for heterosexual couples there. And the Scandinavian couples have had many years to think about the decision, but we have not seen the dramatic surge in couples registering that we might have expected as new relationships form and blossom.

They also propose other possible reasons that are similar to the factors I found relevant, such as opposition to the idea of marriage.[12] But, to really understand why ideological barriers matter, we have to also consider the fact that some couples are eventually able to get around that barrier to marriage, as some couples I spoke with did. Another plausible explanation that Varnell and Eskridge and Spedale raise is that fear of social stigma and discrimination keeps couples in the closet and out of the public registries. However, the couples I spoke with who did not marry or register were quite open in their work and family lives about their relationships, so the closet alone is an insufficient explanation for some couples' decisions to remain unmarried. The one lesbian I interviewed who was not out to her family had married anyway and found that fact no more difficult to conceal than the fact that she is a lesbian.

The difficulty of isolating a particular factor that reduces marriage rates also shows up if we make a more detailed comparison of same-sex partnership or marriage rates across countries instead of relying on data from interviews with a relatively small number of couples. Here I look for patterns by comparing rates of partnership across countries to measures of the practical and cultural value of marriage. Are partnership rates lower where the practical value of marriage is low? Or are they lower in countries that see marriage as outdated? If such patterns emerge, then we might think that same-sex couples' rates of marriage are low because they perceive little benefit from marriage or do not like the institution.

Measuring partnership rates require careful construction and a few adjustments. I added up all of the couples that entered partnerships by country in Denmark, Sweden, Norway, Iceland, the Netherlands, and Belgium. (France does not separate out the numbers of same-sex and different-sex couples entering a PACS [*Pacte Civil de Solidarité*]. Germany and Finland apparently do not publish these figures.) Then I created a measure that adjusts for differences in laws and sizes of countries. To account for the fact that couples marry over time and that some countries have had these laws longer than others, I calculated the average number of registered partners or same-sex married couples per year that the status was available. Next, I divided that figure by the number of unmarried people over the age of fifteen in each country in 2004 to take into account the fact that some countries have larger populations of potential same-sex couples than others. The adjusted rates of registered partners (or marriages) per year per 100,000 unmarried people are: Denmark, 12.5; Iceland, 13.7; Norway, 10.9; Sweden, 13.0; Netherlands (registered partnerships), 25.0; Netherlands (marriage), 39.8; and Belgium (marriage), 77.3.

Next, I plotted each of these adjusted partnership rates on a graph against several factors that might influence marriage or partnership for same-sex couples. If a given factor is closely related to marriage rates, then we should see a clear pattern on the graph: countries that have high same-sex marriage rates will also have high (or low) values of the particular factor we're considering. I also tested the correlations between partnership or marriage rates and the factor for statistical significance.

Unfortunately but perhaps unsurprisingly, the picture that emerges from these comparisons is that no single factor explains much about why couples do or do not marry or register. Consider first the practical consequences of marriage. The legal scholar Kees Waaldijk and his colleagues in Europe created measures of the "level of legal consequences" of marriage and partnership. In the nine countries that granted rights to same-sex couples in 2003, the lawyers compared the rights and responsibilities of legal marriage for different-sex couples on dimensions of parenting, taxation, property division, inheritance, health insurance, pensions, and other factors to those same rights for cohabiting, registered, or married same-sex couples.[13] When I compared partnership ratios to the gain in rights and responsibilities that same-sex couples experienced in marrying or

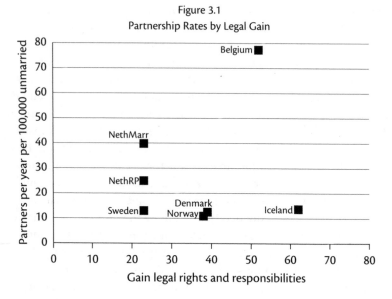

Figure 3.1
Partnership Rates by Legal Gain

registering compared with simply living together, no relationship emerges (see Figure 3.1). The points on the graph appear randomly scattered.

Another comparison that did not pan out looked at social protection spending in each country. Higher levels of social spending did not go with lower rates of partnership registration (see Figure 3.2) (a slight negative correlation was not statistically significant). These two comparisons suggest that a low practical value of marriage does not lead to lower marriage rates in Europe, at any rate.

Another way to assess the value of marriage is to compare same-sex couples' behavior to heterosexual couples' marriage decisions. This comparison gets at the "marriage culture" explanation offered by some commentators. Two good measures are the heterosexual cohabitation rate (see Figure 3.3) and the heterosexual marriage rate (see Figure 3.4).[14] If we leave out Belgium, which has a high same-sex marriage rate but a low cohabitation rate and a low marriage rate, there is no obvious link between the heterosexual couples' cohabitation rate or marriage rate and the rate of registration or marriage among same-sex couples. (Even if we include Belgium, the relationship is not statistically significant, but it comes close for the cohabitation rate.) In other words, the data show no evidence of a link between lack of enthusiasm for marriage among different-sex couples and the registration or marriage rates for same-sex couples.

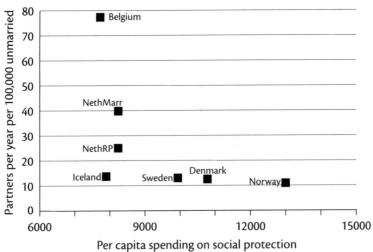

Figure 3.2
Partnership Rates by Social Protection Spending

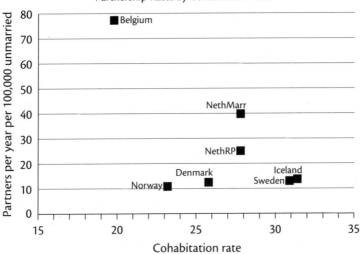

Figure 3.3
Partnership Rates by Cohabitation Rate

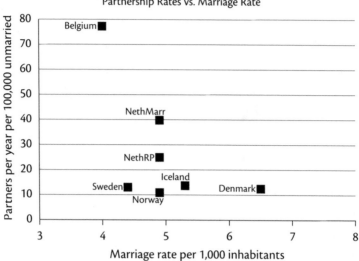

Figure 3.4
Partnership Rates vs. Marriage Rate

However, I did find one intriguing and strong relationship between partnership rates and beliefs about marriage. The World Values Survey asks respondents in many countries whether they believe marriage is an outdated institution. (I look in more detail at these data in chapter 4.) We might reasonably expect to see lower marriage rates in countries where many people see marriage as outdated. Not surprisingly, Figure 3.5 suggests that heterosexual marriage rates are lower in countries where more people believe marriage to be outdated, although the negative correlation is not statistically significant.

What's more surprising is that the pattern for same-sex couples in Figure 3.6 shows just the opposite—their registration or marriage rates are higher in countries where the belief that marriage is outdated is pervasive! Maybe this relationship captures the twist noted by Rachel in chapter 2. Marriage might be square ("*burgerlijk*") for different-sex couples, but same-sex couples find it easier to overlook that given the different political context for their marriages or registered partnerships. Or perhaps same-sex couples are less likely to take these rights for granted than are different-sex couples, given the political battle necessary to win those rights.

One final angle on the numbers confirms the potential importance of beliefs about marriage. Early on in the registration or marriage process in Denmark, Norway, Sweden, Belgium, and the Netherlands, male couples

Figure 3.5
Heterosexual Marriage Rate vs. Belief That Marriage Is Outdated

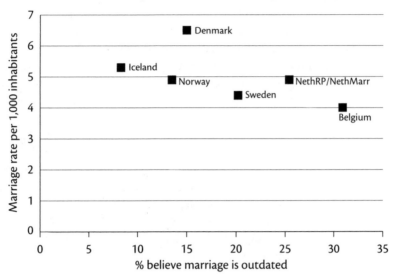

Figure 3.6
Partnership Rates vs. Belief That Marriage Is Outdated

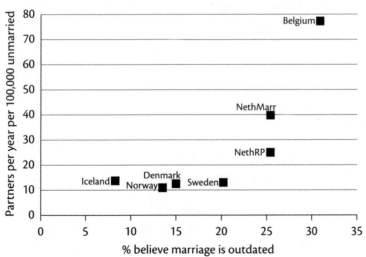

greatly outregistered female couples. Over time, though, women started catching up, and now the numbers of male-couple and female-couple registrations each year are similar. This pattern fits the findings from interviews with Dutch couples, which revealed that certain ideas about marriage act as a barrier to making that choice. The ideological barriers were particularly high for many lesbians to start with, as my interviews found. The big picture suggests that, over time, either women's ideas about marriage shifted or their particular needs changed to make marriage a better option in their lives.

A comparison of GLB people's interest in marriage in Europe and in the United States highlights the potential importance of tangible benefits in the marriage decision. American couples appear more interested in marriage than do European gay couples. In the early 1990s, Gretchen Stiers asked ninety lesbians and gay men in Massachusetts (78% of whom were in relationships) whether they would marry if they could, and 58% said yes. Other evidence suggests that interest in marriage has grown since then in the United States:

- A 2003 online survey of 748 LGB adults by Harris Interactive and Witeck-Combs Communications found that 78% said they would want to get legally married if they were in a committed relationship. Younger and less-educated people were even more likely to say yes than the average gay person.[15]
- A 2001 survey of 405 lesbian, gay, and bisexual Americans in twelve major urban areas found that 74% would like to marry someday.[16]
- A recent survey of LGB teens in the New York area also found enthusiasm for marriage, with 61% of young men and 78% of young women reporting that they are very likely to marry a same-sex partner.[17]

When given the opportunity, same-sex couples in the United States appear to be much more likely to marry or register than do those in Europe. The American Community Survey, conducted by the U.S. Census Bureau, also provides better data on the number of same-sex couples, which is a more appropriate baseline for comparison.[18] In Vermont, 51% of same-sex couples entered civil unions from 2000 to 2007.[19] In Massachusetts, more than 10,385 same-sex couples married in the first three years that marriage was an option, constituting 44% of same-sex couples living in that state. More than 44% of California's same-sex couples entered domestic partnerships before the state briefly opened marriage to gay couples in 2008.

However, heterosexual couples are still more likely than gay or lesbian couples to marry, since 91% of different-sex couples in the United States are married. As the numbers continue to increase for same-sex couples, it is still possible that they will catch up at some point. And, in the United States, female couples are more likely than male couples to marry and to register—just the opposite of the pattern in Europe—suggesting the possible importance of the practical value of marriage related to childrearing. More lesbian than gay male couples are caring for children in their homes in the United States, and the rates of childrearing are higher among U.S. same-sex couples than among same-sex couples in the Netherlands and in Scandinavia.

This chapter suggests some reasons that same-sex couples in the United States are more likely to marry than those in the Netherlands, where only a quarter of same-sex couples are estimated to have married or registered:

- Marriage comes with more benefits in the U.S. than in the Netherlands, such as health insurance through employers.
- Same-sex couples get no clear rights or responsibilities simply by living together in the United States, unlike the Netherlands.
- Same-sex couples in the United States are more likely to be raising children. Roughly one in five male same-sex couples and one in three female same-sex couples are raising children in their homes, according to the U.S. Census. Comparable Dutch data shows that only 9% of same-sex couples have children living at home.[20]
- Marriage rates are higher in the United States, probably because of greater levels of religiousness and other values (see the discussion in chapter 4), which changes the cultural context in which same-sex couples (and heterosexual couples) make decisions.

Overall, the evidence from the Netherlands and from studies of same-sex couples in the United States suggests that the decision not to marry does not reflect disdain for or outright rejection of the institution of marriage. To the contrary, Dutch and American same-sex couples view marriage as a serious step and do not undertake it without feeling a commitment to their partner and an intention to stay together. For many, the decision to have children is linked to marriage through important legal and cultural ties. Those who choose not to marry sometimes disagree with aspects of the institution, but those ideas are malleable and appear to change over time, as I mentioned in chapter 2 and discuss further in chapter 5. The complexity of factors influencing couples' decisions and the variation in the legal and social context in which couples make decisions undoubtedly help to explain the lower rates of marriage so far among gay than among heterosexual couples.

Choosing Among Alternatives to Marriage: "The Real Thing" vs. "a Bit of Nothing"

One obvious way to capture same-sex couples' decisions is to look at the percentage of gay couples that marry or register, but, as this chapter shows so far, it's certainly not equivalent to a referendum on beliefs about marriage. A different perspective on choice is more revealing about gay couples' views on the general value of marriage, in my view. In the Netherlands, all couples have a variety of choices about whether and how to formalize their relationships, as I mentioned in chapter 2. In the second half of this chapter, I look at how gay and heterosexual couples view marriage as compared to its alternatives. Both stories and numbers clearly reveal that marriage ranks highest among formal legal options for couples.

All Dutch couples won the right to register as partners in 1998 as the result of a political compromise that gave same-sex couples most of the rights and responsibilities of marriage without calling it "marriage." Most of the same-sex couples I interviewed were aware of some legal differences between marriage and registered partnership, but they saw those differences as minor. (Interestingly, as noted earlier, they saw the legal and practical differences between cohabiting and marrying as relatively minor, as well.) Most also supported the idea that both gay and heterosexual couples should be allowed to choose between marriage or registered partnership. Nevertheless, almost everyone, regardless of legal status, expressed disdain for registered partnership. They clearly viewed that status as socially and culturally second-rate when compared with marriage.

All four of the couples I interviewed who were registered partners entered that status before marriage was legally available. Of the four, only one couple, Paul and Javier, preferred registered partnership to marriage. Paul was quite clear about why he had made this decision, as noted in chapter 2. "I see marriage as something for your life which you choose for your life and I'm not sure with him," he explained. "And that's for me immediately a reason not to get married." Permanence is a cultural ideal of marriage, not a legal one, and having a different option without that cultural expectation was useful for Paul.

The statements of the other three registered partner couples suggest that they believe that marriage is not just different but is a *better* status in some way. Gert and Willem refer to their registered partnership (and ceremony) as a marriage. They had an elaborate weekend-long wedding celebration to note the occasion, followed by an around-the-world honeymoon sponsored by their wedding guests. These men did not officially convert their partnership to a marriage because the time and the expense (hundreds of euros) of the conversion outweighed the meager legal gains they would achieve, in their view. Laura and Ria were about to convert their partnership to a marriage the week after our discussion. And Ineke and Diana implied that they would have chosen marriage if it had been available because registered partnership "was not the real thing . . . it was to have the Christian parties happy."

Not surprisingly, the couples that had married were the least supportive of registered partnership. They had faced an explicit choice and opted for marriage. But even the couples that were neither married nor registered said that registered partnership was much less desirable to them. In both of these groups of couples, the views of registered partnership ranged from contempt to a more positively stated belief that marriage is superior. "Registered partnership I found really shit. It's really CDA [the Dutch Christian Democratic Party], it's a bit of nothing," according to Margriet, who had married her partner, Miriyam, shortly after they had a child. Rob opposed marriage because he preferred that society be organized around individuals rather than couples, but he still thought that registered partnership was "even more absurd" than marriage.

The dryness of the "registered partner" status contrasts sharply with the rich emotional meaning of marriage: "I thought it was OK as a step forward towards marriage for everybody, so in that way I supported it," recalled Anneke, who was neither registered nor married. "But on a private level I thought, well [I] don't want to get registered—it sounds like the result of an accountant's report: 'I got registered.'"

Otto and Bram's decision to marry was an emotional and spiritual one that did not fit registered partnership, and Otto had little good to say about that alternative: "Because the decision of marriage was really something emotional—I wouldn't say spiritual but it turned out to be very spiritual, but it was something that we decided emotionally—and I think a registered partnership—already [the] name sounds very practical. You write, and you count, and you balance."

Indeed, the 2006 survey by Boele-Woelki et al. supports the idea that registered partnership means something very different to couples that have a choice. The couples they surveyed who had a registered partnership were more likely to have referred to the practical reasons for formalizing their relationships than did the couples that had chosen to marry. Married couples reported more emotional and symbolic reasons for choosing marriage.

Most of the Dutch couples I interviewed found registered partnership to be a good step toward equality in its historical context but believed that marriage was simply better. Either marriage was a more complete legal status or it represented complete legal equality. Ellen and Saskia had considered registered partnership when they began thinking about getting married. But they decided that they wanted the "real thing" that heterosexuals got. "We are exactly the same," Ellen stated forcefully. "We don't do it for less."

Many Dutch couples saw marriage as better because it had an additional social meaning that registered partnership, as a recent political invention, lacked. Martha and Lin chose marriage over registered partnership because marriage "had substance." To Lin, marrying said "This is the woman that I've chosen to be with for the rest of my life," just as it did when her brother married and when her sister married. Registered partnership could not send the same kind of message.

And not only does marriage send a unique signal, but that signal is understood by those who receive it.[21] "One of the amazing things about marriage is people understand it, you know," Martha pointed out. "Two-year-olds understand it. It's a social context, and everyone knows what it means." Other couples pointed out that other countries accept the meaning of marriage, unlike registered partnerships, and in some cases recognize the marriages of Dutch same-sex couples but not registered partnerships.

Although the Netherlands is unique in offering such a wide range of legal options to couples, similar negative feelings about statuses that stop short of marriage may explain the low registration rates in other countries. Eskridge and Spedale dismiss the idea that the low rates of partnership registration in Denmark stem from the fact that it's not a "real" marriage. They argue that Danish couples see the decision to register a partnership as marrying, and registered partnerships are treated as marriages on a social level. But same-sex couples do not have the option of marriage in Denmark (and different-sex couples cannot choose registered partnership), so we have no way to know if the current option would be seen as second-best were marriage available.

In some places, the cultural and political trappings of statuses that are not marriage send a very clear message of difference and inferiority to gay and lesbian couples. The alternatives to marriage generally lack ceremony and are not embedded in cultural or social life in Europe or North America. They do not have cultural rituals or understandings to enhance their meaning, other than in relation to marriage. While gay couples have been resourceful in creating their own ceremonies to honor commitment, the inequality between marriage and informal or lesser legal commitments remains clear.[22] Couples clearly—and accurately—perceive that the alternatives to marriage open to same-sex couples are designed to be inferior to marriage.

To marry in France, for instance, a different-sex couple goes to the town hall with witnesses.[23] The couple waits outside the special room for weddings with other soon-to-be-married couples. When their turn comes, the two exchange vows before the mayor or an appointed deputy. In sharp contrast, the members of a same-sex couple registering a PACS—the strongest form of legal recognition for a same-sex couple in France—go without witnesses to the "tribunal d'instance" to register their pact in the office of the court clerk, with no ritual or special trappings to note the occasion. While waiting to register, the couple might share a waiting room with other people seeking the court's attention on matters related to debts or disputes with landlords. The anthropologist Wilfried Rault calls these reminders of second-class status "symbolic violence." Same-sex couples clearly perceive their inferior position, so they do their best to compensate by dressing up, bringing friends and relatives (who must wait outside the clerk's office), and organizing private ceremonies or celebrations to take place afterward.

Even egalitarian Sweden differentiates between registering a partnership and marrying. Jens Rydström argues that the relatively small differences in the civil ceremonies for marriage and for partnership reinforce a symbolic inequality. For instance, the civil servant who presides "declares" a different-sex couple married, while he or she "informs" a same-sex couple that they are registered: "This gives the partnership more the character of a business agreement, whereas the matrimony transforms the two into one flesh with an almost magic formula."[24] The marriage ceremony affirms heterosexual couples' "responsibility unto coming generations," a role absent and therefore symbolically denied to registered partners.

As the experiences of European couples suggest, without the ability to marry, alternatives to marriage take on some symbolic and expressive meaning as merely the next best thing. In 2008, the California Supreme

Court noted these deficiencies in domestic partnership: when compared to marriage, domestic partnerships may become a mark of second-class citizenship and are less understood socially.[25] In practice, these legal alternatives to marriage are limited because they do not map onto a well-developed social institution that gives the act of marrying its social and cultural meaning. Once marriage is possible, the position on the symbolic ladder is clear: marriage trumps its alternatives for same-sex couples.

The Emerging Ranking of Options

We can also assess the relative value of marriage and registered partnership to couples by comparing the numbers of couples that choose each legal status. Only the Netherlands offers all couples two formal options, plus the options of cohabiting with or without an explicit cohabitation contract (*samenlevingscontract*). In fact, looking at the broader picture painted by international and U.S. statistics reveals a decided lack of enthusiasm for the alternatives, just as we saw in the Dutch couple interviews. Same-sex couples are more willing to use the new legal statuses than are different-sex couples, but that is probably because they want the closest status to marriage that is open to them.

In the Netherlands, 10,401 same-sex couples registered as partners between 1998 and 2007, or 1,040 per year. But, in the much shorter time period that marriage was open to them (2001-2007), almost 10,700 same-sex couples have married, or 1,528 per year. More tellingly, the number of registered partnerships dropped off dramatically, from between 1,500 and 3,000 per year until 2001 to around 500 to 700 per year after 2001, while the number of same-sex couples that married was twice that number, suggesting a strong preference for marriage among gay couples.

When Dutch lawmakers opened marriage to same-sex couples, in 2001, they realized that some same-sex couples who were registered partners might want to marry, so the new law included a conversion process to allow registered partnerships to become marriages and vice versa. We don't know how many partnerships were converted to marriages, so there might be some double-counting in the totals here. The demographer Liesbeth Steenhof uses Dutch population registries (which distinguish between partnerships and marriage) to estimate that by 2005 about 12% of same-sex couples in the Netherlands had married and another 10% were registered partners.[26] So the range of same-sex couples taking up marriage and something almost identical to marriage is at least 22%.

Different-sex couples also vote for marriage. By 2007, only about 37,500 Dutch different-sex couples had registered as new partners in seven years (about 3,700 per year), a fairly small number when compared to the 70,000 to 80,000 marriages that took place each year and in light of the 700,000 cohabiting different-sex couples in Holland.[27] Since there are 3.5 million married Dutch couples, plus the 700,000 unmarried couples, we can calculate a "take-up rate" of registered partnership of only 5.3% for unmarried different-sex couples, or 0.9% of all different-sex couples, whether married or not.

An interesting footnote to the registered partnership alternative for heterosexual couples comes from a curious new phenomenon related to the registered-partner-to-marriage conversion process. To policymakers' surprise, in addition to the 37,000 or so new registered partnerships by heterosexual couples through 2007, 28,567 different-sex married couples converted their marriage into a partnership. Most of those conversions were quickly dissolved in a "flash annulment," or streamlined adminis-trative dissolution that is possible only for registered partners.[28] These flash annulments were an unintended effect of the law that gave same-sex couples the right to marry. However, Dutch demographers note that the number of divorces decreased by more than the number of these flash an-nulments after 2001,[29] so these registered partnership conversions did not increase the number of marriages that ended—they just changed *how* they ended.

Of course, many Dutch heterosexual couples do not bother to marry or register. In the Netherlands, 700,000 couples (presumably mostly dif-ferent-sex couples) lived together outside marriage in 2003, about 17% of all couples. About half of those couples have a cohabitation contract. In other words, about 8.5% of Dutch couples (the vast majority of which are different-sex couples) opt for a cohabitation contract instead of marriage or registered partnership to legally organize their relationship. Judging from the same-sex couples I interviewed, cohabitation contracts are im-portant for getting mortgages and seeking benefits for cohabiting couples, which explains the surprisingly high rate of cohabitation agreements.

From the perspective of heterosexual couples, marriage is clearly the top choice for legally organizing a relationship, followed by cohabitation with and without private cohabitation agreements. Registered partner-ships occupy a distant fourth place. Like their heterosexual counterparts, gay and lesbian couples choose marriage when they decide to formalize their relationships, although so far more same-sex couples have opted to

simply cohabit without a formal legal status. Again, the similarities between same-sex and different-sex couples' attitudes toward marriage are
striking.

No other country provides the same effective referendum on marriage.
France and Belgium come closest, with statuses carved out for same-sex
couples that are also open to different-sex couples. Unfortunately, we
do not have statistics on different-sex couples who became "Pacséed" in
France or on legal cohabitants in Belgium. French law does not even allow the state to track or report the breakdown of PACS into same-sex and
different-sex partners.[30]

In the United States, roughly a quarter of gay and lesbian couples have a
choice of some kind of legal recognition at the state level. American same-
sex couples are most enthusiastic about marriage and statuses very close
to marriage in rights and responsibilities. As noted earlier, gay and lesbian
couples in Massachusetts have married at an impressive pace, with 37%
of couples marrying in the first year.[31] In contrast, only 12% of same-sex
couples entered civil unions in the first year their states (Vermont, New
Jersey, and Connecticut) offered that status, and only 10% entered domestic partnerships in the first year in states that offer that option (California,
Washington, New Jersey, Maine, and the District of Columbia). Another
view compares the proportion of couples that signed up in the first year
for statuses with all or almost all of the rights of marriage (mainly marriage and civil unions) to the proportion that signed up for statuses offering more limited rights. The marriage and near-marriage statuses attracted
21% of couples in year one, while the limited statuses attracted only 10%
of couples in the first year.

In California and New Jersey, older heterosexual couples are also allowed to register as domestic partners, and their actions confirm that most
couples prefer marriage.[32] Very few have taken advantage of this option.
Only 5% to 6% of registered domestic partners in California are different-
sex partners,[33] although at least one partner must be sixty-two or older to
register, limiting the eligible pool. Census 2000 data for California suggests
that this figure accounts for only about 6% of eligible different-sex couples
in that age group, leaving 94% or so unregistered and unmarried. In New
Jersey, only 90 of the 4,111 couples that registered as domestic partners
from July 2004 to May 2006 were different-sex couples.[34] Comparing that
figure to the estimated 3400 age-eligible different-sex unmarried couples in
New Jersey gives a very low take-up rate of 2.7%. Elsewhere in the United
States, another study found that only about 10% of partners registering in

domestic partner registries in college towns were different-sex couples,[35] which also implies a very low level of interest among different-sex couples in something other than marriage.

Interestingly, these small numbers of registration contrast sharply with the experience of U.S. employers that offer benefits to domestic partners. Different-sex partners far outnumber same-sex partners in those situations,[36] although they are a tiny minority in registration systems. Perhaps either the symbolism of these alternative statuses is less meaningful for different-sex couples that can marry when they want full legal and social recognition as a couple, or perhaps the obligations of registration are less desirable and the benefits less tempting for different-sex couples.

Overall, the experience to date with alternative legal statuses for couples in Europe and the United States suggests several conclusions:

- Same-sex couples want their relationships to be legally recognized and prefer the option closest to marriage.
- Both same-sex couples and different-sex couples prefer marriage over other legal forms.
- Very few unmarried different-sex couples take advantage of alternative legal recognition statuses.

As in the preceding chapter, the picture of same-sex couples' decision to marry that emerges here is one of familiarity, not of something radically new. Although the percentage of gay couples choosing to marry in the Netherlands and the United States seems low to some observers, the rates look high to me given the historical and social circumstances. Just like heterosexual couples, Dutch gay couples put marriage at the top of a range of choices for organizing and formalizing their relationships, and we see some evidence that the same thing is happening in the United States. A look across a broader range of countries provides some evidence that gay couples might even be bucking the heterosexual trend of increasing skepticism about marriage.

The next chapter explores more directly the possible links between the marriage choices of gay couples and the decisions about marriage made by heterosexual couples.

4

The Impact of Gay Marriage on Heterosexuals

Dutch winters are notorious for being gloomy, with low gray clouds press-ing down from the sky. But January 1, 1998, was a happy winter day for same-sex couples in the Netherlands, who could finally register their partnerships and receive almost all of the rights and responsibilities of marriage. A little more than three years later, the Dutch parliament had opened up full-fledged marriage to same-sex couples. Did the low Dutch skies drop a bit in response to giving gay couples access to a marriage?

Letting gay and lesbian people marry someone of the same sex obvi-ously changes the gender combinations in married couples by opening up the rules about who may marry whom. In the two preceding chapters, I showed that same-sex couples approach the existing institution of mar-riage carefully as they consider whether to marry, displaying respect for the institution's social power and for its potential personal influence. What would happen to the institution of marriage if same-sex couples were al-lowed to marry everywhere? Some have argued that one good reason to slow down or stop the movement toward marriage equality is the possibil-ity that this change will have a long-lasting negative influence on different-sex couples' decisions about marrying or on the institution of marriage. In other words, some people fear changes in what marriage means in a larger cultural sense. In particular, they worry that opening up marriage poses a threat to children by diminishing heterosexual couples' desire to marry, thereby reducing parents' commitment and attention to childrearing.

One of the most influential writers promoting this view in the United States is the conservative commentator Stanley Kurtz, whose argument is rooted in the assumption that the primary purpose of marriage is to have children. He points to the drop-off in marriage rates over time, the rise in heterosexual cohabitation without marriage, and the rapid increase in nonmarital births in Scandinavian countries and in the Netherlands, the countries that first allowed same-sex couples to register as partners, to bolster his claim that marriage and parenthood have become further sepa-rated in the minds of heterosexual people as a result of gay marriage. He concludes that "gay marriage is both an effect and a cause of the increasing separation between marriage and parenthood" because it accelerates the separation process that had already begun as a result of other causes.[1] His conclusion about the long-term consequence of giving marriage rights to same-sex couples is potentially devastating: "Marriage itself has almost entirely disappeared"; "Marriage has become a minority phenomenon"; "We are witnessing no less than the end of marriage itself in Scandinavia."[2] Kurtz warns that this trend is disastrous for children because of higher rates of break-up among cohabitors and worse outcomes for children raised by unmarried parents.

In many ways, Stanley Kurtz defined what came to be conventional wisdom among conservative opponents of marriage rights for gay couples. Kurtz is an avid reader of demographic research and has assembled a detailed argument based on demographic statistics and on his reading of cultural trends in Scandinavia and in the Netherlands. Over the past few years, I have jousted with Kurtz online and in print on whether the demographic trends truly line up with policy changes, as have other writers and scholars.[3] His perspective is an important one to consider, although I argue that his conclusions are terribly wrong.

Others have piled onto the Kurtz bandwagon, attesting to his influence. The Senate debate on the Federal Marriage Amendment in 2006 showcased charts displayed by several senators that illustrated variations on themes developed by Kurtz.[4] Researchers at the conservative Heritage Foundation argued that demographic data show that "same-sex marriage has not strengthened the family but may have accelerated its decline."[5] In 2004, a group of Dutch scholars who study law and other fields rather distantly related to family studies issued a "statement" that made an argument strikingly similar to that of Kurtz:

> In light of the intense debate elsewhere about the pros and cons of legalizing same-sex marriage it must be observed that there is as yet no definitive scientific evidence to suggest that the long campaign for the legalization of same-sex marriage contributed to these harmful trends. However, there are good reasons to believe that the decline in Dutch marriage may be connected to the successful public campaign for the opening of marriage to same-sex couples.[6]

The Dutch demographers and other social scientists I have spoken with do not agree with this view and tell me that this is a decidedly minority opinion among Dutch scholars. Nevertheless, this statement seems to add to the weight of opinion behind Kurtz's point.

With such a clear-cut assumption about the crucial connection between marriage and procreation—marriage should come first, then children—Kurtz and others can easily point to evidence that ideas about marriage have changed by identifying visible or important people who express a view that marriage is about love, commitment, or anything else—that is, *anything other than procreation*. They argue that the smoking gun in the same-sex marriage debate is a sharp change in the public understanding of marriage that emerged during the debate about rights for gay couples. The public debate in those countries, they argue, provided a highly visible launching pad for ideas about marriage from politicians, academics, clergy, and the media and that these ideas landed in the minds, homes, social institutions, and decisions of heterosexual people. If those potential opinion shapers described marriage as an institution rooted in anything other than procreation, then Kurtz accuses them of contributing to the demise of marriage.[7]

One response from historians and other social scientists is to note that the view of marriage promoted by Kurtz and company is a narrow and incomplete one. The historian Stephanie Coontz shows that marriage has served many other purposes for modern and past cultures beyond simple procreation.[8] She argues that marriage was mainly a way to link families into larger social units. Legal marriage formalized property arrangements that cemented these links. Not until recently did marriage become more about love than about property and in-laws. In the twentieth century, as people have lived longer and spent less of their coupled lives raising children and as economic forces have made both spouses' paid labor increasingly essential, family life and family law have also adapted.

Another possible response is to point to recent demographic research showing that same-sex couples themselves are more involved with procreation than some would expect. In the United States, about one-third of lesbian couples are raising children, and almost one in five gay male couples is raising children.[9] At least 9% of Dutch couples are raising children, while one in six Danish registered partner couples have children.[10] Although we do not know how many of those children were born into the same-sex relationship, clearly same-sex couples are involved in the reproduction of new human beings at some stage of the childrearing process. In chapter 3, we saw that some Dutch same-sex couples married because they were planning to have children, and Eskridge and Spedale report a similar connection for some Danish same-sex couples who registered as partners. In chapter 5, I explore in more detail the possibility that same-sex couples have unorthodox ideas about marriage that might lead to a larger cultural shift, but here I just note that this conservative view of marriage expressed by Kurtz et al. assumes that *heterosexual* people are the only ones who have the capacity to reproduce, when in fact statistics show otherwise, given the variety of ways children can be conceived or raised.

However, the most direct way to respond to the challenge of those who see the "experiment" with same-sex marriage in Europe as a disaster is to look more closely at the evidence on what heterosexuals do with respect to marrying and having children. What has happened to the marriage decisions of heterosexual couples in European countries when they share marriage or marriage-like rights with same-sex couples? Since we see the current meaning of the institution of marriage in both marriage behavior and ideas about marriage, I look at both what people think and what they do about marriage. I use the same data that Kurtz uses (along with some additional sources) but apply some simple but powerful standards to assess Kurtz's argument:

1. Do the trends in family behavior (marriage, divorce, cohabitation and non-marital births) line up with the timing of policies allowing partnership or marriage for gay couples?
2. Do the countries with partnership recognition look different from those without partnership rights for same-sex couples?
3. Is there a logical connection between the policy debate and heterosexual behavior and attitudes toward marriage?

All evidence points to a response of "no" to each question. As a result, my conclusions about the trends and their connection to the issue of marriage rights for gay couples are quite different: what heterosexuals do and think suggests that marriage is still a relevant institution in the lives of most heterosexuals, even though it looks quite different from marriage several decades ago and even though gay couples get similar or identical marriage rights.

Tracking Trends in Marriage and Divorce

Let's start with the basics. One way to assess changes in the meaning of marriage for heterosexuals is to ask whether their willingness to marry or their desire to divorce changed once same-sex couples got partnership or marriage rights. These individual decisions among heterosexuals might have changed if the cultural context for defining marriage or encouraging people to marry changed in some significant way.

We would not necessarily expect such changes to happen quickly, though. Cultures do not change overnight, so it makes the most sense to look at the countries with the longest history of giving rights to same-sex couples. The first five such countries were Denmark, in 1989; Norway, in 1993; Sweden, in 1994; Iceland, in 1996; and the Netherlands, in 1998 (registered partnership) and 2001 (marriage). In those countries, same-sex couples have had rights long enough to allow negative heterosexual behaviors to emerge.

In fact, the numbers do not show any obvious change in marriage behavior once gay couples got partnership or marriage rights. Figure 4.1 tracks the annual number of marriages per thousand residents since 1960 for each of those countries, along with rates for the United States for comparison purposes. The first thing to notice is that the highest marriage rates came in the late 1960s or early 1970s for these countries, followed by a decade or more of falling marriage rates, meaning that marriages became less common. A second oddity is the spike in Sweden's marriage rate, which skyrocketed in 1989 because of a change in the law that abolished widow pensions for couples not married by the end of 1989—a reminder that policy can matter sometimes in marriage decisions, although in the Swedish case the policy change that created such a striking incentive for marriage was a one-time occurrence.[11]

Although the heated rhetoric of the marriage debate might lead one to expect a similar sharp change when same-sex couples can marry or register, clearly we do not see such a dramatic outcome. The big question here is what happened to marriage after same-sex couples received rights. In Denmark, the lowest marriage rates came in the early 1980s, and by 1989—the year of Denmark's pioneering decision to give same-sex couples the right to register their partnerships—the marriage rate had risen to six marriages per one thousand residents. Since that year, the marriage rate has risen and held fairly steady at about seven marriages per thousand residents, the highest marriage rates in the past three decades. The same pattern occurred in Norway and Sweden. The marriage rates reached their historic low points about the time that same-sex couples got their rights, and after that point marriage rates rose. Iceland looks slightly different, with an increase in the marriage rate followed by a return to the level that prevailed before same-sex couples had the right to register.

Figure 4.1
Marriage Rate Comparison

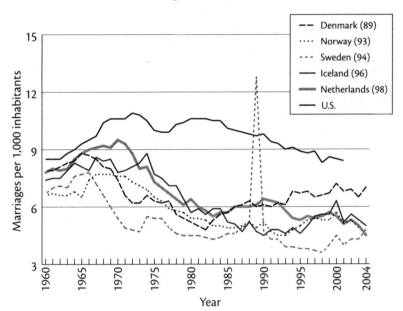

Some writers, such as the legal scholar William Eskridge, point to the rising recent marriage rates in some countries, especially Denmark, as evidence that giving gay couples rights might have actually resuscitated marriage among heterosexuals.[12] A look at the figure should also inject a note of caution into this interpretation, since the increase in the Danish marriage rates was also under way before that country created registered partnerships.

Stanley Kurtz argues that marriage rates are not a good measure, since many marriages are remarriages, not first marriages. The available data do not allow much exploration of this issue. However, data from Sweden suggests that the proportion of first-time marriages has held steady since the late 1970s at about two-thirds of marriages, although the number of first-time marriages per thousand residents of Sweden did not level off until after 1990 because of the odd spike in marriages related to the change in pension policy in 1989. Since 1986, 70% to 75% of Norwegian marriages are between two people who have never married.[13] So the increase in the Swedish and Norwegian marriage rate over the past several years includes a healthy share of first marriages, not just remarriages.

Only the Netherlands shows a somewhat different trend in marriage rates, with a fairly steady decrease since the early 1970s that continued unchanged after same-sex couples were given marriage rights, in 1998. Local Dutch demographers told me that they do not blame the changing recognition of same-sex couples for the drop in marriage, though. Jan Latten argues that the dip since 2001 is the result of a recession-induced cutback on weddings, and Joop Garssen points out that marriages now follow births and that births fell during the recession.[14] A long-term perspective shows that recent Dutch figures reflect mainly a longer-term drop in marriages, whatever the reasons for short-term fluctuations.

One big change in family behavior that is particularly noticeable in Europe is that more heterosexual couples live together without getting married. Marriage rates have declined over the past few decades at least partly because couples are more likely to cohabit. Unfortunately, it is harder to keep track of these less formal family arrangements than it is to track marriage and divorce, but a few countries provide data that give us an idea of the change. In Denmark in 1994, 21.0% of different-sex couples were unmarried; by 2004, 22.1% of couples were unmarried, a very small change. In Iceland, 20% of couples were living together without being married in 2004, about the same percentage as in 1997. The Dutch context was changing more quickly, though. In 1995, 13.1% of different-sex couples were unmarried, and this figure rose to 17.5% in 2004.[15] Some of these cohabiting couples eventually marry, especially when they have children, but not all do. Although we do not have a long series of cohabitation rates to compare for the periods before and after these countries gave rights to same-sex couples, my cross-country comparisons, presented in chapter 9, show that the increase in cohabitation rates for countries that recognize same-sex partners predates the legal change.

Divorce rates also showed little change after same-sex couples began registering, providing no evidence of harm to heterosexual marriage. Figure 4.2 presents "crude divorce rates," or the number of divorces per thousand residents. Divorce rates have not changed much at all in Scandinavian countries or in the Netherlands over the past two decades. Interestingly, Danish demographers have even found that marriages in the early 1990s appear to have been more stable than those in the 1980s, since the proportion of marriages that ended in divorce within five years decreased.[16]

Because some demographic studies have shown that cohabiting couples are more likely to break up than married couples are to divorce,[17] Stanley Kurtz argues that the rise of cohabitation means that the divorce rate

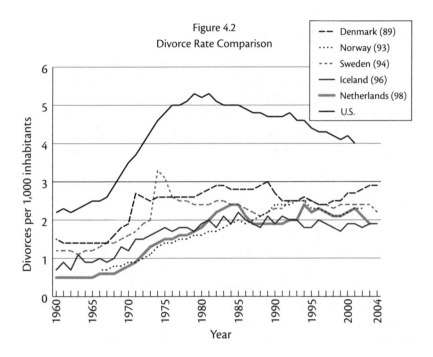

Figure 4.2
Divorce Rate Comparison

understates the full extent of the dissolution of relationships. As a result, we might miss increasing instability in relationships with this measure, which is an important caveat when looking at divorce rates.

Given the scarcity of annual data on cohabitors, it is hard to examine that claim closely. We have one example from Iceland, however, which actually collects and publishes the number of dissolutions of cohabiting couples along with the divorce rate. By combining divorces of married couples and dissolutions of cohabiting couples, we can get a total break-up rate for couples in Iceland. From 1991 to 1996, when registered partnerships began, the yearly break-up rate for couples averaged 4.6 per thousand Icelanders. From 1997 to 2004, the average was 4.7 per thousand couples—not a meaningful difference. Also, a recent study by Michael Svarer finds that couples who live together before marriage in Sweden are now *less* likely to divorce if they marry than if they go straight into marriage.[18] The old assumptions about the stability of cohabiting heterosexual relationships are changing in Scandinavia, increasing doubts about the harm that cohabitation might inflict on European children, regardless of the relationship between trends in cohabitation and marriage rights for gay couples.

Concerns About Children

Setting aside the impact of marriage and divorce on the well-being of adults, most critics of giving gay couples the right to marry worry most about the risks for children. The two big concerns that have emerged relate to the possibility that couples with children will be more likely to divorce if they marry—an outcome that has not materialized in the European countries with partnership recognition—or that the parents will never marry to begin with.

The main measure that critics like Stanley Kurtz point to as evidence of the decline of marriage is the proportion of births to unmarried women, or the nonmarital birth rate. The Scandinavian countries have had high and rising rates of nonmarital births since the 1970s, with roughly half of all babies born to unmarried mothers. Figure 4.3 presents nonmarital birth rates over time for Denmark, Norway, and the Netherlands. In this case, one chart is worth at least a few hundred words. Clearly, the trends were already in place long before these countries gave same-sex couples partnership or marriage rights beginning in 1989, as was true for changes in marriage and divorce. Those rights cannot logically be blamed for high nonmarital birth rates that already existed.

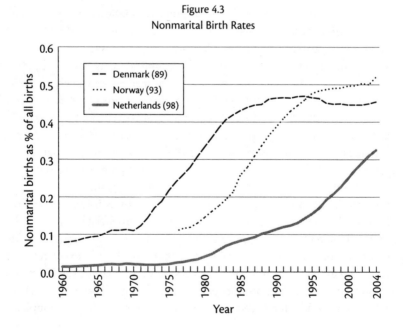

Figure 4.3
Nonmarital Birth Rates

But Kurtz also makes the subtler claim that registered partnerships "*further* undermined the institution" (italics in the original) and that "gay marriage has widened the separation" between marriage and parenthood.[19] In other words, things were already bad, but gay marriage made them worse. However, this argument does not hold up, either, because the nonmarital birth rate began rising in Scandinavian countries in the 1970s, long before any legal recognition of same-sex couples took place, and it has actually slowed down in Scandinavia in recent years.[20]

For example, from 1970 to 1980, a full decade before Denmark adopted its partner registration law, in 1989, the Danish nonmarital birth rate tripled, rising from 11% to 33%. It rose again in the following decade, but by a much smaller amount, to 46% in 1990, before ending its climb. After passage of its partnership law in 1989, Denmark's nonmarital birth rate did not increase at all.[21] In fact, the rate actually decreased somewhat after that date.

Norway's big surge in nonmarital births also occurred well before the passage of its registered partnership law in 1993. In the 1980s, the percentage of births to unmarried parents rose from 16% to 39%.[22] In the first half of the 1990s, the nonmarital birth rate rose more slowly, leveling off at 50% in the mid-1990s.

As I discuss later in this chapter, a focus on the mother's marital status at birth gives a misleading view of the relationship between marriage and parenthood in these countries, since most babies born to an unmarried mother go home to both parents. For example, 91% of Dutch families with children are headed by a couple, either married or unmarried. Also, most of these couples marry when they start having children.

Kurtz claims, though, that the main impact of partner registration laws in Norway was to discourage couples from marrying after the birth of their first child. But the numbers for second, third, and later babies born to unmarried parents tell the same story as the overall trend. In 1985, 10% of second and later babies had unmarried parents, a number that had already tripled to 31% by 1993, when Norway passed its registered partnership law.[23] Over the next ten years, from 1994 to 2003, that figure rose only to 41%, where it appears to have leveled off. The percentage of first births to unmarried parents did not increase at all from 1994 to 2003. If the partnership law had further discouraged parents from marrying even after their first child, as Kurtz has argued, then these rates should have increased faster after 1993, but in fact the rate of increase slowed down considerably (for second and later births) or stopped completely (for first births).

In an attempt to salvage his argument for the Scandinavian countries, Kurtz claims that the leveling off of the nonmarital birth rate is necessary as the shifting culture runs into "the final and toughest pockets of cultural support for marriage."[24] He has no concrete evidence for this, however. He draws heavily on a theory of stages of cohabitation developed by the demographer Kathleen Kiernan, and he simply asserts that Norway is bursting through to the final stages. Mainly he points to nonmarital birth rates that are higher in liberal northern counties in Norway than in more conservative southern counties as further evidence of the correlation between acceptance of gay couples and nonmarital births. The more conservative counties supposedly constituted the cultural wall that once slowed down the rate of nonmarital births but is now crumbling under the onslaught of gay marriage, bringing rising rates of nonmarital births in those counties.

At the risk of sounding repetitive, however, a look at the Norwegian county data shows that the increase in the numbers of babies born to unmarried parents in more conservative counties would have occurred even if gay couples had gotten no rights whatsoever. Figure 4.4 presents nonmarital birth rates for five representative counties going back to 1958, along with more recent annual data. Several now familiar points pop out of the trends for all counties over time:

- First, some counties have always had higher or lower than average nonmarital birth rates, and the relative rankings across county have not changed much for fifty years.
- Second, the big growth in nonmarital births occurred between 1978 and 1988 in every county in Norway. Growth continued in the next decade, the decade in which Norway granted the right of registered partnerships to gay couples (1994). Since then, the trends are similar, with a flattening out in recent years in almost all counties, and, with the possible exception of one county (Aust-Agder), the pace of change has slowed tremendously. If we project the 2002-2005 data into the future, we find nothing like the rate of growth seen in the two prior decades.
- Third, several counties in the south still have rates below 50%, which seems to be a milestone for Kurtz. Any conservative counties that have passed over Kurtz's imaginary threshold were well on their way before 1994, as were the other Norwegian counties that started catching up with their fellow counties.

These patterns simply do not support Kurtz's hypothesis that gay partnerships had different effects across conservative and liberal counties in Norway. Whether the counties started off with relatively high rates or low rates, the later patterns were the same, with the rapid increase occurring well before the registered partnership law was passed and a slowing down since.

The Netherlands shows a slightly different pattern from the Scandinavian countries, but here, too, I can see no correlation between recognition of same-sex partnerships and rising rates of nonmarital births, much less a causal link. Despite high rates of cohabitation, the Dutch have traditionally been much less likely than Scandinavians to have babies before marriage, with fewer than one in ten births occurring to unmarried parents before 1988.[25] Kurtz argues that legal recognition for same-sex couples kicked Holland into the Scandinavian league with respect to nonmarital parenting.[26] As Figure 4.3 shows, the Dutch nonmarital birth rate has been rising steadily since the 1980s, and sometime in the early 1990s the nonmarital birth rate started increasing at a somewhat faster rate. But that acceleration was clear by 1995, well before the Netherlands implemented registered partnerships in 1998, and gave same-sex couples the right to marry in 2001. The trends are also virtually identical for first births and for second and later births.

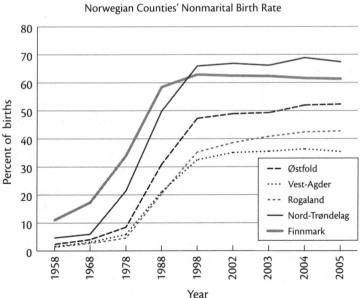

Figure 4.4
Norwegian Counties' Nonmarital Birth Rate

Perhaps because his argument for the Scandinavian countries is so weak, Kurtz has focused his attention on timing of demographic and policy changes: "[I]ntroducing gay marriage to a country with low out-of-wedlock births could kick off a much more rapid rise in the rate. That is exactly what has happened in the Netherlands."[27] However, the timing argument does not work in this case, either. If we place a ruler alongside the data from 1984 to 1994, we see a steady increase in the nonmarital birth rate. The rates after 1995 or 1996 require that we make the ruler's angle a little bit steeper to track the later points, suggesting that rates are rising faster. (Regressions confirm that things changed around 1995.) Since in any given year about three-quarters of babies born were conceived in the prior year, most of these "extra" babies born to unmarried mothers (actually, mostly to two cohabiting parents who will eventually marry) were conceived in 1994 and 1995, or years before the parliament passed registered partnerships in 1997.

Overall, the most basic elements of the sky-is-falling argument fail these simple tests of plausibility. The timing in measured trends in heterosexual behavior does not line up with the timing of changes in policies that recognized same-sex couples' right to marry or to register a partnership. The trends were well established in the 1970s and 1980s, and no adverse changes have occurred since countries recognized rights for same-sex couples: marriage rates are up, divorce rates are down, and (mostly) nonmarital birth rates are not rising in comparison to rates for the years before gay couples could register. In the Netherlands, nonmarital birth rates continue to rise, but the recent trend was clear years before gay couples could register as partners or marry.

For one last check for a connection between same-sex partnership laws and nonmarital births, I compared trends of those countries that had a partner registration law by 2000 with those that did not. If legal recognition of gay partnerships in fact leads to an increase in nonmarital births, then we should see a bigger increase in such births in countries with those laws than in countries without them. That outcome did not happen. In fact, during the 1990s, the eight countries that recognized registered partners at some point in that decade saw an increase in the average nonmarital birth rate from 36% in 1991 to 44% in 2000, for an eight-percentage-point increase,[28] while in the EU countries (plus Switzerland) that did not recognize registered partners, the average rate rose from 15% to 23%, also an eight–percentage-point increase. In other words, the average change in rates was exactly the same in countries that adopted partner registration laws and in those that did not, demonstrating that partner registration laws do not lead to greater increases in nonmarital birth rates.

Even if we distinguish two kinds of countries—separating out those, like the Netherlands, that have traditionally lower nonmarital birth rates from those, like Norway, that have traditionally high rates—we see no connection between partnership recognition and an increase in nonmarital births. The same rapid rise in nonmarital births in the Netherlands (from 12% in 1990 to 29% in 2002) also occurred in other European countries that initially had low nonmarital birth rates. For example, during the 1990s, nonmarital birth rates rose in Ireland (from 17% in 1990 to 31% in 2002), Luxembourg (from 12% to 23%), Hungary (from 14% to 32%), Lithuania (from 7% to 28%), Slovakia (from 9% to 22%), and several other eastern European countries—all countries that do not (or did not until after 2000) allow same-sex couples to marry or register.

Kurtz protests that economic modernization, sexual liberalization, and the lack of access to birth control have combined to raise nonmarital births in those comparison countries but that these factors are not relevant for explaining changes in the Netherlands in the 1990s. Furthermore, he argues that the usual explanations for rising cohabitation rates and nonmarital birth rates, such as the availability of abortion, the entrance of women into the work force, a decline in religiosity, the growth of welfare programs, legal recognition of cohabiting couples, and increasing individualism, do not match up with the timing of the Netherlands' accelerating rate of nonmarital births. Since those usual suspects cannot take the blame for the mid-1990s surge in nonmarital births, he argues, gay marriage is the only other logical explanation.

Argument by process of elimination is not persuasive in this case, however. The complex interplay of cultural forces that has contributed to changes in marriage behavior is not likely to produce a tidy connection in time between cultural change and change in behavior. Controlling for all of these possible causes to dismiss some explanations and to isolate others—the usual social science approach—is not possible with such a small number of countries to compare. All we know is what we see, which is that the Netherlands appears to be following the Scandinavian S-shaped pattern a decade or so later, as are some other countries. Perhaps in time we'll see the Dutch nonmarital birth rate flatten out, too. The bottom line, though, is that the alleged changes in heterosexual behavior in the Netherlands predate the granting of registered partnership rights to same-sex couples.

The detailed debates over the trends are exciting for those of us who want to understand the numbers, but the debate can obscure some of the implications. What do these numbers mean for the well-being of children in those countries, anyway? As I mentioned earlier, the mother's marital status is not a good marker of the strength of children's families in Scandinavia and the Netherlands, for several reasons:

- *Most unmarried mothers who give birth in these countries are living with the father of their children.* For instance, Statistics Norway reports that 48% of Norwegian babies were born to married parents in 2005, and another 42% were born to unmarried cohabiting parents. Statistics Denmark reports that 92% of Danish babies born in 2005 lived with their married or cohabiting parents in 2006, with most (57%) living with married parents. (Statistics Denmark reports that 46% of babies born in 2006 had an unmarried mother, so clearly some married over the course of the year.)
- *Most cohabiting heterosexual couples marry after they start having children.*[29] In Sweden, for example, 70% of cohabiters marry after the birth of the first child, most of them within five years. In the Netherlands, while 30% of children are born outside marriage, only 21% of children under age one live with unmarried parents, and by age five, only 11% live with unmarried parents.[30] In other words, by the time the child is five, two-thirds of unmarried parents have married.
- *The majority of families with children in Scandinavia and in the Netherlands are still headed by married parents.* In 2000, 78% of Danish couples with children were married couples.[31] If we also include single-parent families in the denominator, almost two-thirds of families with children were headed by a married couple. In Norway, 77% of couples with children are married, and 61% of all families with children are headed by married parents.[32] And 79% of Dutch families with children under 17 include married couples.[33] Although the proportion of married couples with children fell in the 1980s or early 1990s in these countries, the drop obviously predates the changes in partnership laws, as Figure 4.5 summarizes. By comparison, 72% of families with children are headed by married couples in the United States.[34] Figure 4.5 shows the proportion of childrearing couples that are married, documenting a decline over time but still suggesting fairly high rates along with a recent leveling off in Denmark.

- *Cohabiting parents who later marry form stable families.* Research shows that unmarried Scandinavian cohabiters' unions are more likely to dissolve than are marriages, as noted earlier, even when the couple has children, although that pattern appears to be changing toward greater stability. But when cohabiting parents marry in Scandinavian countries—as most eventually do—they are not more likely to divorce than are couples who were married when their children were born.[35]

- *Children in Scandinavian countries still spend most of their lives with their parents living together.*[36] In fact, they spend more time living with both parents than kids in the United States do. Gunnar Andersson has calculated how much time the average child spent living with both parents in the same household in the 1980s,[37] the most recent period that allows comparisons across countries.[38] Of the countries he examined, the lowest average was found in the United States, where the time spent with both parents was 67%. The highest was in Italy, where it was 97%. In Sweden, the average was 81%; in Norway, it was 89%; and in Finland, it was 88%. In other words, combining the time that parents are cohabiting and married demonstrates that children are spending the vast majority of their young lives with their parents in the Scandinavian countries.

- *Other policies in these countries appear to be more important for influencing the well-being of children.* If these children are being hurt by higher rates of cohabitation in Scandinavia, the harm is not evident in standard measures of child well-being. Using Sweden as an example, we see that youth suicide rates, homicide deaths, and childhood injury deaths are lower for young people in Sweden than in the United States. Test scores and immunization rates are higher in Sweden than in the United States.[39]

Marriage is not dead in Scandinavia and the Netherlands, so marriage or partnership rights for same-sex couples cannot have killed it. Contrary to some claims in the media, marriage and parenthood are still connected in Scandinavia and the Netherlands, although in a different order than in earlier times. Changes that have occurred in the relationship between marriage and parenthood were already well under way before same-sex couples got rights, though. Stanley Kurtz and I agree that this cultural change probably facilitated the opening up of marriage to gay and lesbian couples, but that does not mean that this opening up has itself changed heterosexual behavior.

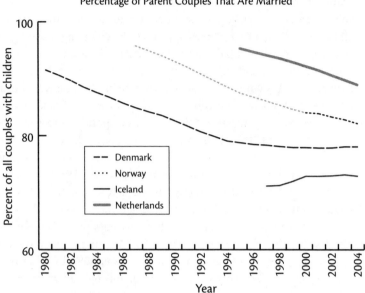

Figure 4.5
Percentage of Parent Couples That Are Married

The Missing Logical Link

The final problem with the sky-is-falling argument concerns the actual mechanism that links marriage rights for same-sex couples to changes in heterosexual behavior. The five Dutch scholars who criticized gay marriage, along with Kurtz, propose that the political debate itself was the main culprit that led to the redefinition of marriage in the minds of the larger population. The debates about same-sex couples have been widely covered in the news media wherever the issue has been considered seriously. In this view, gay organizations and their political and cultural allies who favor opening marriage to same-sex couples contribute to widening the already noticeable gap between marriage and procreation created by increasing access to contraception, individualization, and economic freedom for women.

These critics overexplain cultural change, however. First of all, we have no way of knowing the actual—not hypothetical—impact of a wide variety of conflicting statements about marriage that get broadcast throughout the news media and other cultural institutions. Did Dutch twenty-somethings hear their members of parliament proclaim that marriage is about love (not procreation) and then decide to have babies without marrying? Did young Norwegians have a second child before marrying because favorable media treatment of gay couples meant that marriage and procreation are not linked? Aside from the many issues around the timing of changes that I've already explored, it's clear that different influences send conflicting messages about the seriousness and purpose of marriage.

In the United States context, imagine a time when same-sex couples have the right to marry. Someone is bound to point to some apparent change in marriage-related behavior in the United States that seemed to start around 2003 and to blame it on the debate about same-sex marriage that surrounded events in Massachusetts and San Francisco. They'll mention gay characters on TV shows. They'll quote Congressman Barney Frank and other prominent politicians speaking on C-SPAN about the need to give same-sex couples equal marriage rights. They'll find some academics who predict that giving gay couples marriage rights will not have a harmful effect on heterosexual marriages, and they're sure to find a few gay radicals who would like to abolish marriage altogether.

What they probably won't mention are Britney Spears's momentary marriage or television shows like *The Bachelor* or *Who Wants to Marry a Multimillionaire*—all cultural events that are likely to be far more influential than what a relative handful of same-sex couples might or might not represent. Picking out a few cultural influences in any country that allegedly "explain" a subtle demographic change that started years earlier while ignoring the rest of what went on at that time is not a convincing causal argument, especially when there is no clear behavioral evidence that something big changed.

Oddly enough, focusing on the cultural debate suggests that the political outcome itself would not even matter. Even when gay couples lose votes or court decisions, as Dutch gay marriage advocates did in the early 1990s, people like Kurtz argue that gays still exert the same cultural pressure as long as they have some prominent allies, a visible media campaign, and some minor public victories.[40] If the debates are all that matter, though, then the cat is out of the bag in the United States as well, and those of us involved in the debate about the impact of gay marriage can all go home.

William Eskridge and Darren Spedale point out another big logical flaw in efforts to link gay marriage rights to heterosexual behavior. They argue that same-sex partnership policies are far weaker signals of the separation of marriage and procreation than are childless different-sex marriages, especially since the earliest laws in the Scandinavian countries actually clearly distinguished partnerships from marriage and procreation by not allowing partners to adopt children.[41] The actual factors behind the decline in marriage, the two legal scholars argue, relate to an expansion of choices for couples that developed through the liberalization of laws related to divorce, sexuality, cohabitation, and contraception.[42] All of those changes had expanded heterosexual couples' options and changed their choices long before countries opened eligibility to marriage or a marriage-like status to gay couples. The idea that conservatives could shore up marriage by maintaining a restriction on eligibility—keeping same-sex couples out—rather than by reversing the legal liberalization of marriage and related laws strikes Eskridge and Spedale (and myself) as completely illogical.

Looking for Cultural Change in What People Think About Marriage

Setting aside the illogic of the specific claims by Kurtz and company, it is still possible that looking at individual decisions or political debates might not give us the whole story about cultural changes rooted in changing policies toward same-sex couples. As I noted earlier, the research problem is that we can easily see potential markers of cultural change, like changes in media coverage or politicians' opinions, but usually we see too many of them. Out of the swirl of conflicting and contradictory messages that might appear about marriage, which ones will stick? Which ones are the harbingers of future change at an individual level?

One way to predict the future is to look at what people think about marriage in survey data on attitudes or beliefs about marriage. The World Values Survey has asked thousands of people in selected countries about whether they agree that "marriage is an outdated institution." By comparing what people say at different points in time, we can ask whether the opinions of people in countries with registered partner laws differ from those of people in countries without such laws. A cultural change that makes marriage seem less attractive or relevant to people's lives should show up in their answers to this question.

The World Values Survey has been conducted four times. The 1990 and 1999 surveys nicely bracket the introduction of registered partnership laws in Europe. If we include Denmark, even though technically its law was passed in 1989, six countries (Belgium, Denmark, France, Iceland, the Netherlands, and Sweden) passed such laws between 1990 and 1999

Figure 4.6

Prevalence of Belief That Marriage Is Outdated, by Country in 1990 and 1999

Marriage outdated	1990 % Agree	1999 % Agree	Change
First Partnership Wave			
France	29.1%	34.8%	5.6%
Netherlands	21.1%	25.3%	4.2%
Denmark	18.0%	15.0%	-3.0%
Belgium	23.2%	30.9%	7.7%
Sweden	14.1%	20.2%	6.2%
Iceland	6.3%	8.3%	2.0%
Average			3.8%
Second Partnership Wave			
Germany	14.6%	20.2%	5.6%
United Kingdom	17.8%	27.2%	9.5%
Spain	16.0%	20.9%	5.0%
Canada	12.4%	22.9%	10.5%
Finland	12.5%	19.1%	6.5%
Czech	10.5%	10.4%	-0.2%
Average			6.1%
No Partnership			
Italy	14.1%	17.0%	2.9%
Ireland	9.9%	20.5%	10.7%
Hungary	11.4%	16.2%	4.8%
Poland	7.5%	9.1%	1.6%
Slovenia	17.6%	27.4%	9.8%
Bulgaria	10.5%	17.1%	6.6%
Romania	8.6%	12.5%	3.9%
Portugal	21.9%	24.6%	2.7%
Austria	11.9%	19.0%	7.0%
Russia	14.5%	20.6%	6.1%
Slovakia	8.6%	11.5%	2.9%
Average			5.4%
United States	8.0%	10.0%	2.0%
Turkey	11.3%	8.5%	-2.8%
Japan	7.0%	10.4%	3.4%
Mexico	16.9%	19.8%	2.9%
Average			1.4%
Average all nonpartnership countries			4.8%
Average all nonpartnerhip countries (European)			5.3%

and were surveyed in both years. (Recall that the Netherlands passed its partnership law in 1998, three years before the Dutch opened marriage to same-sex couples.) Sixteen other European countries were surveyed in both years but did not pass partnership laws. Just for comparison purposes, I also analyzed data from the United States, Turkey, Japan, and Mexico.

Figure 4.6 shows how many people in these twenty-six countries agree that marriage is outdated.[43] Maybe the most surprising thing to notice is how few agree, given the obvious changes in marriage behavior discussed earlier. The French are the biggest marriage skeptics, according to this survey. In 1990, 29.1% of the French agreed that marriage was outdated. The other thing to note in Figure 4.6 is that the proportion of people agreeing that marriage is outdated has been rising over time in most countries.[44] In 1999, 34.8% of French people agreed, suggesting that 5.7% of French people had changed their opinion about marriage's current relevance since 1990.

If giving rights to same-sex couples undermines the relevance and attractiveness of marriage, then the proportion of respondents who see marriage as outdated should *increase more* in countries with such laws than in countries without them. The first block of countries in Figure 4.6 lists those with partnership laws. In those six countries, the proportion that believed marriage was outdated rose by 3.8 percentage points on average. The countries without partnerships saw a faster rise in the proportion of those who saw marriage as outdated, though. The average change within that group of countries was 5.3 percentage points between 1990 and 1999. Beliefs about marriage changed faster in the countries without registered partnership laws. In other words, the belief that marriage is outdated was becoming relatively *less* common in countries that recognized same-sex partners than in other European countries that did not. This finding contradicts the prediction that recognizing same-sex couples will somehow undermine marriage in the minds of heterosexual people.

As a check on this simple comparison, I also used statistical procedures designed to take into account other factors that predict opinions about marriage. Because questions included in each country's survey varied from year to year and from country to country, I was able to adjust for a limited set of individual characteristics: age, frequent attendance at religious services (at least once a month), sex, and marital status, along with the country of each respondent. Women, religious people, married people, and older people tend to disagree that marriage is outdated more often than men, infrequent church-goers, currently unmarried people, and young people. On average, people surveyed in 1999 were more likely to agree that marriage is outdated than people surveyed in 1990, and people in registered partnership countries were more likely to agree in 1999 than people not in partnership countries. Even after taking those factors into account, though, agreement in the registered partnership countries rose significantly less between 1990 and 1999 than in the nonpartnership countries.

Another revealing angle on these surveys comes from focusing on the countries in the survey that passed partnership or same-sex marriage laws after 1999. Those six "second-wave" countries (Germany, the United Kingdom, Spain, Canada, Finland, and the Czech Republic) were different both from the first wave of partnership countries and the countries that have still not passed such laws. Opinions about marriage held by people living in the second-wave countries changed much more than opinions in either the first-wave countries or the no-partnership-yet countries. On average, 6.1% more people living in the second-wave countries said that marriage was outdated in 1999 than in 1990. That change was much bigger than in the first-wave countries (3.8% more residents) and the not-yet countries (5.4% more residents). Perhaps the increasing numbers of people who viewed marriage as outdated and old-fashioned were also more likely to support proposals giving partnership or marriage rights to same-sex couples. This possibility links beliefs as a cause of later policy change, though, rather than suggesting that the change in beliefs was an effect of policy changes.

Overall, whether we look at marriage behavior or marriage beliefs, none of the data convincingly link the recognition of same-sex partners to either fewer marriages or a declining belief in the current relevance of marriage. The findings from survey data, demographic trends, and logical analysis in this chapter all fail to support the idea that policy change led to cultural change in the meaning of marriage. In chapter 9, I come back to the possibility of a political link between changes in marriage behavior and beliefs and openness to same-sex couples' demand for recognition. But that is a very different kind of link from the sky-is-falling claim of same-sex marriage critics in the United States and other countries.

5

Something Borrowed

Trying Marriage On

After Rachel and Marianne made the decision to marry, they invited Rachel's mother, Judith, to lunch at a restaurant to give her the news about their plans. According to Rachel, Judith's first reaction was not delight. "Nah. . . nah. . . nah. What should I tell my friends, my girlfriends?" Judith exclaimed. "And if I say my daughter is getting married, and they all ask, 'What does her husband do?' Then I have to say it's a woman. Well, what should I say?" she demanded to know in dismay. Judith had long accepted Rachel's relationship with Marianne but was not happy about the plan to marry and thought marriage unnecessary.

But, according to Rachel, that night Judith called a friend and hesitantly confided, "Well, guess what happened today. My daughter said she is going to marry." And the friend said, "Oh, well, that's amazing! Congratulations!" Then she called another friend who reacted the same way. After one more call to another friend who accepted the news enthusiastically, Judith thought, "Well, hmmph, this might be fun." At that point she called Rachel and Marianne and said, "Oh, it's so lovely that you're getting married!" After this turnaround, Rachel said her mother was very enthusiastic about the marriage.

This story illustrates how the change in the marriage law led to one woman's strong negative emotional reaction to the prospect of her daughter's same-sex marriage. Judith's negative reaction was not the end of the story, though. Within a larger social and cultural context that included at least some vocal support for same-sex marriage, Judith's immediate negative reaction morphed quickly into support for the marriage.

What exactly changed for Judith in the larger context? Judith's friends' warm and supportive reaction removed the fear of social disapproval that had apparently shaped her initial reaction. Perhaps more important, these friends also recognized Rachel's impending wedding as a marriage that is entitled to the same degree of excitement as other marriages. Judith adopted her friends' approach, expressing excitement and approval for Rachel's upcoming wedding. Either Judith's understanding of "marriage" changed to let Rachel and Marianne in, or perhaps Judith shifted how she thought about her daughter's relationship.

Judith's changing reactions remind us that the end of the political debate over marriage equality for same-sex couples means the beginning of cultural adjustment. The misgivings of parents and others add up to resistance to the idea of same-sex marriage, even when it is legal, although those opinions will likely be challenged and perhaps influenced by those who are supportive of same-sex marriage. Similarly, individual changes in perception and acceptance over time may shape the cultural definition of what marriage means. This process of cultural adjustment is complex and not yet well understood for the marriage issue.

In contrast, the political debate is usually presented as a relatively simple process of legal recognition. When they speak of recognition, same-sex couples mean that they want the state to formally acknowledge their relationships by granting them the legal option of being married. Recognition also has another relevant meaning that we could usefully apply to the process of cultural adaptation: the perception of "something or someone previously known."[1] One way to reframe the question about whether gay people will change marriage in the sense of cultural change (not the kind of behavioral change in marriage discussed in the previous chapter) is to ask whether the heterosexuals who make up and define the larger culture *recognize* same-sex couples as marriageable and married, as Judith's friends did.

It might seem odd to think that a relatively small number of people—the roughly 20,000 same-sex couples who have married or registered in the Netherlands over ten years (during which time period there were almost 800,000 heterosexual marriages)—could make a dent in the cultural understanding of marriage. Theoretically, heterosexual people might never even notice a married gay couple in the course of their daily life. In fact, some demographers I have spoken with point to the small number of gay couples marrying to argue that same-sex marriage will have no cultural impact. However, I believe that the potential for cultural change is real, although not for the same reasons that Stanley Kurtz, Maggie Gallagher, or other gay marriage critics offer, which highlight the political debate *before* gay couples can even marry. The preceding chapter picked apart the claims about the impact of the gay marriage debate on heterosexual marriage in the Netherlands and Scandinavia. In my view, the more interesting and challenging question asks what happened in the Netherlands when same-sex couples could actually marry—and what will happen in the United States when that right becomes widely available here.

Marriage is, after all, a public act. Marriage comes with highly visible accoutrements, including public ceremonies, big parties, a new legal marital status, and (sometimes) name changes. The public nature of marriage itself is the key to understanding the possible cultural leverage that even a small number of couples might have as they come into contact with many other people in the course of their married lives. Instead of focusing on the politicians, celebrities, and news media whose opinions about marriage might or might not directly influence the larger cultural understandings of marriage, here I turn to the grass roots to look at the lives of Dutch couples for signs of change in the meaning of marriage. If same-sex couples are changing the institution of marriage in the Netherlands, then at least some of those effects should show up in the lives of the couples whom I interviewed and in their communities. We can see the effects in how heterosexuals think about marriage by drawing both on national survey data and on the interactions that gay couples have had with heterosexuals.

How might gay and lesbian couples alter the current cultural understandings of marriage? I think about this question from two directions, looking at it first from the perspective of gay and lesbian people and then from the perspective of heterosexual people. As part of a culture, people develop ideas about the meaning and relevance of marriage for themselves and others. Anthropologists and sociologists who study marriage sometimes call these deeply rooted ideas "cultural schemas," which reflect a complex process of learning by individuals and are shared by and transmitted among members of a group who have common experiences.[2] *For same-sex couples to change or dislodge those ideas, gay couples who marry must first display or express some profound differences in the idea about what marriage means.* If the institution of marriage fits, same-sex couples can wear it without any alterations. If the institution does not fit, though, then something must change. Either the idea will change, same-sex couples will change, or same-sex couples will not try to use that idea and legal institution to structure their lives.

But same-sex couples, or even gay, lesbian, and bisexual people more broadly considered, are obviously not the only cultural players when it comes to same-sex marriage. *Heterosexual people might perceive a difference in the meaning of marriage for same-sex couples, or a different meaning for an institution of "marriage" that includes same-sex couples, that will eventually alter the meaning of marriage for heterosexuals.* "Cross-cultural" dissonance related to marriage (if it exists) should be visible in heterosexual people's reactions to the marriages of their gay and lesbian friends, family, neighbors, and coworkers. Using the example that opened this chapter, we can ask whether Judith's initial dismay reflected a conflict between the future marriage of Rachel and Marianne and the Dutch cultural understanding of marriage, as well as whether the resolution of her concerns reflected a change in the meaning of marriage (an alteration of the cultural schema) or something else. When same-sex couples marry and have access to the outward and visible signs of being married, the potential emerges for conflict, confusion, and wrenching cultural change—or for a relatively seamless integration. The experiences of the couples I interviewed included all of those possibilities.

Recognizable:
Cultural Change From the Perspective of Same-Sex Couples

The first way to assess whether the idea or institution of marriage changes when same-sex couples can marry is to infer some of their ideas about marriage from their actions and statements about marriage. Same-sex couples want a choice—not a social obligation—to marry, and clearly not all choose to marry, as chapters 2 and 3 made clear. The decision-making factors for same-sex couples ended up sounding a lot like those expressed by Dutch different-sex couples.

In taking another look at those reasons for marrying in this chapter, I want to focus on what they tell us about the meaning of marriage for same-sex couples as a way to start. The couples I interviewed had several main reasons for choosing to marry or for at least considering marriage:

- To express a commitment to the relationship and an intention to stay together
- To express that commitment both to each other and to their families and friends
- To establish a legal bond that addresses the practical issues related to living a joint economic life together and pooling some or all of their financial resources
- To ensure the well-being of their current or future children
- To cement this bond at a meaningful time in their relationships
- To make a political statement about the equality of gay men and lesbians or a feminist statement related to the equality of men and women.

Most of those reasons include elements that should be instantly familiar even to those with traditional views: marriage is about commitment, children, economic partnership, and family ties. On one hand, these are familiar elements of a contemporary cultural idea of marriage in the Netherlands, as Anna Korteweg's study of young Dutch heterosexual couples shows. On the other hand, some differences emerge in how these more traditional elements look or work among same-sex couples. For instance, same-sex couples are more likely than heterosexual couples to rely on adoption or alternative reproductive technologies for producing children to raise. Same-sex couples do not seek to replicate roles of "wife" or "husband" with their definitions of who does what within the family, although several couples told me stories of clueless acquaintances who wanted to know which one of them was the wife and which was the husband.

Overall, while same-sex couples do not adhere precisely to a particular traditional simplistic view that the purpose of marriage is procreation, neither do heterosexual people in the Netherlands, or in many other European and North American countries, for that matter. Therefore, most elements of the idea of marriage expressed by same-sex couples would be recognizable to their heterosexual friends and siblings. To compare gay and lesbian couples with heterosexual couples more convincingly, I first look in more detail at the apparent similarities and differences that emerge from my interviews. To provide a broader context from a representative sample of Dutch heterosexuals, I also draw on survey evidence from the European Values Survey on Dutch beliefs about marriage.

A Choice, Not an Obligation

As I discussed in chapter 2, the fact that same-sex couples see marriage as a choice comes out of the historical and legal context of marriage in the Netherlands and of the gay and lesbian political movement. In fact, lesbian and gay couples probably would not have sought the right to marry if marriage still meant a social obligation to enter a legal institution that reinforced restrictive social roles for husbands and wives.[3] Demographers, historians, and other social scientists have long noted that the trends in marriage and divorce in Western Europe and the United States reflect a clear movement away from marriage as a traditional social institution that involves distinct roles for men and women and an expectation of lifelong marriage. Marriage has become thought of primarily as a relationship that two individuals freely choose to enter but might later choose to exit if the relationship does not meet the needs of individuals.[4] These changes in heterosexual ideas are not just theoretical, since the preceding chapter showed that increasing numbers of Dutch heterosexual couples choose not to marry and instead live together outside marriage.[5]

Procreation

Marriage is tied to procreation for same-sex couples, but mainly as an effect of procreation rather than a cause, at least for the couples I spoke with. When a lesbian couple plans to have children, they see marriage as a way to enhance the legal ties between parents and children and to formalize the corresponding rights and responsibilities for both the child and the parents. Heterosexual couples in the Netherlands also often have kids first and then marry, as noted in chapter 4. A third of children born in the Netherlands have unmarried parents, many of whom marry within a few years of the child's arrival. Among younger cohorts of Dutch people, same-sex couples and different-sex couples clearly share a sense of the relationship between marriage and procreation.

Living a Joint Economic Life

Same-sex couples did not explicitly talk about their relationships as economic partnerships, but the couples I spoke with had mingled their economic lives rather than remaining financially separate and independent:

- In every couple, whether married or not, both partners contributed to the household income through their jobs.
- Several had bought homes together, and some explicitly tied the consideration of marriage to buying a house.
- Their interdependence was also evident in how they pooled their incomes for daily life expenses. While most of the couples had separate accounts, almost all had a joint bank account so that they could share some or all of the expenses of living together. Five couples had completely pooled their incomes and assets, while many others pooled significant parts.
- Some couples also revealed their economic ties when they noted that the contributions to household and other expenses depended on each partner's income. When one partner earned more, he or she often carried more of the financial load, even when the couple was not married.
- The main economic decision related to marriage concerned what to do with premarital assets. A few couples had chosen to sign a

prenuptial agreement to keep premarital assets legally separate as allowed by Dutch law, but in each of those cases one partner had his or her own business that needed to be kept separate from the family finances.

Taken as a whole, the evidence suggests that same-sex couples mingle economic resources to a significant degree, which fits with many cultural assumptions about marriage.

The last few items on the earlier list of ideas about marriage seem to suggest some important differences in how same-sex couples see marriage, however.

Timing of Marriage

In traditional terms, marriage represents a transition for a young couple from their parents' households to their own joint household. After a courtship, two young people walk down the aisle to establish a new life together as adults. However, the married same-sex couples I spoke with were much further along in their relationships when they finally decided to marry than would be true in the old traditional pattern. On one level, the timing of marriage reflected the legal reality that same-sex couples in the Netherlands had no option to register as partners until 1998 or to marry until 2001. What will happen to couples whose relationships have formed since 1998 or 2001? Time will tell. My sample does not allow me to look at that question, unfortunately, since almost all of the couples I spoke with were already living together by 1998.

In chapter 6, I address this issue of how the option of marriage might change the timing of marriage as gay people's ideas and lives change. Here I will simply note that the same-sex couples I interviewed might be more traditional in terms of their thinking about the appropriate timing of marriage than they first seem. Some of the couples who rejected marriage for various ideological reasons told me that they might have overcome that opposition had marriage been possible early in their relationships, since marriage offers many practical advantages for relatively new couples. The events that triggered thinking about marriage for these couples had already occurred by the time marriage became possible for them, especially the purchase of a house and the mingling of economic resources. Those couples had used other ways to formalize their relationships to satisfy mortgage lenders and other necessary authorities, so marriage had little practical value to them at the time that it became an option. If marriage had been available earlier, then we probably would have seen more couples marrying earlier in their relationships.

Political and Ideological Aspects

Some of the political aspects of gay couples' marriage decisions differentiate them from marriage among heterosexuals. The marriages of different-sex couples do not, in and of themselves, make a statement about the equality of gay people, although heterosexual weddings make some gay men and lesbians more conscious of their exclusion in places where gay couples cannot marry.[6] However, some Dutch couples told stories of heterosexual friends, mostly feminists, who saw their own legal ability to marry as a conservative statement and, therefore, boycotted marriage out of solidarity with their lesbian and gay friends for many years. Martha and Lin told me the story of a prominent Dutch politician who remained legally single until gay couples could also marry, at which point she also finally married her long-time male partner.

The only way to open up access to marriage for same-sex couples is to make marriage political, even though it might make heterosexuals with more traditional beliefs nervous.[7] But the same-sex marriage debate is not the first time politics and marriage have come together, and the politicization began long ago with heterosexual people, not gay people. Over the years, in many countries in Europe and in North America, debates about changing marriage and divorce laws revealed how politics and the state create marriage in a legal sense, just as the larger culture contributes other elements of our understanding of marriage. Historians like Mary Ann Glendon, Stephanie Coontz, and Nancy Cott have shown that no natural, consistent definition and understanding of marriage has existed.[8] Both the legal and the social meanings of marriage have changed and adapted to the reality of family life and the needs of society. Politics has always been involved in the adaptation. The most recent political debate related to marriage in the Netherlands concerns the rules for the immigration of foreign spouses, a debate prompted by concerns about low rates of intermarriage between immigrants and ethnically native Dutch people, as noted later.

In one significant way, same-sex couples' messages about gay and lesbian equality actually reinforce the traditional position of marriage atop the relationship hierarchy, as I mentioned in chapter 3. In principle, most people I interviewed thought it was a positive thing to give both same-sex and different-sex couples the option of registered partnership as well as marriage. In practice, only one of the couples who were legally united after

April 2001 chose registered partnership, since most saw that status as inferior to marriage. Even those who refused to marry agreed that registered partnership was a second-class status that was simply a useful temporary compromise position on the way to full equality.

The most ambitious and explicit political claim of some lesbian feminist activists is that same-sex couples can help dismantle the gender roles still present in heterosexual marriages. According to this prediction, same-sex couples are the poster children for egalitarian marriages, since marriages between two husbands or two wives involve different dynamics from those of heterosexual couples and do not impose hierarchical roles or expectations on spouses. Growing evidence from the United States supports the idea that same-sex couples are less gender-bound and more egalitarian in determining how much each partner will contribute to the household earnings and housework, although some inequalities exist within gay couples, too.[9] Even if same-sex couples carry this egalitarian potential, though, the necessarily small number of same-sex couples suggests that the internal differences in the organization of gay family life will not be visible to a large number of heterosexuals.

In particular, same-sex couples do not appear to assign particular roles to partners or spouses as breadwinner or caregiver. All of the people I interviewed were employed, including all of the parents, with many employed at a job less than full-time. But heterosexuals are also already in the process of "de-gendering" their marriages in the sense of breaking down a strict division of family roles between men and women, with most heterosexual women now contributing to the family income in the Netherlands and in the United States. In 1975, only 28% of Dutch women ages 25-54 were employed. In 2004, 74% of women in the same age group had jobs—a smaller proportion than for men (89%) but still a clear majority of Dutch prime-age women. More Dutch women (60%) work part-time, whereas only 15% of men do so,[10] suggesting that Dutch women still have more household responsibilities than men do. Nevertheless, the changes over time suggest that husbands' and wives' roles have become much less gender-specific, even though some gender differences remain.

The small number of married gay couples also significantly dilutes the potential cultural threat to monogamy that worries many marriage equality foes. At least some gay men (now) openly disagree with the norm of monogamy in their relationships.[11] Some gay marriage advocates predict that marriage will lead to more monogamy among gay men, since the commitment implied by the marriage bond will reduce men's desire to seek out additional sex partners.[12] Advocates on the other side worry that any nonmonogamous behavior in the context of marriage will undermine the traditional view that monogamy is a good thing to preserve.[13] Given the dramatic difference in the size of the gay and heterosexual populations, surely more nonmonogamy occurs in the context of straight relationships in a numerical sense, although finding reliable statistics on the actual extent of heterosexual nonmonogamy is difficult.

In the cultural context of marriage, the norm seems more important than a potential but small increase in nonmonogamous behavior within marriage. The evidence from the Dutch couples I interviewed is somewhat mixed with respect to the norm. Marriage and monogamy seemed fairly separate in the minds of most of the gay men. On one hand, most of the married and unmarried male couples I spoke with were not monogamous, and some distinguished their norms related to monogamy from those attached to traditional marriage. On the other hand, evidence of more traditional norms was also present.

For example, Bram decided that he would become monogamous after he and his partner, Otto, married. And even male couples who were sexually nonmonogamous had their own definitions of fidelity that focused on love and honesty. As Willem, who was married, put it, "Fidelity is not between your legs but between your ears." Rob, who was unmarried, noted that his nonmonogamous relationship with his partner, Piet, was sometimes confusing for their friends, including some gay men, who seemed to expect that a long-term committed relationship would be—and perhaps should be—monogamous. In other words, while gay men may not always behave monogamously, they clearly recognize the existence of the monogamy norm and have felt its power.

Evidence from other countries on the role of monogamy among gay men in legal relationships is complicated to interpret. William Eskridge and Darren Spedale also found that some but not all Danish gay male couples embraced monogamy after registering their partnerships, although they also found that the nonmonogamous couples became more likely to use safer sex practices to protect their registered partners.[14] The research of economist Thomas Dee supports the possibility that gay men become more monogamous when registered or married. He found that rates of syphilis and gonorrhea, both sexually transmitted infections, decreased markedly in the European countries that recognize same-sex partners, possibly because more gay male couples became monogamous after their relationships were legally recognized.[15] While rates of HIV infection also fell, that result was not statistically significant, but Eskridge and Spedale note that that rates of HIV infections fell in Denmark, Norway, and Sweden more than in other European countries after registered partnership was implemented in those countries.[16]

From the cultural perspective, expectations and aspirations are probably more important than actual behavior. In the Netherlands, perhaps my most important finding related to monogamy is that the men I interviewed did not seek to marry to overturn the cultural expectation of monogamy in marriage. In that way, norms about monogamy among same-sex couples appear to be quite different from norms about egalitarian gender roles: the same-sex couples I interviewed sometimes used their marriages to spread the gospel of gender equality, but they did not use marriage to try to undermine monogamy.

The complexity of interpreting data on gay men's sexual behavior and its relationship to cultural expectations also emerges in studies of the United States experience. Solomon et al.'s study of couples entering civil unions in Vermont shows that gay men in civil unions were not more likely to be monogamous than gay couples who weren't in civil unions, and most of those couples were not monogamous.[17] However, gay men in civil unions were more likely than those not in civil unions to have agreements with each other that outside sex was not acceptable. In other words, men in civil unions were more likely to hold the ideal of monogamy for their relationships even if they didn't practice it consistently.

What Heterosexuals Think

Overall, the ideas expressed by same-sex couples about what marriage is and what marriage is good for turn out to be quite similar to those expressed by their heterosexual counterparts of the same age. The 1999 European Values Survey of Dutch people gave each participant a list of factors that make for a successful marriage and asked the participants how important those qualities were.[18] While the factors in the survey do not match up precisely with the elements of marriage expressed in my open-ended interviews of same-sex couples, the survey provides a context for thinking about the range of views of heterosexual people and the similarities with the views of gay and lesbian people. (Although the survey did not ask about the sexual orientation of those surveyed, we can reasonably assume that the vast majority are heterosexual people.)

Figure 5.1 presents the opinions of Dutch people ages 30–50, the age range of the people I interviewed. The factors that almost all agree are very important relate to the quality of the relationship of the spouses: mutual respect, willingness to discuss problems, understanding, and faithfulness. The participants also generally agree that similarities of spouses in terms of social, religious, political, and ethnic background were not important for most people.

Turning from general relationship characteristics to day-to-day life, though, the Dutch are much more diverse in their perspectives on what marriages should look like. Within the questions about the importance of children, sex, chores, time together, and income, we can see a wide variety of choices and situations that could make for successful marriages for a substantial number of Dutch people.

What we do not see in the opinions of Dutch heterosexuals is a shared notion of the traditional family that same-sex couples might be seen as rejecting. Producing children does not alone define a successful marriage:

Figure 5.1

Importance of Factors That Make for a Successful Marriage, Dutch Respondents, ages 30–50, in 1999 (n = 506)

Factors that make for successful marriage	Very important	Rather important	Not very important
Mutual respect and appreciation	95.9	4.1	0.0
Willingness to discuss the problems that come up between husband and wife	88.4	10.9	0.7
Understanding and tolerance	87.4	12.6	0.0
Faithfulness	83.6	14.4	2.0
Living apart from your in-laws	55.0	20.2	24.8
Having a happy sexual relationship	48.2	47.9	4.0
Having children	44.8	28.4	26.8
Sharing household chores	30.8	53.8	15.4
Talking a lot about mutual interests	26.3	63.7	9.9
Spending as much time together as possible	22.9	58.3	18.7
Having an adequate income	19.2	55.1	25.7
Having good housing	18.7	64.3	17.0
Being of the same social background	9.4	47.4	43.2
Sharing religious beliefs	5.1	19.5	75.4
Sharing the same ethnic background	2.9	23.3	73.9
Agreeing on politics	2.0	21.9	76.1

Source: Author's tabulations from European Values Survey.

fewer than half of Dutch people in this age range think that having children is very important, and a quarter think it is not important. Building an economic partnership no longer means a strict division of labor between husbands and wives; sharing household, childrearing, and income responsibilities is the new economic marriage partnership. Fulfilling traditional roles of husbands and wives does not make a good marriage; having a warm, committed relationship with good communication and time together does.

Answers to other questions in the survey also reflect the changes in roles for husbands and wives that have occurred in recent decades. The breadwinner-homemaker household model appears to be on the way out. Fewer than a quarter (23%) of Dutch people agree that "A job is all right but most women want a home and children." Four in five (82%) agree that fathers are as well suited as mothers to look after children. Along with the data on women's employment suggested earlier, the survey shows that Dutch heterosexual men's and women's lives are becoming more similar both in principle and in practice.

The same-sex couples who married shared a personal commitment to each other and to their relationship that fits within the mainstream ideas about marriage expressed by their heterosexual peers. Pushing at the boundaries of gender norms and, to a lesser extent, questioning monogamy is perhaps more noticeable among same-sex couples. But we see those changes in gender roles as important to their heterosexual peers, as well. The range of experiences in same-sex couples' lives—having children or not, sharing incomes, buying houses, joining each other's families, planning for the future, deciding whether to marry—would also be recognizable to Dutch heterosexuals.

Dutch same-sex couples' understanding of marriage also lines up well with that of heterosexual couples in the United States. Indeed, the anthropologist Gilbert Herdt and the psychiatrist Robert Kertzner note that gay couples in the United States propose reasons for marriage or commitment ceremonies that "fall within the historically normative cultural range of what Americans in general expect of marriage and why they desire to have public declarations of marriage."[19] The anthropologist Naomi Quinn describes the American cultural model of marriage, or the "core expectations and assumptions," that emerges from her research: "Americans expect their marriages to be lasting, mutually beneficial, and shared."[20] The main benefit that adults get from marriage is psychological fulfillment of individual needs through the relationship, but they also know that they may have to work hard to create marriages that achieve compatibility and meet both

Figure 5.2

Attitudes Toward Marriage and Family by Sexual Orientation in the United States
(percentage of 18–44-year-olds agreeing)

Statement	Women		Men	
	Hetero-sexual	Lesbian & bisexual	Hetero-sexual	Gay & bisexual
1. Better to get married than stay single	50.3	33.9	66.8	35.7
2. Divorce best if can't work out problems	45.3	49.2	43.7	52.4
3. OK for unmarried female to have child	70.5	83.1	59.7	76.4
4. Young couple should not live together unless married	34.7	14.5	31.7	13.8
5. Rewards of being parent worth cost and work	94.8	91.2	95.0	90.5
6. Working mother can have warm and secure relationship	83.2	85.7	72.3	81.1
7. Better if man earns main living and woman takes care of home	34.0	22.7	36.1	24.2
8. More important for man to spend time with family than career success	73.7	67.7	77.3	69.9
N	6,235	314	3,807	228

Source: Author's tabulations from the National Survey of Family Growth (United States).

partners' needs. Quinn argues that various other kinds of motivations are attached to marriage, such as fulfilling adult sex roles, achieving maturity, having children, meeting family pressures, acting on religious beliefs, and meeting economic needs, but that "people recognize that fulfillment is what you are *supposed* to marry for, first and foremost."[21] The Dutch couples I spoke with expressed views of marriage that resonate closely with this model of marriage.

We can get a more direct comparison of gay and heterosexual attitudes related to marriage and family life in the United States. The U.S. government surveyed more than 12,600 men and women ages 18-44 in the National Survey of Family Growth in 2002. This survey included numerous questions about fertility and childrearing, as well as questions about attitudes and sexual orientation. Figure 5.2 compares the percentage of people who agree with statements about marriage, divorce, parenting, and gender roles for four groups: heterosexual women, lesbian and bisexual women, heterosexual men, and gay and bisexual men.

Several points pop out of the figures in Figure 5.2. Half of heterosexual women and two-thirds of heterosexual men agree that it's better to marry than to go through life single, but only a third of gay, lesbian, and bisexual people agree with that statement. Such a big difference is not surprising when one considers that no GLB people were allowed to marry in the United States in 2002 and that the only way for a gay person to marry would have been to marry someone of the other sex.

In the rest of the statements about marriage and childbearing, however, the most striking feature is how similar gay people are to heterosexual people of the same sex. While gay people's opinions are somewhat less traditional than those of heterosexuals, the differences are fairly small, and the majority of gay and heterosexual people share broad agreement on family matters.[22] Roughly half of people in each group agree that divorce is the "best solution when a couple can't seem to work out their marriage problems." A large majority in each group agrees that it's acceptable for an unmarried woman to have a child. Few people agree that young couples should not live together unless they are married. Almost everyone agrees that "the rewards of being a parent are worth it, despite the cost and the work it takes."

Gay and heterosexual people are also hard to tell apart when it comes to attitudes about gender roles, as the last three lines of Figure 5.2 demonstrate. Just about everyone agrees that "a working mother can establish just as warm and secure a relationship with her children as a mother who does not work," although heterosexual men are the least likely to agree. Less than one-third of any group in this age range agrees that a man should be the breadwinner while the woman takes care of the home and family. Between two-thirds and three-quarters of each group agree that "it is more important for a man to spend a lot of time with his family than to be successful at his career."

Both survey data and my interviews show that in both the Netherlands and the United States, gay men and lesbians share understandings about marriage with their heterosexual peers. No matter which group holds the modern marriage mirror, gay and straight married couples are likely to recognize themselves.

Recognizing: From the Perspective of Heterosexual People

We can also look more directly at how heterosexuals see same-sex marriages. To start with the broadest measure of cultural acceptance, the couples I spoke with believed that the Dutch public now largely approves of the idea that same-sex couples can marry. Public opinion polls bear out this impression. In 2003, a Gallup Europe poll found that 80% of Dutch participants agreed that marriage should be possible for same-sex couples throughout Europe.[23] The Dutch were second only to the Danes in their support for same-sex marriage. All of the other European countries that now let gay couples marry or register their partnerships also showed majority agreement with the idea on a European level, with the exception of the Czech Republic, which was evenly split at 50% agreement, and the United Kingdom at 47% agreement.

However, pockets of resistance remain, even in liberal Holland. The most obvious tension concerns the increasing number and visibility of Muslim residents and immigrants, some of whom hold conservative religious ideas about the immorality of homosexuality. Almost every gay man and lesbian I spoke with in the Netherlands mentioned this political tension. While I lived in Amsterdam, a local conservative mosque was found to be distributing a book that advocated throwing gay men off of tall buildings, generating vocal protests and demonstrations by gay men and lesbians.

But immigration has itself generated a new marriage debate that reveals how accepted gay marriage has become. Roughly half of marriages involving Moroccan and Turkish immigrants or their children are "migration marriages" in which the new spouse comes from the Dutch partner's country of origin.[24] This pattern has raised new concerns about the assimilation of immigrants. Dutch politicians—even (or perhaps especially) conservative ones—have used acceptance of gay marriage as a litmus test. Potential migrants to the Netherlands from the Middle East or Asia are now required to watch a DVD about Dutch life—including shots of a gay wedding—and to take a test that includes questions about whether gay marriage is legal.[25] Apparently the goal is to make sure that migrants know about the culture of the country they hope to live in, perhaps weeding out those who cannot accept open and equal displays of affection by gay people or at least warning them that gays have equal rights and that migrants will be expected to respect them. The controversies over immigration make it clear that policymakers do not intend to downplay or revisit the issue of gay marriage in order to make immigrants feel more culturally comfortable but that limitation of immigration is the more likely policy outcome.

Of course, not all Muslim people in the Netherlands oppose gay marriage, but there is very little discussion of actual same-sex marriages among immigrants or among Muslim residents. Dutch gay people are also usually quick to note that opposition to gay marriage is not limited to ethnic minorities. Smaller conservative Christian groups have long existed in Holland, and some of the couples I spoke with pointed to those groups as examples of Dutch people who disapprove of same-sex marriage. Nevertheless, the opinion polls suggest that the pockets of opposition to the idea of gay marriage are small, even though they are sometimes highly visible.

Public approval at a broad level, though, is not enough to answer the question about whether gay couples will change marriage in some way. The fact that heterosexual marriage behavior did not appear to change as a result of same-sex marriage or partnership rights also might not fully answer the question about changes in the institution of marriage. Instead, I will use the interactions between same-sex couples and heterosexual people to assess how much of a stretch heterosexuals have to make to incorporate same-sex couples in their ideas of marriage.

Heterosexuals Recognize Same-Sex Marriages as Marriage

Whether married or not, many of the couples I interviewed experienced the power of inclusion in an important social institution, although in varying ways. Access to this social institution opened up new sources of support and understanding for same-sex couples that suggest same-sex couples were easily accommodated and brought into the fold.

Friends and family are curious about the intentions of unmarried same-sex couples and sometimes even pressure them to marry, just as they pressure different-sex couples to marry.[26] Dutch heterosexual people expect people in same-sex couples who have been together for a while to be thinking about marriage. Anna and Joke's friends ask Joke (not Anna, who opposes marriage) whether they will marry, although she does not feel much pressure from this. When Erik goes to other people's weddings, his friends ask whether he and James will marry. Isabelle's work colleagues, who are more "traditional" than her friends, ask her when she will marry. Even though she does not plan to marry Anneke, Isabelle likes the fact that her colleagues ask: "I think, OK, it's good because these are straight people and they show that gay marriage is a serious option. . . . They show they accept the idea of gay marriage and they take our relationship that serious[ly] as being worth marriage."

In chapter 2, I told how Marianne's grandfather campaigned to convince Marianne and Rachel to marry. Marianne said, "He talked about it the whole night. He had all these questions: 'Well, you two love each other and why not? And, 'It's possible now, and it's the best thing you could do!'

So we got really convinced." Clearly he saw the parallels between his own relationship and that of his granddaughter.

Once couples make plans to marry, other people sometimes insert their own ideas of marriage and weddings. For instance, when Margriet and Miriyam ordered a cake for their wedding, the baker (without asking) added pink icing roses to denote the occasion, much to the couple's dismay. In other examples, staff at restaurants and hotels involved in weddings noted the celebrations when they found out that their customers were celebrating a wedding.

Later, family and friends in the larger community support the married couples in different ways that also show that the same-sex marriage was the same as a different-sex one. For instance, friends of Jan and Paul like to celebrate their wedding anniversary. "We keep forgetting it," Jan laughed. "Other people remember, though." Their friends send cards, visit, or even bring cakes to celebrate the occasion, even though they were not invited to the actual wedding in 2001.

Most of the married same-sex couples found that heterosexual family members, friends, and work colleagues took their relationship more seriously after they married. Heterosexuals more easily "understand" a relationship once the couple marries. Margriet reported that even her conservative Belgian aunts and the blue-collar male workers she works with accepted her relationship more readily: "I think it is more clear that you belong together. . . . Or it's very serious or something like that. . . . And it's easier for them to accept when you are married because they understand that part of it." Or, as Martha puts it about Lin's family members,

> Absolutely being married makes a difference. I mean it just clicks. . . .
> I mean, it's not like I wasn't accepted in her family before, but everybody understands what marriage is. They understand now that we've got what they've got, and you know, even if on some level they try to make it different—they can't. It's marriage.

Positive Parental Reactions

Maybe the most discerning viewers of same-sex couples are parents—mothers, in particular, as we saw in the opening story about Rachel's mother, Judith. Mothers were the most-mentioned relative by the same-sex couples I interviewed. In general, mothers seemed genuinely supportive and happy for their children, even when they had some ambivalent feelings about a same-sex couple marrying. Mothers saw marriage as a positive step for their gay sons and lesbian daughters. The sense of commitment played a particularly important role, but mothers also wanted to see a happy and cared-for adult child, as several comments make clear.

- *Liz*: Well my mom is pretty religious, but she was very happy about it. I think . . . she's really into the commitment aspect of it. So I think she's been really, really supportive about that.
- *Ria*: I think for my parents it really was like OK, they are really committed to each other. It did make a difference I think. . . . We really are committed, and we really made a decision of staying together through better and worse times, you know. I mean it sounds old-fashioned, but I do think that they like that idea.
- *Gert*: My mother was so happy that I got married. Finally! So all the kids . . . are taken care of.

Parents recognize their children's wedding on a material level, with wedding presents and financial support, and on an emotional level, with blessings and toasts.

One reason that parents were often thrilled by their gay or lesbian child's wedding was the shortage of recent family weddings. Two people I spoke with mentioned that they had fulfilled their parents' wish to attend the wedding of at least one of their children. Saskia's siblings had married their different-sex spouses but had not invited their parents for one reason or another. As a result, her parents were very happy that they could attend the wedding of Saskia and Ellen—so much so that they kept increasing their financial contribution to the wedding. Marta thought that Tineke's father was "a little proud that he has at least one married child." Joke suspected that her mother would be pleased if she and Anna married and gave a big traditional party, since Joke's sister lived with her boyfriend and was not planning to marry. These comments suggest that parents see the marriages of their gay or lesbian children to same-sex partners as equivalent to those of their heterosexual children, and perhaps even better in some ways than those of their heterosexual children who simply lived with a partner.

Parents who were not invited to their child's wedding were sometimes upset to miss the big event. I began this book describing Stephanie's heartbroken father, who was not invited to the wedding of Stephanie and Ingrid. One other couple I spoke with experienced a similar reaction. Andrea and Katherine married without anyone present other than their two friends, who were the required witnesses. They told no one, although word leaked out. When Andrea's parents learned of the wedding, they were angry that they had not been invited. The anger in this case reflected the significance that Andrea's family attached to weddings in general and to the meaning of a marriage for Andrea and Katherine, in particular. Families know their role—to witness the commitment of the couple and to officially welcome a new family member—and they may be angry when deprived of it.

Neutral Parental Reactions

Some families did not react noticeably or did not seem to see the couple as different after their marriage. One reason may be that most couples were together for years before marrying. Several couples noted that an alternative route to family acceptance is time instead of marriage. In fact, until registered partnership and marriage were available, being together for many years was the most visible way for same-sex couples to express commitment to outsiders. So one reason that these same-sex couples were easily accepted as "married" may have been that their families had time to get used to the idea of their relationship.

Negative Parental Reactions

Gay and lesbian couples usually have experience dealing with social disapproval for their relationships. Some couples mentioned that their parents' initial negative reactions to their relationships had smoothed out or mellowed—or even changed completely—over time. Many respondents noted that their parents had eventually "gotten used to" their son's or daughter's bringing home a same-sex partner. As Laura put it about her American family, "In the abstract, I think [my lesbianism] was even more strange and difficult for them, but now that it's connected to a person who they know and really love, I think it's gotten easier." In some cases, that prior process of coming to terms with a gay son's or lesbian daughter's sexual orientation and same-sex relationship made for an easier transition to seeing the couple marry.

For others, though, marriage threatened to upset the precarious balance of parental acceptance. Martha knew that her mother opposed same-sex marriage, but her mother still sent a gift of a cookbook and got up at 4 a.m. in her time zone to call Martha and Lin on their wedding day. Reconciling this apparent ambivalence might be stressful or hurtful for some gay and lesbian people, although Martha interpreted it matter-of-factly: "But I just accept the fact that she says she's against same-sex marriage in the same way she says she's a Republican and then votes Democrat, you know?" And, given her mother's somewhat positive reactions to the same-sex weddings that took place in San Francisco in early 2004, Martha wondered aloud, "Having said she's against it, I have to ask her again to see if she's still against it." Also, recall the happy ending to Ellen's story of overcoming her mother's objections as described in chapter 2, which is in contrast to Willem's continuing conflict with his mother long after his wedding was over.

It's hard to know how to interpret parents' negative reactions, although they are clearly evidence that cultural recognition and acceptance of same-sex marriage are not universal. In some cases, opposition to the *idea* of a same-sex couple marrying was clear—a few parents did not want to recognize their child and his or her partner as marriageable or married. But most came around to the idea, raising the question of how this reconciliation occurred. One possibility is that the mothers changed their ideas about marriage in some profound way. Because I did not interview those parents who objected, I cannot say for sure that such a change did not happen. But the relatively short length of time that it took to reconcile a child's marriage to a same-sex partner (in less than a day, for Rachel's mother, Judith) suggests that some other process was at work.

I would argue that these parents instead changed the cultural schema or idea of same-sex relationships that they apply to their child's particular relationship. In the absence of marriage, parents might have been applying some other kind of schema or set of expectations to the couple. (Such a process could also occur for people not so closely related to a particular couple.) To my knowledge, no existing research has explored the ways that the heterosexual world might conceptualize the meaning of a relationship between two people of the same sex. On the basis of my observations of cultural representations of same-sex relationships, as well as my reading and hearing accounts of parental reactions to their gay and lesbian children's lives, I suggest several possible ideas that parents might use to think about their child's same-sex relationship:

- *A sinful relationship that is to be tolerated because of the love and bond between the disapproving parent and the gay or lesbian child.* The partner is not considered a family member.[27] The partner could be seen as an evil temptress and therefore shunned or, more benignly, treated as just another friend of the child.
- *A close relationship that is short term and more akin to a casual cohabitation, although closer than the relationship with a roommate.* Again,

the partner is not a family member and develops no close ties to the parents.

- *An intimate relationship that has survived over many years and through life challenges, suggesting that it will last indefinitely during the child's life.* Family members treat the partner as family, although the relationship to the partner is mediated through the child. However, no independent status accompanies the relationship between partner and parents, unlike that of a son-in-law or daughter-in-law. Parents might not understand or continue to recognize the relationship without the presence of the child, such as continuing to invite the partner to family events after the child's death.
- *A relationship that will not produce grandchildren.* This expectation might also be combined with the others and might heighten the contrast between a lesbian daughter's relationship and a married heterosexual daughter's relationship.

Contrast my sketchy outlines of these categories with the evocative specificity of the internal workings of marriage as described by Naomi Quinn, the anthropologist mentioned earlier: marriage is "lasting, mutually beneficial, and shared." My guess is that most parents (and perhaps heterosexual people more generally) do not have a detailed or textured way of understanding same-sex relationships. If parents put their lesbian daughter's or gay son's relationship into one of these alternative boxes in order to understand it, the need to shift and apply the otherwise familiar schema of marriage, with its differing public and private elements and expectations, will require adjustment when applied to an unfamiliar context and might lead to anxiety and conflict.

This way of thinking about the information embedded in parents' reactions also captures the idea that cultural schemas serve important practical purposes, namely by solving a recurring task.[28] In the case of families, such "tasks" for parents might include choosing from among their child's broad social network whom to invite to family events or deciding who gets a birthday present. A child's marriage clearly defines the spouse as a family member, but parents must decide if a child's boyfriend, cohabiting partner, best friend, or roommate will also get the same treatment.

Understanding these changes of mind and heart more fully will require further exploration by researchers. Certainly, one other important factor that is distinct from the definition of marriage relates to discomfort with the public acknowledgment that a child is gay or lesbian. Parents who had gotten used to the idea of their children being in same-sex relationships might have simply been resistant to bringing those relationships out into the open through marriage. Just as being married increases the public visibility of gay men and lesbians, a factor I will return to shortly, talking about a son or daughter who is married to someone of the same sex is also a very public kind of coming out for parents.

Curiosity and Gay Weddings as Spectacle

Beyond close family members, the married couples I spoke with reported generally positive interactions with heterosexual people. But, for some heterosexual Dutch people, a same-sex couple's marriage provokes a reaction of surprise or curiosity, neither of which clearly falls into a "positive" or "negative" reaction category but which supports my argument that a redefinition of same-sex relationships is under way. Weddings of same-sex couples attracted a lot of public attention in the early days. Several couples reported that they were either the first same-sex couple to marry in their particular town hall or were the first same-sex couple to be married by their wedding official. This was especially true in smaller towns. Julia and Hester noticed some funny looks coming from the guests of the couple marrying just before them, as if the guests were wondering where the men were.

Even a few years after marriage was opened to same-sex couples, mentioning a same-sex spouse could still shock an unsuspecting acquaintance or bureaucrat. Martha had recently had such an encounter with a friend. "We were talking, and I said something about my wife," Martha recalled. "And she said, 'Your wife?!' That kind of interested smile. 'Your wife?!' Like I guess she hadn't met one yet to know somebody who married someone of the same sex." Similarly, I asked Jan whether he had experienced any negative reactions. "No one ever said anything nasty," he responded. "Well, they're surprised and they say, 'Yes, that is possible,' and that is all they say. There's very little discussion about it."

The New Ambiguity: Nobody's Normal and Nobody's Weird

So far, I have argued that relatively little changed in the larger cultural landscape of marriage once same-sex couples could marry. Heterosexuals, in general, are able to apply the usual cultural understanding of marriage to gay couples. Although the general social understanding of what marriage means does not appear to have been altered, some things have changed in the wake of same-sex marriage. When same-sex couples have access to the public insignia of marriage, like the terms "husband" or "wife," social confusion can result. As the end of the previous section implies, same-sex couples have shaken up the meanings of the terms "husband" and "wife." Such a finding might not seem particularly profound. After all, the same-sex marriage debate was about eliminating the sex restriction on who may marry whom. At the very least, however, the issue of terminology provides another prism through which to see whether heterosexuals are willing and able to integrate same-sex couples into the institution.

Terms are a challenge for same-sex couples everywhere, including the ones I interviewed. Despite some grumbling about the businesslike sound of "partner," that term has become very common in Europe and North America in defining an unmarried partner of either sex. "Partner" or the Dutch equivalent of "girlfriend" or "boyfriend" does not always fit with the weight that respondents give to their relationships, however. Words like "wife" or "husband" have more cultural weight but come with understandings and social meanings that are too heterosexual-sounding and too associated with roles that same-sex couples are not eager to take on.

Dutch same-sex couples sometimes, but not always, expressed some discomfort with using "wife" and "husband" when I asked how they referred to each other. Several angles emerged from our discussion of terms. First, married respondents often use these terms with other people, but many use them only in a joking way between themselves. Second, they also often use these terms even if they are not legally married, both in joking and serious ways. For instance, Pauline used the term "wife" before she and Liz could legally marry as a way to signal the equivalence between her relationship and those of married couples. The joking and discomfort come mainly from the couples' unwillingness to take on the traditional gender roles associated with "wife" or "husband." The humor reflects the fact that, in some ways, either legally or practically, the partner is like a wife or husband but does not fit the traditional image. Isabelle further points out that there is a problematic possessiveness associated with introducing Anneke as "my wife": "She isn't *mine.*"

Aside from the concerns about gender roles, visibility was the other big problem related to marriage terminology that I heard about. Since most people who are married are heterosexual, a gay man or lesbian who says "I am married" is likely to be assumed heterosexual until proven otherwise. Using the term "husband" or "wife" for a same-sex partner, on the other hand, is equivalent to coming out. The couples I talked to were acutely aware of how these terms can mask or unmask a gay identity. The lesbians and gay men who did not intend to be closeted found that they came out more frequently than they used to.[29] Not all gay people wanted to be out all the time in every context, though, and Liz even noted that her reluctance to use the term "wife" revealed her own lingering internalized homophobia. In those cases, people selectively chose when to use the term "husband" or "wife" depending on their desire to be visibly gay in a particular context.

New jobs, new colleagues, new clients, new students—all require a new kind of coming out for married people. Tineke, a health care provider, described an awkward situation at work with a blind patient. She wasn't sure how her elderly patient would react to the news that she was going to marry a woman, so she left that part out when announcing her marriage. When the patient gave her a congratulatory card that was designed for a man and a woman marrying, Tineke knew she had to come out, but she put it off. She thought, "Oh, gee, when am I going to tell her?" When Marta gave birth to their son, Tineke knew the time had come: "I had to tell her, 'OK, I am getting a son, but, no, I'm not pregnant.'" Fortunately, her patient reacted well.

Many people I interviewed had a story of coming out through the use of "wife" or "husband," especially in dealings with businesses or bureaucracies where being married gave one person the right to speak on behalf of his or her spouse. In the case of businesses, customer service representatives or others who deal with the public sometimes react with surprise or embarrassment when called on their assumptions. This pressure on businesses might be leading the way to more change. According to Willem, who works in the airline industry, and to Julia, who works for a large international clothing company, there is less and less a presumption in corporate situations that being married means being married to a different-sex partner. In dealing with government bureaucracies in other countries, Dutch couples used "wife" or "husband" as convenient badges of political pride. Binational couples, in particular, liked to use the traditional terms while traveling to remind officials in less gay-welcoming countries (like the United States) that same-sex marriage is an accepted reality in at least one country.

For gay and lesbian people, coming out is at least a familiar issue, even when it is still stressful. But the visibility issue also now works in an unexpected direction: heterosexual married people must sometimes even come out as heterosexual. For example, Pauline makes sure that people know that they no longer signal their heterosexuality simply through marriage. When she is working with new people in her law enforcement job, she gets to know them by asking whether they're in a relationship. But Pauline now finds that the typical "I'm married" reply doesn't give enough information:

> And I say, "I'm married, but it doesn't tell me if you are involved with a man or with a woman." "Oh, yeah, yeah, yeah, I'm married with a man," you know. And they're like, "Don't think that I am gay." Because the whole implication of when you're married then you are normal—it's gone. . . . So nobody's normal anymore and nobody's weird anymore.

Some married heterosexuals might feel uncomfortable with the occasional need to come out as straight, although they obviously do not face social stigma when doing so.

In the other direction, the gay couples I spoke with found that heterosexuals naturally apply the traditional terms to same-sex spouses and sometimes even act as the terminology police. Rachel and Marianne admit that they mostly use the term "girlfriend," since they were not comfortable with using "wife" in a serious way. They find that heterosexuals often enforce the appropriate term, reminding them when they use the wrong one. "Sometimes colleagues or friends correct me," Marianne laughed. "'No, that's not your girlfriend, that's your wife!'" Perhaps surprisingly, Rachel even hears her mother enforcing the appropriate terms: "But my mother, who was against this whole marriage stuff, now constantly says, 'Well, Rachel's wife said. . . .' But it's true we did it ourselves. She is right!"

In thinking about terminology, maybe these examples show that we have a clear reason to worry about whether gay and lesbian couples are a good fit with marriage. The terms and corresponding expectations are part of the standard package when a same-sex couple gets married, even if they do not want them. Same-sex couples do not seem to easily fit into the institution's linguistic or cultural conventions denoting the new social and legal status of a married man or woman. Maggie Gallagher, a critic of opening marriage to gay couples, expresses exactly this concern:

> One thing same-sex marriage indubitably does is displace certain formerly core public understandings about marriage: such as, that it has something to do with bringing together male and female, men with

women, husbands and wives, mothers with fathers. Husband will no longer point to or imply wife. Mother no longer implies father.[30]

The economist and judge Richard Posner's concern is similar—that the term "marriage" will convey less information if gay couples can marry. He appears to worry that planning a dinner party will be much more complicated if the host does not know which sex an invitee's spouse is.[31] Parents will also be confused: "If our son or daughter tells us that he or she is getting married, we know the sex of the prospective spouse. All these understandings would be upset by permitting homosexual marriage."[32]

In the Netherlands, it is true that the word "husband" certainly no longer points to or implies the existence of a wife. The amount of information lost seems relatively trivial, though. Not only would a consistent guess that a married stranger has a different-sex spouse be right 99.7% of the time of the time, but anyone talking about a "husband" or "wife" can be instantly classified.[33] In the few cases of remaining confusion, a simple follow-up question should suffice.

Of course, Gallagher's bigger concern about the cultural implication of gay couples marrying is the last sentence of her excerpt: "Mother no longer implies father." Since same-sex couples can now also adopt each other's children, potentially confusing situations like Tineke's encounter with her blind patient also occur, confirming Gallagher's "prediction." But, again, this definitional change seems relatively easy to adapt to, given that it reflects the expanded legal reality of who may marry whom and who may adopt a child.

In her writing and public speaking, Gallagher is not very direct and prefers to frame her concern in terms of the ability to publicly encourage mothers and fathers to marry, stay together, and raise their children. If same-sex couples can marry, Gallagher worries that anyone who focuses on encouraging different-sex couples to marry for the sake of their children will be called a bigot, thus cutting off social pressure on heterosexuals to marry. But why not simply encourage all married couples to have children and stay together, including gay couples? I suspect that the reason Gallagher does not advocate such a position is that she does not think same-sex couples *should* raise children, although she does not say so directly. Her real concern, as I interpret her statements, is not the implication of a term but the social reality—that some children will have two mothers or two fathers—and the possibility that those families will be equally accepted by society. Both the social reality of same-sex couples' relationships and childrearing and the terms that point to the reality will change, of course. That's the point of changing the marriage law.

The question of whether the change in the lives of married same-sex couples' children is good or bad is a different one, though. A growing body of evidence in the United States and the Netherlands suggests that children raised by lesbian and gay parents are faring well; they suffer no harm compared to children raised by heterosexual parents.[34] Marriage is likely to strengthen the social, legal, and material support for same-sex couples who are raising their children, which is logically more likely to improve their children's lives than to harm them.

Conclusions So Far

Overall, the findings from my interviews and analysis of surveys provide one new data-driven perspective on whether and how same-sex couples might have changed marriage. It is true that I'm getting some of this "evidence" filtered through the perspective of same-sex couples. Maybe they are painting a rosier picture about their own ideas of marriage and the reactions to their marriages than the reality warrants. The fact that some couples talked about actual conflict with heterosexual family members, including conflict that was not always resolved, suggests to me that same-sex couples are not papering over real differences for self-serving motives. These Dutch couples already have a right to marry, a policy that is not in any serious political doubt, reducing their incentives to try to hide the truth from an inquisitive foreign researcher.

The lives of Dutch same-sex couples who have married suggest that the meaning of marriage has not changed as a result of access for gay couples. Same-sex couples recognize themselves in the modern idea and practice of marriage. Dutch heterosexual people recognize same-sex couples as marriageable, and they apply the same cultural model of marriage to gay couples. In fact, my couples' experiences suggest that most heterosexuals recognize and affirm gay couples' marriages. Furthermore, both gay and heterosexual Dutch people share a marriage agenda that is changing the roles for men and women within marriage. As in many other Western countries, including the United States, the new Dutch marriage is a "companionate" marriage that is defined by the commitment and emotional bond between mature spouses rather than an obligatory rite of passage to adulthood, compulsory parenthood, and restrictive gender roles. Marriage for same-sex couples easily fits into this modern understanding but might require a shift in the cultural lens that others use to understand such relationships.

The places that marriage does not have an easy fit for same-sex couples are few and should generate little concern. Resting a case against gay marriage on the declining quality of "information" conveyed by marriage or on the possibility of a radical redefinition of marriage is a very weak one, as the Dutch couples show. Terms are, however, another example of the power of the social institution of marriage that transcends any individual couple's intentions. In language, as in legal rights, same-sex couples who marry find themselves in the middle of an institution that still comes with behavioral expectations for the couple, such as the terms they use to talk about each other and their new relationship. This power means that, while gay people might not change marriage, the institution may have profound implications for how gay and lesbian people think about themselves, as I discuss in the next two chapters.

6

Something New

Will Marriage Change Gay People?

Up to this point in this book, I have mainly considered the impact of same-sex marriage on the larger culture. This chapter and the next turn the causal arrows around and explore what we know and might reasonably predict about the effects of marriage on lesbian and gay people, looking at Europe and the United States for insights. This chapter focuses on the impact of the right to marry on lesbian and gay people as individuals and as members of same-sex couples.

When my Dutch friends Stephanie and Ingrid married without inviting Stephanie's father, he reacted with anger and a deep sadness. Even though Stephanie and Ingrid claimed to have married purely as a practical matter on the advice of their accountant, they could not control how other people interpreted their act. "Their" marriage was no longer their own private matter. To Stephanie's father, his daughter's marriage was a significant life event that he should have been invited to and involved in. The Dutch state would also now treat them differently, giving each inheritance rights, reducing inheritance taxation, and creating rights to joint property and alimony if the relationship ends. Even though marriage appeared to change nothing in their day-to-day lives, a simple bureaucratic act transformed two individuals into a married couple in the eyes of the law and their families.

Analyzing how marriage matters for individuals like Stephanie or Ingrid and for couples' relationships will help us understand how a gay community that was created and shaped by legal inequality will adjust in an era of legal equality that was almost unimaginable even a decade ago. The evidence suggests that a political victory in the marriage debate might well come with some tradeoffs for lesbians and gay men. However, I also believe that to the extent these tradeoffs exist, they are very much overstated. Individuals might lose some personal autonomy but gain in terms of health and social inclusion. Same-sex couples will find that the state and larger culture have something to say about how they form and end relationships, but they will also have a clear legal framework for those transitions and a cultural framework for defining their commitment to one another. The critics of gay marriage underestimate the positive gains to the community while overstating the potential downsides, as I will argue later.

Why Might Marriage Change Gay People?

Some peculiar aspects of the marriage debates emerge when looking at the full range of participants in the debate, which includes both conservatives who oppose gay marriage and gay people who oppose prioritizing the goal of gay marriage and sometimes oppose the institution of marriage itself. (In the next chapter, I call those gay people the "marriage dissidents.") Although they reach different conclusions about whether marriage will change gay people—"It will," say the gay marriage dissidents; "It won't," insist religious conservatives—the dissidents and conservatives are, oddly, more alike than they first seem. Conservatives have an idealized picture of heterosexual marriage that focuses on the old breadwinner dad/caretaker mom/multiple children ideal marriage, with marriage as an institution that tames the baser instincts of men. Some gay marriage dissidents also as- sume an old-fashioned view of heterosexual marriage: two people giving up their individuality to become one undifferentiated couple that is guided by a strict gender code, with marriage "domesticating" gay men and lesbi- ans—in short, the conservatives' marriage dressed up in fancier language.

This historically frozen perspective contrasts sharply with the dynamic view of marriage sketched out in the work of demographers, sociologists, historians, and economists who study marriage and modern families. The broad range of modern family forms, including marriage, remarriage, co- habitation, blended families, and single parenting, suggest that marriage has a very different social and personal meaning today than it did a hun- dred—or even fifty—years ago.

The intense focus on whether gay people will be changed in some way by marriage might seem odd to some academics who study marriage for a living. For most of those social scientists, the issue of same-sex marriage has barely made the intellectual radar screen, much to my surprise. One exception is the noted demographer Andrew Cherlin. He argues that mar- riage has become "deinstitutionalized" in the sense that there are no lon- ger any "shared understandings of how to act," that is, social rules, embed- ded in marriage now to tell married people what to do.[1] In his view, the individual couple now largely stands alone to negotiate roles and behavior that meet the individual emotional needs of the two spouses, rather than simply adopting and fulfilling traditional expectations for husbands, wives, and married couples (such as permanence, procreation, and monogamy, to name a few that are highlighted in the same-sex marriage debate).

Cherlin views same-sex couples as the poster children of deinstitution-alization. Without institutions like distinct gender roles for husbands and wives, same-sex couples must go it alone as they decide who will care for children or will do housework.[2] Without a clear set of institutions to con-struct and define kinship, married gay couples will need to figure out how to integrate their marital relationship into the complex social relationships described as "families we choose" by the anthropologist Kath Weston, as well as into the couple's families of origin. Same-sex couples float free of the constraints and supports of the legal institution in a kind of "pure re-lationship," in the words of another sociologist, Anthony Giddens, so they must construct their own customized marriage through "discussion, nego-tiation, and experiment."[3] Cherlin's argument casts doubt on the prediction that access to "deinstitutionalized" marriage will change gay people at all.

However, I believe that Cherlin underestimates the continuing power of marriage, especially when it comes to gay and lesbian couples. In fact, any lingering power of an ancient institution like marriage might be more visible when it is suddenly available to a group previously excluded from its formal reach. After all, marriage is a complex, multilayered institution that is deeply embedded in legal, psychological, social, and economic lay-ers of life. When same-sex couples marry, they take on legal obligations and rights, new social expectations, and expanded kin networks. They also take on a cultural framework for understanding their relationship that did not emerge from the historical development of lesbian and gay culture, unlike the "families we choose" rubric developed by Kath Weston. When same-sex couples can finally experience the full force of the lived institu-tion from the inside, rather than looking on an idealized institution from the outside, we have the opportunity to study whether these newly felt forces still matter and why.

Who has the edge in a clash of intentions between individuals and institutions? One couple, like Stephanie and Ingrid, and their particular needs, beliefs, desires, and expectations? Or the adaptable millenia-old in-stitution, with its socially reinforced set of rules and expectations about what marriage means and how married people should act? The stories from Dutch couples suggest that even in a society where traditional mar-riage is on the wane, marriage triggers expectations among the couple's friends and family members, and probably within the couple's larger social networks. Even in my relatively short interviews, many people in same-sex couples clearly expressed examples of direct messages they had received from friends and family members:

- When two people love each other and plan to stay together, they should marry.
- Marriage means commitment to a lifelong—or at least long-lasting—relationship.
- Marriage means monogamy.
- Anniversaries are important occasions to celebrate because marriage is a significant event.
- Spouses become family members and are sometimes treated differently from unmarried partners, girlfriends, or boyfriends.
- Married people take on a new identity, and they should refer to their spouses properly: as a "husband" or a "wife."

We can take this investigation a step further by looking for other significant influences of marriage in same-sex couples' family life. The new cultural, legal, and social forces might either reinforce or contradict the cultural ideas, economic incentives, and social norms that shaped those couples' unmarried lives. In the end, we are likely to see in same-sex couples evidence of the lessening pressure on married couples to conform to well-defined norms and traditional expectations, but I doubt whether the influence of the institution of marriage has disappeared as completely as Cherlin makes it sound. As I noted earlier, though, I think the gay marriage dissidents and perhaps even the gay conservatives also go too far in their predictions about how gay lives will change once marriage is a possibility. The evidence suggests that married gay couples live somewhere between the extremes, becoming participants in the lively ongoing process—begun by heterosexuals—of identifying the functions of marriage and the meaning of marriage in the twenty-first century, both for themselves and for their communities and larger societies.

Being Invited to the Party: The Potential Tradeoffs for Individuals

The idea of uniting two individuals in legal matrimony generates a two-becoming-one image that troubles marriage critics who are suspicious of the state and protective of individuality.[4] Some of the Dutch couples I spoke with mentioned their concern about a loss of privacy. They wanted to retain the ability to form, craft, and end relationships beyond public scrutiny and the reach of the law. The first few chapters of this book make the argument that marriage gives others, both the state and society, a role in recognizing the relationship that affects how couples are perceived and in defining their legal rights and obligations, so here I would not argue that the marriage critics are wrong. Research in the United States documents that some American couples avoid marriage because of concerns about loss of individuality and independence, suggesting that people perceive marriage to involve binding constraints.[5] However, individual flourishing is a complex matter, and marriage can provide concrete and emotional resources that enhance the lives of men and women as individuals, even if they consciously (or unconsciously) give up some of their autonomy.

From a legal perspective, while marriage involves state-defined responsibilities toward a spouse, American law also sees marriage as creating an important zone of privacy. That zone is crucial in Supreme Court decisions that carved out new rights related to sexuality, such as the 1965 *Griswold v. Connecticut* decision that said states cannot intrude on a married couple's privacy when they decide to use contraceptives. Similarly, in the United States, spouses cannot be compelled to give testimony about each other in criminal and civil matters.

Remaining unmarried no longer means being outside the reach of the law, either. Increasingly, the law imposes some obligations on individuals who are *not* married, most directly in European countries where simply living together for a period of time generates legal expectations about responsibilities of partners to each other. Somewhat oddly, the gay marriage dissidents tend to ignore the concerns of heterosexual cohabiters vis-à-vis privacy and individuality when they advocate completely equal legal treatment of unmarried and married couples, a topic taken up in chapter 8.

A longer historical view of marriage should reassure those who worry about the loss of individuality. The historian Stephanie Coontz points out that the feelings, needs, and even rights of the individual have assumed more importance over time in marriage.[6] Marriage was once a social obligation controlled by families and communities, but now we see marriage as a personal choice made by individuals. Similarly, marriage as baby factory gave way to marriage as an emotional relationship that must meet the needs of two separate individuals. Even the rise of divorce confirms the new idea that individuals should not be trapped in suffocating or troubled marriages, and people now have options for a life outside marriage.

Despite these historical shifts, marriage still plays a role in mediating the needs of individuals within society. Many argue that marriage promotes a healthy balance between our individual needs and the needs of others. From a philosophical perspective, Milton C. Regan contends that marriage offers an opportunity to make and maintain an intimate commitment to another person that helps individuals "lead lives that they can call their own."[7] The legal scholar Chai Feldblum endorses this view, arguing that marriage promotes an important social good by demanding a kind of "thick interdependence" that forces individuals to grow in ways that total independence does not.[8]

The interplay between the individual and the couple might lead to positive effects on individuals who marry. Decades of research on the impact of marriage on health and economic well-being suggest that marriage equality might provide material and psychological resources that support lesbian, gay, and bisexual people as individuals and as part of same-sex couples. Married people live longer, smoke less, earn more, and are less depressed than single people.[9] Many other outcomes also appear to be affected by marriage, mostly in positive ways, although marriages sometimes break up or involve domestic violence.[10]

The argument here is not that unmarried people are mentally unhealthy but that the institutional and social supports provided by marriage are often good for individuals. A healthy academic debate continues as to the reason for the link between marriage and these outcomes. Some argue that people who are happier, healthier, and wealthier are more likely to marry (what social scientists call the "selection" effect), creating the link. The smaller number of studies that can pull out that selection effect usually find that marriage still appears to have a causal impact on health and other measures of well-being. Spouses monitor each others' health and may exert pressure or other kinds of control to get their spouses to adopt a healthier lifestyle.[11] Marriage might enhance the support of extended family members and sometimes leads to access to helpful material support, such as health insurance.

Like several other social scientists who have written about this question, I believe that same-sex couples who marry are also likely to receive these gains from marriage.[12] To the extent that the marriage advantage comes from the support and companionship of a partner in a committed relationship, gay couples might already be reaping some marriage-like gains. But if marriage enhances commitment among couples (as the evidence from chapter 2 suggests) and the support of family and the larger community (as chapter 5 suggests), then it seems likely that marriage could improve the health of GLB people, even among couples who marry after having lived together for a while.

When it comes to being married, a big prize sought by some in the United States is health insurance. Like it or not, most nonelderly people in the United States get health insurance through their own jobs or through a family member's employer. People in unmarried couples, whether same-sex or different-sex, are much more likely to lack health care coverage than are married people.[13] In the United States, one in five people in same-sex couples is uninsured, and one in three people with different-sex unmarried partners is uninsured. People with same-sex partners are almost twice as likely to be uninsured as are married people, and people with different-sex unmarried partners are three times more likely to be uninsured. Marriage matters for access to health care, although many people (myself included) wish that it did not. In the next chapter I argue that the debate about marriage in the United States focuses too much on the health insurance link, since the political links between marriage and health care are not as fixed as some people might think. Health insurance is one direct connection between marriage and married people's health, but other research on marriage suggests that it is not the only source of the marriage effect.

Reducing Minority Stress: The Value of Inclusion

Most people—sometimes including gay and lesbian people themselves—do not realize the extent of the sense of difference that is embedded in many gay people's lives and, consequently, in most social interactions. In a given day or even hour, the context of difference means that we might travel back and forth between feeling affirmation and alienation, connection and rejection, understanding and confusion. Not all of us operate at the extremes, of course, at least not all the time. Maintaining one's mental health in a world that legally treats gay people as second-class citizens, with no protection against employment discrimination in thirty states and very little legal recognition of relationships, means learning to distinguish ordinary unfriendliness from prejudiced behavior, to choose battles carefully but bravely, and to depersonalize institutionalized discrimination, including exclusion from marriage.[14]

The limitations of these personal strategies are probably evident in the higher rates of depression and anxiety that are seen in studies of the mental health of LGB people.[15] Social science research suggests that experiences of discrimination or unequal treatment can have harmful effects on physical and mental health. This "minority stress" has been linked to higher blood pressure and other outcomes among African Americans and to other negative health outcomes for lesbian, gay, and bisexual people.[16] The psychologist Glenda Russell's research shows that life in an atmosphere of antigay politics has similar negative effects on the mental health of LGB people.[17] Recent studies show that stigma and homophobia reduce the quality of same-sex relationships.[18]

In this context, it seems reasonable to predict that removing formal discrimination through policies such as opening up marriage to same-sex couples will have positive mental health effects on individual LGB people (including those who are single), and those effects will not cost anyone a cent, unlike the expansion of health insurance coverage. The toll taken by shutting gay people out of marriage was apparent in the Netherlands. Many of the people I interviewed were angry about having been excluded from an important social institution. Lin remembered, "I was already kind of really pissed off about marriage because it excluded me. And I stayed that way for a long time." It will take time and highly detailed studies before we can directly assess the impact of cultural acceptance on a wide range of lesbian, gay, and bisexual people who have the right to marry. Right now, however, the lessening of anger and the growth of a feeling of greater acceptance is clear, even in a country like the Netherlands that has long been known for its tolerance of homosexuality.

I suspect that, in most cases, lesbian, gay, and bisexual people learn to live with these low-grade feelings of difference or alienation in the background of our lives, with an occasional jarring experience of prejudice to remind us of our vulnerability and outsider status.[19] But every now and then, a more positive moment of connection can powerfully remind us of both the low-grade difference and the potential for bridging the gap.

The most profound and hopeful moments of awareness I have had of a sense of difference came in the context of planning my own wedding. My partner, Elizabeth, and I walked into our local florist shop to order flowers for our wedding. A bunch of women scurried around behind the counter to fill orders for the next day's weddings, the bread and butter of that business. Even though I had been in a couple of wedding parties earlier in my life, I was (admittedly somewhat willfully) never fully privy to the logistical complexity of this rite, but there we were in the belly of the beast in a downtown corner shop. Elizabeth and I discussed the possibilities within our budget with the owner, and we filled out the order form after crossing out the "bride" and "groom" designations. The florist laughed and admitted that she needed to order new forms that would include same-sex couples. Other businesspeople and bureaucrats were more gushingly congratulatory about our upcoming marriage than was our florist, whom we suspected to be of the rare Republican species in Massachusetts. But the matter-of-factness of our encounter with her made me feel normal, not unusual or special or like a pioneer—just like one of the marrying crowd.

And I was moved to read a letter from my conservative eighty-year old Uncle Henry, who could not attend our wedding because of his poor health. He did not focus on the fact that Elizabeth was a woman but instead focused on the value of marriage. "I do hope that you and Elizabeth will have a very happy marriage," he wrote. "It will not be too easy, but what really good things are easy? The more you invest in it (both of you) the more it will mean to you and your families." The political took a backseat to the personal for most of my family members, who were supportive of us and eager to be included in our celebration of an occasion they recognized as significant, even if they were not all so supportive of the political proposal to give same-sex couples the right to marry. To be treated just like my sister and cousins who had married was something that I never expected. Although my head told me that I was a worthy, productive adult citizen whether married or not, my heart was touched to be accepted as entitled to this rite of passage.

An acquaintance noted that she had never had the experience of being totally ordinary and normal until she married her partner in Canada. "We couldn't shock people," she laughed. This recognition of same-sex couples as fitting the idea of "marriage" that I explored in chapter 5 creates a social and psychological climate of acceptance for same-sex couples that makes gay and lesbian people feel equal and supported.

In the absence of the right to marry, same-sex couples in the United States have often created their own commitment ceremonies to publicly and privately acknowledge their relationships. As Ellen Lewin points out, those rituals are often consciously designed to proclaim the equal legitimacy of same-sex and different-sex relationships, and those ceremonies generate the same kind of emotional intensity and community approval that mark legal weddings.[20] Yet, as real as those feelings are, and as powerful as the commitment ceremonies may be in recognizing the worth of those relationships, the ceremonies lack not only the legal recognition but also the broadly recognized social understanding of the meaning of that particular statement. Just as Dutch couples distinguished registered partnership from marriage by the fact that everyone understands what marriage means, so too might same-sex couples contrast commitment ceremonies with marriage when given the choice.

On a personal, psychological level, as well as on a cultural level, my own experience makes me wonder how the ability to marry could not change LGB people in some profound and positive way, especially for those LGB people who decide to marry or to take on whatever form of committed legal relationship is open to them. Moving from a position of exclusion to one of inclusion is a change that is likely to have a positive psychological effect on some people.

The Effect of Marriage on Relationships

Because marriage is a ritual that involves a pledge of commitment between two people that is backed up in the law and in the culture, those who marry may end up with relationships that are different than those they had before. Since most of the Dutch couples I spoke with had been together for many years, they already felt quite committed to their relationships before they had the option to marry. Even so, several spoke of an immediate effect of marrying and, in particular, of expressing their commitment in front of other people.[21] Beyond saying that they felt more committed, the Dutch couples had trouble putting words to the emotional effects of marriage. Many married people reported feeling "different," "responsible," or "a special feeling" after the ceremony and celebrations were over.

If marriage has an effect on the feelings that at least one partner has for the other, then maybe other kinds of changes in the relationship occur, too. The psychologist Robert-Jay Green writes about the stressful "commitment ambiguity" that same-sex couples experience about what partners can expect from each other in terms of mutual responsibilities, such as monogamy or combining assets, or even involvement in broader family life.[22] Marriage can help resolve or reduce such ambiguity, and an enhanced feeling of commitment related to marriage can lead a couple to make longer term plans, such as buying a house or having a child, that make sense only if the couple expects to stay together. Economists call these commitment-related events "relationship-specific capital" that tend to reduce the likelihood that a couple will split up.

Married couples may also receive more support from families and friends. Surveys of same-sex couples in the United States suggest that gay and lesbian couples perceive less support from their families of origin than their heterosexual married family members receive.[23] Solomon et al. find that lesbian couples in civil unions report more family support than do lesbian couples not in civil unions, though.[24]

Perhaps for all of these reasons—social, economic, and legal—marriage is also more complicated to end than a non-formalized relationship. Several people who had married among the Dutch couples pointed out their potential liability for alimony and other legal costs if they decided to divorce. They were well aware of the potential legal complications should their marriages end. By increasing the cost to splitting up and by creating a public forum for expressing commitment, marriage can lead to longer relationships among gay couples who are married than among those who do not marry, even if those couples are otherwise similar.

As yet the jury is still out on whether the break-up rates for same-sex couples who marry will be different from those for same-sex couples who do not marry, as they are for different-sex couples who marry and those who do not. That would be the best test of whether marriage makes relationships more stable, which at least gives us a sense that the relationship is stronger.[25] The existing evidence on the impact of formalization same-sex relationships is not yet well developed and is not completely consistent. In a three-year longitudinal study, Balsam et al. found similar break-up rates for same-sex couples in civil unions in Vermont and for heterosexual married couples, and both groups were less likely to break up than same-sex couples who were not in civil unions.[26] Divorce rates are roughly similar for same-sex and different-sex married couples in the Netherlands, with about 1% of both kinds of couples who married between 2001 and 2003 getting divorced (von Metzke, 2005).[27] In Sweden, same-sex couples were more likely to end registered partnerships than married different-sex couples were to divorce.[28] The same factors made divorce more likely among both gay and heterosexual couples in the Swedish study, such as age differences between partners, having one noncitizen partner, and being young. However, we don't know if the registered partners were less likely to split up than were same-sex couples that did not register, and it's possible that marriage would have an effect different from that of registered partnership. Although Eskridge and Spedale argue that same-sex couples in Denmark see registered partnership as equivalent to marriage, it would also be important to know whether the rest of society also sees the two as the same and treats married couples and registered partners in the same way.[29]

No one I spoke with in the Netherlands mentioned any obvious changes in their day-to-day life as a result of marriage. Because the marriage debate highlights sexual behavior and old-fashioned gender roles, I paid particularly close attention to monogamy among the gay male couples and the development of traditional-looking patterns of family responsibilities among both male and female couples. As I discussed in chapter 5, monogamy was an issue for some gay men. Only one male couple said that they had become monogamous specifically because of their marriage. While other married male couples had decided not to incorporate a policy or practice of monogamy into their lives, the fact that one couple did so suggests that marriage might change at least some gay men's behavior, as some commentators have predicted, both happily and unhappily.[30]

Another change often attributed to marriage (especially by economists) is that heterosexual couples decide to *specialize* when they divide up household tasks so that the family gets more use out of the time, energy, and money that family members need to live and thrive. In the more traditional (but now rarer) situations, husbands took on the job of earning money as the breadwinner, while wives were supposed to concentrate on the unpaid work of running the household and raising the kids. The common pattern now in Western countries like the United States and the Netherlands is for women to work for wages, too, while still shouldering most of the household responsibilities.[31] Women may cut back on their market work while children are young, either dropping out of the labor force entirely or taking a part-time job.

In contrast to traditional expectations, the Dutch same-sex couples I met had not taken on the old male-female patterns of dividing up family labor after marrying or registering. Some men and some women worked part-time, but none had cut back their market labor time after marrying. (Some of the unmarried people also worked part-time.) One or two mentioned that they had cut back their hours somewhat when they had children, but in no case did a couple tell me that the division of household or wage-earning responsibilities had changed because they were married.

That I found no obvious evidence of specialization among same-sex couples as a result of marriage should probably not be too surprising. Indeed, several studies in the United States show that same-sex couples are more egalitarian in assigning housework than are different-sex couples, both in intentions and in practice, although, as mentioned in the previous chapter, some studies find that same-sex couples do engage in some specialization in the division of housework and other domestic duties.[32] Several researchers find that lesbian couples divide childcare much more evenly than do heterosexual couples, although one recent study of African American lesbian couples found that children's biological mothers have more responsibility for and authority over children than do their partners.[33] Much of the heterosexual division of labor likely stems from cultural ideas about what work men and women should do, rather than from economic incentives to send the higher (male) earner out into the labor force and to keep the lower (female) earner as the homemaker and caregiver. Those understandings are not likely to be strong for same-sex couples, if they exist at all.

Over time, same-sex couples might take advantage of the security that marriage provides to a nonearning spouse, as some have wondered.[34] That spouse might retain some claim on the couple's joint property should the marriage break-up and could take advantage of spousal benefits, such as health insurance. Taking time out of the workforce is not always a bad idea. One spouse might want to stop working temporarily to go back to get a college or graduate degree, take care of a small child, start a new business, or retool for a different career. A temporary cutback in work hours would not necessarily put the nonearning spouse in a permanently precarious and dependent position should the marriage end. In fact, in some cases, taking time off could *increase* that person's earning potential rather than increasing the risk of postdivorce poverty.

The scenarios that might lead to more dramatic and obvious forms of specialization may take time to develop and unfold over many years of marriage. With more time, maybe a future study will see more specialization among same-sex couples than we see now, but it's hard to imagine that the levels will ever be as high they are as for traditional heterosexual couples.

As noted earlier, expectations for husbands and wives have changed dramatically in heterosexual marriages. Ironically, some scholars point out that heterosexual couples are looking more like gay couples as gender roles diminish for husbands and wives.[35] So, if same-sex couples start looking more like different-sex couples, who are looking more like same-sex couples, it seems reasonable to project that there will be little change in what same-sex relationships look like from the perspective of the family's division of labor. The changes that married same-sex couples have experienced have less to do with economic factors and more to do with personal and cultural factors: an enhanced sense of commitment to the relationship and acceptance or support from the larger community.

So far, on both the individual and the relationship level, having the right to marry seems to have some benefits and only a few downsides. But, if marriage is an institution that still has the power to influence behavior and well-being, then changes in individuals and in couples must ultimately affect the larger gay culture. The next chapter ties the changes discussed here to the larger debate in the lesbian, gay, and bisexual community. While that debate was once academic, both in tone and relevance, the current political climate has made it a vital one.

7

Marriage Dissent in the Gay Community

Given the heated debate about same-sex marriage, maybe it's no surprise that public disputes have trickled down into conflict on a personal level. Dinner parties are divided by passionate opposing positions. Old friends who disagree intensely must finally agree not to talk about the same-sex marriage issue anymore. Guests attend same-sex weddings grudgingly and even duck out to read magazines during wedding parties. And that's *within* the lesbian and gay community—those are scenes from my own personal network of friends and family. Perhaps ironically, gay people working on the front lines of the marriage debate get pushback from lesbian and gay people who are not thrilled about the prospect of marriage, as well as from nongay opponents of the right to marry. Those gay people worry that marriage will irrevocably change lesbian, gay, and bisexual people, relationships, and communities for the worse.

The long-simmering political debate in the gay and lesbian community over whether gay people really want marriage boiled over into the headlines in the summer of 2006. A group of lesbian, gay, and bisexual activists released a public statement signed by more than two hundred people, both notable and unknown, calling on gay community leaders to turn away from a narrow focus on same-sex marriage. These marriage dissidents (my name for them) want to make same-sex marriage "just one option on a menu of choices" for people in constructing families, with all options treated equally by the state.

But the signers released the statement the on the same day that the State of Washington's Supreme Court upheld a ban on same-sex marriage, sharpening the sense of a gay community division between those pursuing the right to marry and those who'd prefer to get rid of marriage altogether—or at least to drop or downplay the issue. Some gay people are upset that the dispute over marriage is hijacking gay support for other issues and movements. Joseph DeFilippis, who organized the statement, argued, "[Same-sex marriage] is a limited goal, and to see that goal suck up all the resources and money has been very concerning to many of us."[1]

Many of the signers object to marriage for other reasons. Lisa Duggan, Richard Kim, Katherine Franke, Michael Warner, and Nancy Polikoff, for instance, have resisted the gay marriage movement in print for years. The signers of the "Beyond Same-Sex Marriage" statement and other similar thinkers argue that the efforts to win the right to marry create three big problems for the lesbian, gay, and bisexual community:

1. On a cultural level, marriage means adopting heterosexual forms of family and giving up distinctively gay family forms and perhaps even gay and lesbian culture.
2. On a political level, winning marriage equality means either compromises that edit out noncouple family forms or the risk of political backlash that will delay changes that would benefit many other family structures.
3. On an ethical level, having and exercising the option to marry means creating a hierarchy of relationships within the GLBT community that will marginalize and stigmatize some families.

The debate certainly generates public confusion: What do gay people really want? Who speaks for the gay community on the subject of marriage? Most heterosexual people I talk with don't really understand the concerns of the marriage dissidents. Regardless of their own experiences with marriage, many heterosexual allies of gay people scratch their heads and say, "How bad can equality be?" And yet the politics and prospect of marriage tap into a deep well of anger, uncertainty, irritation, and other emotions among some of my LGBT friends and acquaintances, and a few even signed the "Beyond Same-Sex Marriage" statement that criticizes the marriage equality movement.

These old debates and new fears stirred up within the gay community have fed back into the political debate with opponents of gay marriage. In the United States, the marriage dissidents in the gay community seem to confirm conservatives' worst fears about the gay movement, which then prompts a different group of gay people to claim that marriage will change gay people in positive ways, further inflaming the marriage dissidents, and so on. For example, after "Beyond Same-Sex Marriage" was released, the conservatives Robert George and Stanley Kurtz jumped on one line that advocated recognition of families "in which there is more than one conjugal partner," raising the specter of polygamy as the inevitable next step down the slippery slope.[2] Liberal and conservative pro-gay marriage writers jumped in to object, arguing that this segment of the gay community represented neither the larger community nor the intentions of the gay marriage movement.[3]

Like the discussions in earlier chapters, this debate highlights the question of the *consequences* of allowing same-sex couples to marry, although this time the debate focuses on consequences for the gay community itself. Unlike the discussion presented in chapter 6, the debate framed here has particularly high stakes because of the strong emotions it arouses. Although my own preference in a disagreement is to analyze the issue in a careful, reasoned way, my experience is that this internal debate cannot be resolved through reason alone. My response in this chapter is to dig deeper into the fears and claims of the dissidents, holding them up to the same standard of evidence that I proposed for the fears and claims of conservatives in earlier chapters. Beyond rationality, we should also try to better understand what is behind the emotions. On that level, I hope to find some common ground that may promote peace in the gay community and a more constructive and practical approach to dealing with family diversity in our larger culture.

Will Marriage Lead to the End of Gay Culture?

Maybe even more is at stake than friendships in the debate over marriage in the gay community. Might we be planting the seeds of the destruction of gay identity and culture by pursuing the right to marry? The lesbian and gay community as we know it might wither away if gay people win the right to enter all social institutions on their own terms, including jobs, marriages, and the military. The gay writer Andrew Sullivan makes this very argument about the "end of gay culture." Access to marriage, like other advances in gay rights, reduces the gap between the experiences and options of gay and heterosexual people. Over time, new generations of gay men and lesbians will have options and will make choices that many of today's LGB people have only begun to imagine. Sullivan sounds only a tiny bit wistful about the loss of the old gay culture, which he describes as a gilded "cage of exclusion." He takes a clear stand in the end: "But, if there is a real choice between a culture built on oppression and a culture built on freedom, the decision is an easy one."

The dissidents would probably quickly respond that gay people would simply be winning the freedom to act like heterosexual people—the complete "assimilation" so dreaded by the marriage dissidents—and would leave behind healthy and valuable kinds of family relationships that do not conform to marriage. However, the choice between complete immersion in mainstream culture made possible by legal equality and a distinctive subculture created and maintained by inequality will not be so stark, I suspect. Looking into the crystal ball over the next few decades at least, I predict that the future for gay men and lesbians in parts of the United States may look a lot like the gay community in the Netherlands.

On one level, my discussions with Dutch couples led to some doubts about the long-run survivability of the concept of a gay identity or community. Certainly, the Dutch gay men and lesbians with whom I spoke felt more normal and accepted when offered the option of marriage. Martha said, "So it was really a way to let people appreciate us and treat us like we . . . don't have horns growing out of our heads." In her words, gay couples can be part of what she called a "totally normal tradition." Even people who did not want to marry felt this sense of inclusion. As Anna put it, "I think [the ability to marry] makes us feel more normal and more accepted. More a part of society, for good and for worse, of course, but still more part of society."

Feeling more normal might also lead to feeling less "like a lesbian," too, as several Dutch lesbians who had married discovered. Although Andrea thinks of herself as being "very left" politically, she saw no contradiction between her political principles and her marriage to Katherine. Andrea refused to see her relationship as a "same-sex marriage"—it was just marriage, and she liked thinking about it that way. "You don't want to be busy with the idea of being a lesbian," she said forcefully. "No—you just want to be you." Or, as Katherine put it when describing what it meant to have equal marriage rights, "Coincidentally we met each other, and we happened to be the same sex."

Other people I spoke with also described how marriage allowed the fact of being gay or lesbian to at least temporarily fade into the background in the context of their marrying. Combine these personal feelings with the sense of some gay activists that political complacency has taken hold of the Dutch gay and lesbian community,[4] and the Netherlands begins to look like a "post-identity" world. Erik reports that many heterosexual people also perceive a dramatic change, telling him, "Now that you can get married, the job is done. . . . You are not a minority anymore."

It's far too early to pronounce the complete death of gay culture in the Netherlands, though. I interpret the experiences of same-sex couples not as a full-fledged gay cultural shift but as a brief *personal* glimpse of a post-identity world. Alongside the sense of fading into normalcy was an awareness that marriage made them more visibly gay to the rest of the world, as their stories related in chapter 5 showed. The Dutch gay men and lesbians I met were still aware of how contentious the same-sex marriage issue remains on the global political stage. They saw that the right to marry, and even the fact of marriage, is no guarantee of complete and immediate social and legal equality.

For instance, almost all had experienced the limits of their equality at home once they crossed borders. Just as gay couples marrying in Massachusetts lose their wedded status when they cross the border into any state other than New York, California, or Connecticut, same-sex couples married in Canada, the Netherlands, Belgium, or Spain lose that status when they travel to most other countries. Total complacency is far from an option on a global level, although perhaps the international nature of the marriage debate is not always apparent in the more globally isolated U.S. debate.

Even in the confines of gay-friendly Holland, the equality revolution is not complete. Paul and Jan went to their town hall to marry soon after the law changed, but the computer system could not accept the idea of two men marrying. To accommodate their marriage, first the clerk had to give bureaucratic birth to a Ms. Paul DeVries in the system so that "she" could marry Mr. Jan Smit. Although Paul and Jan now laugh about the temporary bureaucratic glitch and the clerk's creative solution, vestiges of antigay prejudice related to marriage continue to trouble many Dutch lesbians and gay men. The continuing refusal of some court clerks to marry gay couples and the intense debate over the antigay attitudes of some immigrants remind Dutch gay couples of the persistence of prejudice. Several same-sex couples I spoke with felt uncomfortable kissing in public or even just holding hands in more conservative towns because they had been yelled at or received hostile looks. Family members still occasionally oppose the marriages of same-sex couples, as I discussed in chapter 6. Even with complete legal equality in the Netherlands, enough social prejudice persists to help hold the lesbian and gay community together.

Over a longer period of time, maybe as early as a decade or two from today, the cultural change in the lesbian and gay community might be more profound. I expect marriage to become more common among same-sex couples in the Netherlands and the United States than it is today. Gay and lesbian relationships are likely to shift from the do-it-yourself "being together" model that most of the couples I spoke with experienced to the off-the-rack "marriage." Marriage will become both a means to gain important resources for a relationship, mainly social acceptance and legal recognition, and an important end in itself for couples. Pamela Lannutti has found a shift and heightened consciousness among gay and lesbian people in Massachusetts as they think about evolving relationships, wondering if their potential romantic partner is "marriage material."[5]

For one thing, younger gay men and lesbians will grow up in a society that allows marriage, and that possibility expands the social scripts or plans that they might follow in their relationships. Younger gay couples might not have the same ideological commitments that block the way to marriage for some older couples. Marianne, who at age 29 was the youngest person I interviewed, confirmed that she and lesbian friends her age were much less opposed to marriage on principle than the older lesbians she knew.

We see similar variation across age cohorts in the United States. One survey found that younger lesbian, gay, and bisexual people are much more likely than older LGB people to say they would marry if they could, as are less educated LGB people.[6] The opinion difference is large: an eighteen-year-old gay person was 31 percentage points more likely to want to get legally married than a sixty-five-year-old gay person. A survey of LGB teens in the New York area also found enthusiasm for marriage, with 61% of young men and 78% of young women reporting that they are very likely to want to marry a same-sex partner.[7]

Another reason that marriage is likely to become more common is the changing attitudes toward marriage among committed lesbian feminists and others who see marriage as a patriarchal, outdated, or bourgeois institution. In chapter 2 I showed how discovering a good reason to consider marriage, either for romantic or practical reasons, sometimes led to changes in ideas about marriage. Similarly, one part of the feminist critique of marriage was that it excluded lesbians and gay men. With the legal reforms that made the roles of husband and wife more equal, and with the extension of marriage to same-sex couples, much of the political and intellectual rationale for rejecting marriage on principle disappeared.

Although feeling some tension with marriage as feminists, Margriet and Miriyam viewed marriage by same-sex couples as a strategy for changing what marriage means for all women. As weddings became less common among heterosexual couples, Rachel and Marianne could see marriage as an expression of an alternative sensibility rather than as capitulation to traditional norms. Martha and Lin are now enthusiastic proponents of marriage and of the right to marry, but they once held very different opinions, rejecting marriage as an institution, partly because it excluded lesbians and gay men. The new political context might even push feminists toward marriage, rather than away from it. Ellen and Saskia crafted their reasons for marrying around the emerging international political backlash of conservative religious and political forces in the Netherlands and elsewhere. Likewise, the political context inspired some feminists in Massachusetts to marry despite their earlier feminist opposition to marriage. As one friend of mine put it in describing her political conversion, "I'll be damned if I'll let [then-Governor Mitt] Romney make me get a divorce!" (Romney favored a state constitutional amendment to stop same-sex couples from marrying.)

Finally, aging might also shift ardent feminists' priorities and commitments in other directions. Ellen admitted that her own principles about marriage and other political commitments had shifted as she got older. "Actually the only two principles I still have left now [are] going to a biological (organic) shop and buying recycled toilet paper and cleaning products!" she joked. I also expect the relative value of marriage to increase as people get older and have to face issues of inheritance and health care.

I am arguing here that marriage will eventually blur the line between what it means to be heterosexual and what it means to be gay or lesbian. But that's not the same thing as saying that gay couples will simply adopt the traditional heterosexual form of marriage. I argue that the desire to marry, or even the choice to marry, is not the kind of destructive assimilation feared by marriage dissidents.

First of all, same-sex couples who marry are already couples. In other words, they already look a lot like heterosexual married couples in terms of how they live their lives; they're just missing the legal status and the support it provides. Whether you call it assimilation, imitation, integration, or just a historically common form of creating relationships between adults, the issue isn't marriage per se, since gay coupling long predates any claim or right to legal recognition.

Second, more than once in this book I have mentioned that the same-sex couples I spoke with consciously reject the rigid traditional expectations of the roles of "husband" and "wife." That point bears repeating in the context of fears of "assimilation" of gay couples to the expectations and practices of heterosexual couples. I see little sign that gay couples are interested in re-creating the strict gender roles that many heterosexual couples themselves are dismantling or abandoning, nor did any of the married couples I interviewed slip into these roles once they had a piece of paper saying that they were married.

In some cases, though, what the dissidents mean by "distinctive" gay family forms that will be lost includes kinds of family relationships that are found among heterosexuals, too. Extended families that include friends and relationships with ex-partners and even having more than one partner are forms found across sexual orientations.[8] And, because there are so many more heterosexually identified people than gay, lesbian, or bisexual people in the United States, gay people are probably a minority among those family forms, too, so it's not clear to me what is truly distinctive about "gay families" that will be lost. For instance, the 600,000 same-sex couples counted in Census 2000 in the United States are dwarfed in number by the nearly 5 million different-sex unmarried partners.[9] Some of the marriage dissidents also have a nostalgic preoccupation with some forms of relationship that I suspect are largely mythical. For example, the legal scholar Katherine Franke mourns the lost "opportunity to explore the possibilities of a 'lawless homosexuality,'" although she never defines that term.[10] Any lesbian or gay man interested in lawless sexuality will still have legal institutions to resist or boycott.

Overall, from the perspective of my study in the Netherlands and my own experience in Massachusetts, I agree that the cultural fear of marriage dissidents and the hope of marriage promoters are rooted in some reasonable predictions about the prospect of change ahead in gay culture, although my own predictions based on the Dutch experience are far less dramatic. Access to marriage will eventually change the way some gay men and lesbians think of and formalize their relationships. However, there is little evidence that gay couples will blindly imitate the traditional models for marriage. Eventually, gay culture will incorporate the changing options for couples to include marriage, and that change might reduce (but probably not eliminate) the need for a separate gay identity and community. Finally, marriage is a moving target, so any assimilation into this previously heterosexual institution will move LGB people into a very different legal and social institution than existed even forty years ago.

Will the Marriage Campaign Impede Progress on Other Important Political Issues?

The political concerns of the marriage dissidents are mainly practical. They argue that funneling financial and volunteer resources to the marriage equality effort siphons off resources that could instead be used to create large-scale policy changes that will benefit all kinds of family without regard to marital status, including single people.[11] The dissidents call for political action to untie marriage from the health and pension benefits that often go along with marriage or for action to end the war in Iraq, to promote immigration reform, or to work on whatever other issue seems more pressing to a particular critic. Ironically, another fairly common argument among marriage dissidents is a call to drop the same-sex marriage issue and instead to seek to abolish marriage completely,[12] although such an effort would also take significant time and resources away from other worthy issues. Fortunately, the evidence suggests that there's enough political energy and activism to go around for lots of issues.

Much of the critics' focus is on the health care system, which is a very pressing issue in the United States, given the 46 million people who lack health insurance coverage. As I discussed earlier, health care is indeed closely linked to marriage in the United States through employer compensation policies that include health insurance as a fringe benefit. Wage and price controls during World War II led to the provision of health benefits for a family's wage earner instead of direct pay increases, a practice spread by growing union power and demands.[13] This odd historical linkage of marriage and health insurance in the United States is an unfortunate policy anomaly in the international context.

The logical independence of marriage and health care policy is clear when we look at European countries that recognize same-sex partnerships, though. Many of those countries provide health care coverage to everyone, delinking it almost completely from marriage. The Scandinavian countries, the home(s) of the most supportive social welfare and health care systems in Europe, were the first to grant marriage or a marriage-like relationship to same-sex couples. However, it seems unlikely that the order is fixed. A strong social welfare system might have appeared necessary before the recognition of same-sex couples, but it seems more likely that egalitarian beliefs and a concern for the welfare of all citizens led to both kinds of policy (see more in chapter 9). And, finally, note that marriage and partnership rights showed up on European gay agendas even though gays and lesbians had access to some of the benefits sought by gay couples in the United States.

The claim that same-sex marriage is holding back health care reform in the United States just doesn't hold up to scrutiny. Some of the states with the most successful marriage equality movements are also the current leaders in health care reform. Vermont, Massachusetts, and California aren't just three of the first states to give same-sex couples access to marriage or another kind of partnership recognition. They're the three states with recent legislation that would provide universal coverage for state residents through a single-payer plan (Senator Sheila Kuehl's bill in California, unfortunately, was vetoed by the governor) or would significantly expand subsidized coverage for uninsured people in other ways (Vermont, Connecticut, Massachusetts, and California). These recent efforts are, I hope, just the beginning of large-scale health care reform that will improve access to health care for all Americans, but clearly the movement for marriage equality has not significantly stood in the way of change. Likewise, activists in many of the states with gay marriage on the agenda are also pushing hard for changes that would benefit all families and single people through increases in the minimum wage and paid family leave.

Another concern of marriage critics is that a political focus on marriage will detract from the current efforts aimed at recognizing unmarried different-sex couples and other kinds of family forms. Since 75% of the U.S. population lives in states that do not recognize same-sex couples, domestic partner benefits, in particular, will likely remain high on the agendas of gay organizations and individuals. And that's good for heterosexuals, as well as for unmarried gay couples. For every lesbian or gay man who covers his or her partner through domestic partner benefits, roughly nine people with different-sex partners also get coverage—mostly thanks to the efforts of LGB workplace activists who have led the charge for domestic partner benefits in workplaces across the country.[14]

Many people, both marriage dissidents and marriage supporters, were dismayed when some Massachusetts employers announced that they would withdraw domestic partner benefits once gay couples could marry. Some of those employers had covered unmarried different-sex partners, who also stood to lose benefits. However, most companies that floated the idea ended up *not* dropping partner coverage.[15] Only a handful of employers, usually those with only a local workforce and those that had not given unmarried partner benefits to heterosexual employees, abolished partner benefits. The evidence so far demonstrates that improving the lives of all kinds of families and single people does not require a zero-sum mentality or the deferral of the dream of equality for the tens of thousands of same-sex couples who've tied the civil union or marriage knot so far and the many others who want to.

The diversion of political efforts has additional consequences, the dissidents argue, reducing financial resources that could be spent on other issues and weakening those efforts significantly. But would the alternative strategy to decouple benefits and marriage result in significantly quicker achievement of social goals like universal health coverage or lower poverty, for instance? It's hard to imagine. The evidence suggests that the critics are dramatically overestimating the resources that are going to support the marriage effort, both in absolute terms and in relative terms.

Money is a convenient measure of the investment being made in the GLB movement, which includes issues well beyond marriage. Several recent studies document that the amount of funding for gay organizations is quite small when compared with political support and funding for other issues. In 2004, foundations and other grantmakers provided $50 million of support for GLB issues and organizations.[16] It looks like a lot of money, but it constituted only 0.1% of the almost $32 billion in grants tracked by the Foundation Center. Of course, not all funding comes from foundations. If we look at the total budgets of sixty-three of the largest GLBT advocacy organizations, we find that they had only about $38 million in revenue in 2001.[17]

Isolating the money that supports the marriage effort is more difficult, but two studies suggest that only a small fraction of those grants and organizational budgets goes into the marriage effort. Only one-tenth of foundation funding to gay organizations went to support work on the marriage issue, or about $5.6 million.[18] That figure is probably the minimum amount going to the same-sex marriage movement, though, since funding also comes from individuals and other sources besides foundations. Recent data on large gay organizations collected by the Movement Advancement Project shows that sixteen organizations listed a goal for 2006 that included the marriage issue, and their 2006 budgets totaled $81 million. Only two of those organizations work exclusively on marriage. The rest of the organizations included many other goals related to health, discrimination, youth, and other issues. Weighting the budgets of the multi-issue groups by the proportion of goals that involved marriage gives us a higher figure of about $28 million as a very generous estimate of what might be spent on marriage. Adding a few million to account for spending on the antigay (and one pro-gay) ballot measures in 2006 gives us a number around $30 million or so. Gay marriage defenders spent more than $33 million in 2008 to preserve the right to marry in California.

Now imagine what would happen if all of that money were to be spent on other important issues. In 2002, $1.8 billion in foundation funding went to support social justice issues related to economic development, health care access, housing, or civil rights.[19] A shift of $5 million or even

$50 million per year in spending would be a drop in the bucket for social justice funding. If almost $2 billion in foundation spending isn't enough to end homelessness or discrimination, then even $50 million more isn't likely to lead to big gains on those issues.

Or consider health care reform. What would $5 million or $50 million buy in the effort to create universal health insurance? Not much. The Robert Wood Johnson Foundation funds a variety of programs to improve health care and research to meet several goals, including "To assure that all Americans have access to quality health care at reasonable cost."[20] This one organization involved in health care reform spent almost $370 million in 2005 on such programs. Health care, like poverty, homelessness, and other social justice issues, is a complex public policy issue that attracts advocacy resources that dwarf the resources supporting same-sex marriage.

From pretty much any perspective, the idea that the money spent on same-sex marriage could make a significant political dent on other issues is quite farfetched. Of course, shifting even that small amount of money away from marriage to other issues could be satisfying for the marriage dissidents. On a personal level, I can understand the feeling of some gay men and lesbians that they would rather work on other political issues that they rate as more important or pressing. Time is precious, and choosing issues that arouse one's passions makes sense for any political activist, regardless of sexual orientation. However, in my view, the marriage dissidents make a mistake in applying what I would characterize as a *personal decision* about whether to be actively involved in the marriage movement to the growth of the segment of the LGB movement that is focused on marriage equality.

If the political movement for marriage equality disbanded today, would same-sex couples ever win that right? *How* would they do it? The marriage dissidents point to the European countries that have won marriage rights or registered partnership for same-sex couples as proof that deinstitutionalization of marriage leads to advances for same-sex couples.[21] Some argue that a better strategy for achieving many of the needs addressed by marriage is to stress support for household diversity in order to ride that wave of deinstitutionalization.[22]

I agree that the two big social and policy trends are related, and in chapter 9 I will show that the proportion of cohabiting couples is one of the best predictors of which countries have those laws. However, the declining marriage rate was not a gay movement strategy—it was a demographic reality for heterosexual people that led to family policy changes without a political movement to promote those changes. And every European country in which same-sex couples have won the right to marry or to have registered partnerships has also had a lesbian and gay movement that led the effort. In chapter 9, I also show how that political involvement was crucial to the policy change, since politicians would not have acted otherwise.

In this debate over priorities for the gay movement, I can't help but think of the often-quoted words of Rabbi Hillel: *If I am not for myself, then who will be for me? And when I am only for myself, what am I? And if not now, when?* For gay and lesbian activists, abandoning an explicit commitment to winning the right to marry would mean abandoning gay couples who value and seek the social recognition, cultural connection, and legal tie that marriage provides. More than 80,000 same-sex couples in the United States, and many more around the world, have voted with their feet, heading to the altar or county clerk's desk to take advantage of the marriage equality movement's successes. Many more are working for marriage equality, and many hundreds of thousands of others would surely marry if they could.

The three hundred or so signers of the Beyond Same-Sex Marriage statement claim, in effect, that the marriage equality movement has forgotten the second part of Hillel's famous quote. They speak for the many families not headed by gay couples or married heterosexuals, arguing that those families have been forgotten in all the work to win recognition and rights for same-sex couples. As I discussed earlier, the dissidents conveniently omit the fact that some of the early successes of the developing marriage movement, in the form of domestic partner benefits, actually helped more heterosexuals than gay people. Furthermore, almost all of the gay organizations that work for marriage equality also battle other sources of inequality based on sexual orientation related to workplace discrimination, parenting issues, youth issues, and so on.

And if now is not the time for activists to pursue marriage equality, then when? As Evan Wolfson has pointed out, those compromise statuses of registered partnership, civil unions, and pumped-up domestic partnerships came about only when gay people demanded marriage.[23] The glass is already 25% full: the marriage movement has succeeded in gaining some significant legal recognition for same-sex couples in eighteen countries and in states that hold one-fourth of the U.S. population. The claim that marriage equality will not come to the United States until marriage has no legal or social value does a disservice both to the continuing cultural value of marriage (as judged by gay and heterosexual couples alike) and to those whose lives would be improved by access to the rights and responsibilities of marriage.

I think that history will eventually reveal a different view of the marriage movement as a school for activists. In Massachusetts and other active states across the country, gay, lesbian, and bisexual people have learned the names, addresses, and even faces of their elected representatives. They know where to find their elected officials, and a little political experience now may well come in handy when gay couples find out that their marriage certificates don't guarantee them decent wages, health care, or other public services that their families need.

Marriage equality is surely not the solution to all of the political challenges faced by a very diverse group of gay, lesbian, bisexual, and transgender people, especially those challenges that heterosexual people share. But marriage isn't the problem, either. In my view, the political fears and predictions of the gay marriage dissidents are as blown out of proportion as the fears of the conservative religious opponents of marriage equality.

Will Marriage Marginalize Unmarried LGB People?

The third general concern voiced by the marriage dissidents—the marginalization of unmarried LGB people—is one I also worry about. If one kind of gay family becomes socially acceptable when couples can and do choose to marry, what happens to the rest?

Single gay men and lesbians, singles raising children, people who do not marry their partners, families with transgender people,[24] people who do not live with their partner, people who count more than one other adult as a family member (whether sexually involved or not) are all forms of family seen in the LGB community in addition to cohabiting same-sex couples.[25] Once marriage is an option, the dissidents fear that these other families will be marginalized and stigmatized as "bad" gay people in contrast to the "good" gay people who marry. At the very least, marriage could elevate the status of some gay people and gay families above others.[26] This concern is perhaps the most personal issue behind my friends' coolness to marriage, I suspect. As one single friend complained to me, "You'll get privilege by marrying that I won't have."

To start with, I can't help but note that this argument runs perilously close to that of conservative opponents of gay people's right to marry. Rather than accept the possibility of giving same-sex couples the same rights as married different-sex couples, conservatives sometimes create new legal statuses that instead equate long-term, committed same-sex couples with adult siblings who live together or with two roommates (see chapter 8 for a longer discussion). In either case, whether acting on an aversion to gay people (the conservatives) or an aversion to marriage (the dissidents), the outcome is the same: gay and lesbians couples remain in an unequal position vis-à-vis heterosexuals.

Still, it seems reasonable to consider whether gay people will exacerbate inequality by marrying. Once some gay couples marry, other LGB people who are not married (whether because they have no partner or because they do not wish to marry a partner) may feel more conspicuous and vulnerable to being seen as less socially virtuous than the visibly married couples. In the United Kingdom, the legal scholar Rosemary Auchmuty sees little threat of stigma, since heterosexual unmarried couples are now common and accepted as one of many types of legitimate family. She points out that in the U.K., as in many other European countries, unmarried couples are increasingly recognized within the law, as well, further reducing any gap in legal and social status between married and unmarried people.

The legal recognition of unmarried couples has not progressed nearly as far in the United States, but surveys of opinions on family matters suggest that Americans have become much more accepting of family diversity over time. The family scholars Arland Thornton and Linda Young-DeMarco have tracked attitudes toward premarital sex, divorce, and unmarried cohabitation since the 1970s. They found that Americans have become much more open to a range of family configurations in recent years.[27] The change is most striking among young people, among whom fewer than 20% see cohabitation as socially destructive or morally bad, for instance.[28] Young people are almost as supportive of having children outside marriage, and only a minority—about a third—believes it to be destructive or morally problematic. (The survey results I report in chapter 5 support these findings.)

The one exception to the trend of increasing acceptance of nonmarital families concerns monogamy, or exclusivity in relationships. A growing number of Americans in that study support the concept of exclusivity, including a large majority of women and a somewhat smaller majority of men. Such a trend probably helps explain the harsh reaction to the single line in the Beyond Same-Sex Marriage statement that sought equal rights for "committed, loving households in which there is more than one conjugal partner." The dissidents' fear that polygamous or polyamorous relationships will not be swept along toward respectability together with marriages by same-sex couples is probably correct, given the strength of opinion against nonmonogamy in the United States. (Also note that the fears of conservatives that same-sex marriage will lead down a slippery slope to polygamous marriage seem quite farfetched given these same survey findings.)

Marriage may also be implicated in economic or class hierarchies, another source of potential concern, given that we live in an era of widening income gaps between rich families and poor families. Some scholars have worried that recent trends in marriage might be contributing to that widening gap. Research on heterosexual couples confirms that marriage pulls together people who are alike, and, over the last few decades, that pull has gotten stronger. Highly educated men are now even more likely to marry highly educated women than they once were, and, from another angle, high-income men increasingly marry high-income women.[29] Some economic studies seem to support the idea that more marriages—at least if they follow current patterns of like marrying like—will contribute to pushing richer and poorer families further apart.[30]

I don't think that marriage equality for same-sex couples will widen income gaps within the gay community, however. For one thing, same-sex couples also already show similar patterns of like pairing with like, even without marriage.[31] Heterosexual couples who live together also look a lot like married couples in many ways—like pairing with like, higher incomes than single households, and so on.

Another reason is that marriage can *reduce* inequality across families, too.[32] Two people who marry have another person's income to provide support for the household because the spouses share income with each other and because the expenses of two people living together are lower than the expenses of two people living separately (economists call this "economies of scale"). Those factors reduce inequality between families by moving two relatively low-income households into one higher income family. This contrasting effect of marriage highlights the fact that marriage is itself a form of income redistribution. Several economic studies show that the shift *away* from marriage among families contributed even more to the increase in inequality than the increasing correlation of husbands' and wives' earnings did.[33]

Therefore, more marriages by same-sex couples would not exacerbate inequality; to the extent that the married couples would already be living together, not much would change in the short run. The biggest economic gain to couples comes not from marriage at all but from coupling. In fact, I think the main community issue starts with coupling per se and the fact that marriage makes couples more conspicuous. The concern related to marriage may be less that people in families that aren't two adults (with or without children) will look bad by comparison; it's that *single* people will stick out more and will *feel* different, even though their relative economic and political position has not changed significantly vis-à-vis the newly married couples.

Rosemary Auchmuty offers a similar reason for why, even setting aside the material benefits of marriage, the prospect of friends marrying might be emotionally distressing. "[Happily coupled people] live each day in the comfortable assurance that they have succeeded in finding love and *being chosen*—in contrast to the undesirable uncoupled or unfortunate de-coupled," she summarizes one possible perspective. "Do they deserve extra privileges when they are already so richly served?" Those of us, like myself, who have spent long parts of their lives being single but also have been in wonderful relationships can appreciate that the sense of well-being and security that can come from a healthy, supportive, and committed relationship is a true gift not to be taken for granted.

I wonder if some of these concerns are present at the emotional core of the marriage debate within the gay community. Here I mean something very different from envy or the idea that someone without a partner would prefer to have a partner and a long-term relationship. Without marriage, same-sex couples are legally and symbolically single, a situation as well as a legal status that is not so different from that of truly single people. Same-sex couples were (and mostly still are), in a sense, in symbolic solidarity with their single friends as legally single individuals—not necessarily by choice, but at least in legal status. Marriage, then, could seem like an abandonment of solidarity, an explicit acknowledgment that one has a relationship with someone that is different from one's relationships with friends. These negative feelings that single people might experience are obviously different in substance from an economic effect of marriage, but the feelings are no less real and meaningful as an outcome of cultural change related to marriage equality.

The emotional reaction might be tied to other social aspects of life, too. Some sociologists have argued that marriage is "greedy," increasing the time that spouses spend with each other by taking time away from parents, friends, and other family members. Not all studies have found this pattern, apparently, but some recent and careful research in the United

States by Naomi Gerstel and Natalia Sarkisian shows that married people on average spend less time socializing, supporting, and helping other people than do never-married or previously married people.[34] Married people also *receive* less help from others, too. It's not clear why married people are more independent of their larger family and friend networks than are single people, though. An alternative explanation is that others see married couples as less needy and treat them accordingly.[35] Regardless, the study reminds us that coupling—and perhaps marriage—might pull couples inward toward each other and away from friends and community activities.

On a cultural level, the forging of stronger legal and social ties between two people might mean the weakening of other ties that some LGB people think of as family. Kath Weston's study of gay kinship in the San Francisco area in 1980s found a rich web of family ties across households between close friends, extended family members, and even ex-lovers. She worried that increasing attention to the couple and children would cause the other kinds of "chosen" family ties to wither away or that perhaps such family ties would stop forming in the first place.[36]

It's difficult to use Weston's study to argue that distinctive gay families are threatened by marriage, however. For one thing, we don't know how common the San Francisco family model has been in the larger American gay community. Such family formations might simply reflect a particular time and local culture, as well as being a response to a legal and political environment that has changed dramatically. It's also easy to exaggerate the strength of the bonds between all of the members of a given kinship network. Her study showed more intense ties, especially economic ones, among couples, even when they were part of extended gay chosen families. In other words, partners appeared to have a different status in these larger family configurations well before domestic partnership and marriage were on the horizon for the gay community.

Aside from those empirical issues, the vision of uniquely gay family forms clearly animates much of the concern among the marriage dissidents discussed in this chapter. In my view, even if such families were once common and strong in many places, it would be hard to pin a decline in "families we choose" on marriage. Many other aspects of gay life have changed that would have the same privatizing pull. LGB people are increasingly raising children. Opportunities for housing and employment that allow gay people to live openly have improved as antidiscrimination laws and public attitudes have created space for LGB people in the larger society. The extraordinary need for community in the early days of the HIV/AIDS epidemic has, perhaps, diminished with improvements in treatment and public policy. And the aging of the gay baby boomers in twenty-first century America creates many life and job demands on time and other resources—like relocation decisions, saving for retirement, caring for aging parents, or saving for a child's education—that might make larger families more difficult to create and maintain.[37] In other words, there are reasons other than marriage that explain why heterosexuals don't live in similar larger "chosen family" contexts, and gay people live in the same society. As inequality recedes, I would expect gay life to evolve in an increasingly parallel way with heterosexual families.

One could make a political choice to buck the trends and other social or economic pressures to try to create a different sort of community. My point here, though, isn't to say that one of these family choices is better than another as much as to disagree with the dissidents' premise. To oppose a fight for marriage equality in an effort to preserve chosen families presumes that *not* pursuing or winning the right to marry (or perhaps not choosing to marry if one could) would preserve chosen families, but I see other pressures that could still undermine those ties.

Likewise, to fight for marriage equality would not necessarily mean that one wants to give up those other important family connections outside the nuclear family. Marriage derives much of its meaning from its social context and public nature. One function of marriage has always been to create new social ties across family lines, although that function has become weaker as families have become less important sources of economic and political support.[38] From that perspective, perhaps marriage could be a way to create new social and cultural connections that will link broader family networks instead of drawing lines around a narrower nuclear form of family. In other words, marriage for same-sex couples does not have to be isolating and exclusionary. Just as same-sex couples challenge the old sexist roles for husbands and wives, at least within their own relationships, perhaps gay couples can provide a new model of marriage that reintegrates married people into their larger communities.

The history of gay community and family life suggests that same-sex couples might well feel social and ethical pulls toward incorporating others in their lives in deep ways, even as they marry. The anthropologist Ellen Lewin's book on same-sex couples' commitment ceremonies demonstrates the desire of gay couples to acknowledge, strengthen, and even create ties between biological and chosen families, as well as between the couple and its multiple communities.[39]

The most obvious way that I observed couples doing this in the Netherlands was their incorporation of friends and family members in wedding ceremonies. For example, Otto and Bram married onstage after a performance at a theater festival. They gave their friends and family members heart-shaped lighted buttons to wear during the performance to set them off from the strangers who would be leaving before the wedding, symbolically uniting their friends and family and distinguishing them from the nonfamily members in the audience. Ellen and Saskia wanted to bring together the globally far-flung children in their lives—nieces, nephews, and godchildren—and involve them in their wedding. Some other couples marrying had sisters or friends (or both) conduct part of the ceremony. Symbolically, the joint participation of chosen family and traditional family could be seen as a broadening of the couple's circle of family members, not a narrowing.

At the same time, I recognize that this view of marriage as uniting the broad chosen and traditional families of the two individuals involves institutional expectations and is, therefore, in tension with the idea of deinstitutionalization and an emerging reconsideration of the contemporary meaning of marriage. Andrew Cherlin wonders why marriage is still so common, at least in the United States, and argues that its meaning has changed:

> [Marriage] has evolved from a marker of conformity to a marker of prestige. Marriage is a status one builds up to. . . . It used to be the foundation of adult personal life; now it is sometimes the capstone. It is something to be achieved through one's own efforts rather than something to which one routinely accedes.[40]

From Cherlin's perspective, marriages (and weddings in particular) focus attention on this life achievement of the two individuals getting married, rather than on the blending of families or other purposes of marriage. While marriage can be both at the same time—an institution that shapes changes in relationships as well as an achievement—its ambiguity means that friends of a gay couple marrying might not feel a part of the process, even though the couple might intend marriage to widen, not narrow, their families.

These political, cultural, and demographic whirlwinds that swirl about the gay marriage debate create a volatile context for change. The gay community's transition from exclusion to inclusion in the larger culture may not be a smooth one, since some of the values that once seemed to define a gay "community" appear to be challenged by marriage. What can be done about the cultural and ideological divisions and sense of pain that marriage might create within the lesbian and gay community? I am not sure, to be honest, and this is difficult territory for an economist to explore. An awareness of the divisions and different perspectives is an important first step, as is an agreement to disagree respectfully with others' opinions in the context of the current debate.

Over time, marriage proponents within the community will probably demonstrate that they have not abandoned their unmarried gay friends or their other political principles, perhaps alleviating some of the dissidents' concerns. The views of individuals on both sides might also change over time as relationships begin, evolve, and end or as other cultural and political circumstances lead them to reassess marriage as an institution. I predict that tensions within the community related to marriage will eventually diminish, although, in a world with complete legal equality, lesbian, gay, and bisexual people might need to search for new understandings about what those identities mean. As the social and political battles over marriage fade away post-equality, the political might eventually assume less importance in defining what it means to be lesbian, gay, or bisexual.

This chapter and the previous one show that the research on marriage and the experiences of married same-sex couples in the Netherlands and elsewhere all suggest that marriage will improve the lives of LGB people, whether that improvement comes from better health, a more solid financial picture, a sense of inclusion in larger society, or stronger relationships with partners. The right to marry might come at some cost, though. While I doubt that married same-sex couples will fall into traditional patterns of marriage with the associated problems (such as vulnerability to postdivorce poverty or pressure to accept restrictive gender roles), there is already heightened conflict within the gay community. However, as I've argued, the facts suggest that the political costs to the LGB community are relatively small, if they exist at all, and the cultural conflict cost is an unavoidable by-product of political gains in achieving formal legal equality. The psychological and ethical solidarity of the community might well be at stake, although I suspect that, as marriage becomes more common and its effects are seen as minor in comparison to the effects of living in couples, the rifts will heal. Redefining what it means to be gay, lesbian, or bisexual in a world of equality will require some working out.

In this broad context, some individual lesbian, gay, and bisexual people will experience the policy change—gaining the right to marry—as a net gain, whereas others will see it as a net loss. LGB people and same-sex couples will struggle in a new legal context with the old conflict between individual autonomy and new social expectations and between the demands of relationships and involvement in communities. Although some argue that the importance of marriage has diminished for heterosexual couples, the debate within the community and even within individuals' heads suggests that marriage still holds more meaning than some scholars believe. The road to change is not a simple or smooth one, either for heterosexual people or for LGB people.

8

Strange Bedfellows

Assessing Alternatives to Marriage

In the winter of 2006, a curious political debate developed in Colorado. The group Coloradans for Marriage, backed by two conservative religious organizations, the National Association of Evangelicals and Focus on the Family, began collecting signatures to place a constitutional amendment to ban same-sex marriages on the November ballot. A different organization, Coloradans for Fairness and Equality, began promoting a comprehensive domestic partnership bill for same-sex couples that would also go on the ballot in November.

But then Shawn Mitchell, a conservative state senator, took center stage. Mitchell introduced a bill to create a new "reciprocal beneficiary" status to provide an alternative to the domestic partnership bill. Any two adults, including a same-sex couple, two siblings, or two friends, could become reciprocal beneficiaries and establish several rights, including inheritance and medical decision-making rights—as long as that couple could not legally marry. Although the bill never made it out of committee, Colorado could have been on its way to offering three different legal statuses to Colorado families: marriage for different-sex couples, domestic partnerships for same-sex couples, and reciprocal beneficiary status for any two relatives or same-sex friends who are not allowed to marry but are willing to enter that status together.

This range of possibilities led to a confusing and odd set of alliances and conflicts in Colorado. Political support for the reciprocal beneficiary bill was led by Focus on the Family, the well-funded conservative religious group headed by James Dobson. Dobson and his organization endorsed the reciprocal beneficiary bill, even though the group had seemed to condemn policies giving any rights or benefits to gay and lesbian couples only two years before in a "position statement":

> Focus on the Family holds [marriage] in the highest esteem, and strongly opposes any legal sanction of marriage counterfeits, such as

the legalization of same-sex "marriage" or the granting of marriage-like benefits to same-sex couples, cohabiting couples, or any other non-marital relationship.[1]

Interestingly, Equal Rights Colorado, an organization that supports giving gay and lesbian couples the right to marry, did not oppose this bill (but they did not endorse it either).[2]

What led Dobson to endorse Mitchell's bill that would have given rights to same-sex couples? At least on the surface, Dobson and his crew sounded supportive of fair treatment for same-sex couples. As Focus on the Family spokesperson Jim Pfaff testified before a legislative committee, "We do not believe that homosexual couples should be given special rights nor do we believe that they should be set aside for special discrimination."[3] Dobson himself argued, "What this bill is that we have endorsed is a fairness bill with regard to need, not sexual relationships."[4]

Dobson's endorsement for the bill earned approval from the *Denver Post* as an expression of tolerance, but opposition quickly mounted, both against the bill and against Dobson.[5] Paul Cameron, an antigay researcher, criticized the bill, as did Concerned Women for America and other antigay conservative organizations. Cameron went further, though, generating an angry war of words with Dobson over the apparent sell-out to give even a few marriage-like rights to gay couples, a change that Cameron adamantly opposes.[6]

In yet another odd twist, Cameron himself took a rhetorical position that set him up with an unlikely ally in the form of Thomas Coleman, who leads a group called Unmarried America and who seeks to reduce benefits of marriage that are denied to unmarried people. Both Coleman and Cameron criticized the Colorado bill for discriminating against unmarried heterosexual couples:

> *From Coleman*: Left out of the debate in Hawaii and Vermont, and now Colorado, is the legal status of unmarried heterosexual couples. They have been consistently excluded from the definition of "reciprocal beneficiaries" in these states since they are eligible to marry. They are also excluded from "domestic partnerships" or "civil unions" because they are not gay. Like it or not, to the scores of opposite-sex couples who are delaying marriage or who would prefer being considered domestic partners rather than spouses, the political message seems apparent: let them eat wedding cake.[7]

From Cameron: Dr. Dobson claims that the proposed legislation has "nothing to do with sexual orientation," and while the phrase "sexual orientation" may not be used, the bill actually discriminates against cohabiting heterosexuals. Because of their "orientation," they are not eligible to receive the same benefits as cohabiting homosexuals.[8]

Coleman's (and maybe even Cameron's) concern would be a familiar one for readers of feminist and gay scholars who oppose a political focus on winning the right to marry, as I discussed in the previous chapter. Gay and lesbian critics of the push for same-sex marriage, such as Michael Warner and Nancy Polikoff, challenge marriage activists to broaden their imaginations to create policies that would reflect the needs and desires of individuals living in many forms of family.[9]

While scholars' opinions do not always lead or even track those of their communities, other evidence discussed in earlier chapters seems to confirm that not all lesbian, gay, and bisexual people in the United States seek or prioritize the right to marry. A sizable minority of 25% to 30% of same-sex couples says they prefer a different option, and many same-sex couples in states and countries that offer the right to marry or register have chosen not to do so (see chapter 3). In the historical and ongoing context of inequality for most gay couples, they have had to think seriously on a practical and ethical level about alternatives to marriage, and they have had to create their own alternatives in the absence of the option to marry.

So maybe it is not surprising that the marriage equality debate has sparked new thinking about the needs of different kinds of family relationships and new ways to meet those needs. Once fairness for same-sex couples hits the policy agenda, the list of political options for legislators and citizens to choose from is now a surprisingly long one if we draw on legal developments both in Europe and the United States:

- Equal access to marriage for different-sex and same-sex couples
- Civil unions or registered partnerships with virtually all of the benefits and obligations of marriage for same-sex couples only
- Civil unions for same-sex and different-sex couples
- Idiosyncratic packages of benefits and obligations for same-sex and/or different-sex couples (such as the French PACS or the German life partnership)
- "Reciprocal beneficiary" status with a very limited set of rights and responsibilities for any two adults

- Private civil contracts that would replace marriage for all couples
- Recognition of degrees of family relationship (such as parent, sister, or niece) in inheritance and other laws
- Recognition of (unregistered and unmarried) cohabiting partners for some purposes.

In theory, we could consider separately these options and the kinds of family needs they address, instead of folding the long list into the debate about marriage equality for same-sex couples. But debates like the one in Colorado are common enough now that I consider them an inevitable part of the same-sex marriage discussion. As soon as one side says "marriage rights," somebody else says, "recognize all families" or "let's start with something more palatable than marriage equality."[10] I started this chapter by showing how the debate about the importance of the brand "marriage" can set us rolling down what I call *the slippery equity slope,* as one equity or fairness comparison generates another. The danger is that we might end up in an undesirable position at the bottom of that slope.

Policymakers, activists, and even voters must be able to decide on the right way to approach the issue of fairness for same-sex couples. Can we and should we try to meet the needs of same-sex couples by crafting new legal relationships that might apply to other kinds of couples, too? If such a broader approach is proposed, should people concerned about equity for gay couples support it? Isn't partial recognition better than no recognition for same-sex couples, especially if we see these new statuses as political compromises that will someday lead the way to full equality?

Answering these questions is not easy, especially if one looks to potential allies for guidance about the appropriate course of action. As the Colorado case shows, political lines blur when the options multiply. To call feminist scholars and radical gay activists "strange bedfellows" with James Dobson would surely be an understatement. Obviously, the equity comparisons do not happen in a vacuum. Often, politics shape the comparisons and the eventual political choices more than does a careful discussion of the ethics and practicalities of those alternatives.

And that turns out to be the problem with alternatives to marriage. When same-sex couples end up with an alternative to marriage instead of access to marriage, the happiest people are usually those who oppose rights for same-sex couples. Same-sex couples often feel like they have won a second-class form of marriage, or even "a bit of nothing," as some of the Dutch people I interviewed called it in chapter 3. The story that emerges from a look at experiences in Europe and in a handful of U.S. states is a cautionary tale about policymakers' ability to create alternatives that address fairness without sacrificing some other important policy goal, such as expression, privacy, autonomy, or practicality. At best, most of these alternatives appear to offer same-sex couples some useful legal benefits and rights. At worst, the alternatives become a stopping point rather than a compromise that leads to further change.

The Slippery Equity Slope

Thinking about fairness always involves comparisons. In the marriage equality debate, the comparisons start simply but multiply quickly.[11] I summarize all of these comparisons in Figure 8.1 to keep track of the details and compare them directly in this section.

Figure 8.1

Equity-based Comparisons of Different Family Structures

Group: Comparison	A (married diff- sex couples)	B (same-sex couples)	C (other couples or relationships)	Policy remedy
(1)	Married diff-sex couples	Same-sex couples		Allow SS couples to marry
(2)	Married diff-sex couples	(B1) SS couples who would marry		Allow SS couples to marry; rights based on cohabitation; alternative legal status
(3)		(B2) SS couples who would not marry	(C1) Diff-sex cohabiting couples	Rights based on cohabitation; alternative legal status; universal benefits
(4)			(C2) Other related couples, e.g., siblings, aunt-nephew	Alternative status; statutory protection; universal benefits
			(C3) Other unrelated couples, e.g., best friends, close neighbors	Alternative status; universal benefits
			(C4) Larger extended families; intentional families	Alternative status; universal benefits
(5)			(D) Truly single	Universal benefits

Married Couples—Same-Sex Couples

Of course, this whole debate about same-sex marriage begins when someone compares legally married different-sex couples and same-sex couples who cannot marry. The first line of the comparisons in Figure 8.1 shows married different-sex couples in group A and same-sex couples in group B. This is the comparison that lawyers make when challenging laws that forbid same-sex marriage. With the exceptions of Canada, Massachusetts, Connecticut, California (depending on the outcome of a lawsuit challenging an antigay marriage amendment), the Netherlands, Belgium, Spain, Norway, and South Africa, in general different-sex couples are the only ones allowed to enter the one widely recognized legal institution of marriage that comes with a culturally validated package of state and third-party rights, benefits, and obligations.

From the mainstream gay political perspective, this is an unfair difference in the way same-sex couples who want to marry but can't and different-sex couples who want to marry and can are treated. Same-sex couples should have the right to marry because they are similarly situated to different-sex married couples: people in group A and in group B are in a committed, intimate (presumed sexual) relationship of indefinite duration with one other person that is characterized by mutual emotional and material interdependence. To treat group B differently from group A deprives members of group B of the legal rights and benefits that go with marriage, along with the social status accorded to married couples.

Fixing this form of unfairness can be simple: give same-sex couples the right to marry. Others argue that it's not that simple, however. We should reserve marriage for different-sex couples, some policymakers and commentators argue, either because of the political infeasibility of letting gay couples marry or because of the religious and cultural roots of marriage.

One alternative to marriage is to give same-sex couples access to virtually the same legal rights and responsibilities of marriage but to call the status something else. European countries have created a legal status called "registered partnership." In the United States, this new status is typically called "civil unions." Denmark and the other Nordic countries began the movement down this path when they created registered partnerships for same-sex couples only.

In the United States, the Vermont State Supreme Court ruled that same-sex couples had to have equal access to the benefits of marriage, although not necessarily through marriage per se. The Vermont legislature responded, in 2000, by creating civil unions for same-sex couples that have the same legal implications as marriage in state law. California gradually added on to the package of rights and responsibilities for registered domestic partners until that status was effectively the same as a civil union. In 2005, the Connecticut legislature also created a civil union status that is identical to marriage with respect to state-granted benefits (without the impetus of a Supreme Court decision, though). New Jersey followed the same path in 2006 after a state Supreme Court decision similar to the Vermont decision. The group Coloradans for Fairness and Equality was pursuing this strategic path via a referendum, at least as a temporary stop on the way to full marriage equality, but Colorado voters turned down a comprehensive domestic partnership proposal in 2006.

But supporters of marriage rights for gay couples in the United States argue that civil unions are a classic case of a "separate-but-equal" policy that leaves same-sex couples second-class citizens. On a legal level, civil unions are not valid outside the state that creates them, and the federal government does not recognize the status.[12] On a social level, civil unions are, by definition, distinct from marriage, depriving same-sex couples of social equality as well as legal equality. People understand marriage, as Dutch couples noted in chapter 3; however, they might not know or recognize the meaning of a civil union. Finally, segregating same-sex couples into a separate status merely allows the continuation of social stigma and a sense of inferiority related to being nonheterosexual.[13] As I was completing this book, the California Supreme Court's 2008 majority opinion requiring the state to allow same-sex couples to marry (*In re Marriage Cases*) made quite similar arguments in rejecting the view that domestic partnership was adequate:

> [A]ffording same-sex couples access only to the separate institution of domestic partnership, and denying such couples access to the established institution of marriage, properly must be viewed as impinging upon the right of those couples to have their family relationship accorded respect and dignity equal to that accorded the family relationship of opposite-sex couples.

Many gay people and organizations do not see the civil union approach as creating equality or equity, and they resist civil unions as a goal while sometimes seeing them as a useful political compromise on the road to change. This debate raged in Connecticut when the state legislature moved toward passage of a civil union bill in 2005. Some marriage equality activists, such as those in the Love Makes a Family organization, initially opposed that bill because it stopped short of full equality. Controversy within the group ensued, culminating in the resignation of that organization's long-time lobbyist and the alienation of key legislative allies.[14] After much internal debate, and after seeing that a marriage bill would not pass, Love Makes a Family reversed its initial decision and supported the bill in the end as a stepping-stone to the group's true goal.[15]

And it's worth noting that, to achieve a significant "compromise" position like civil unions, advocates might need to seek marriage. The attorney and marriage equality leader Evan Wolfson points out that the right to lesser compromise statuses, like domestic partnership, would not have been achieved if the gay community had not started out seeking the right to marry:

> When well-meaning allies and politicians in the middle proffer the suggestion that gay Americans will accomplish more by "compromising" or settling for the purportedly more palatable civil unions, all-but-marriage, gay marriage, or piecemeal partnership protections, it's important to remember that you don't get even half a loaf by asking for half a loaf. Americans have learned to ask for, and indeed demand, the whole loaf we all deserve.[16]

A slightly different equity argument in this simplest comparison is that "marriage" is best left to religious communities. In this view, the state should create and sanction only civil unions—as distinct from religious "marriage" or even from civil marriage per se—for both same-sex and different-sex couples.[17] In other words, we can create legal equality between groups A and B by changing the status of different-sex couples rather than by elevating the status of same-sex couples. No state or country has yet taken such an approach, probably because it requires abolishing legal marriage. Presumably, this course is different from making a civil status more removed from religion than marriage already is in the United States. In France and the Netherlands, for instance, all marriages must take place at city hall in front of a civil servant, but it's still called "marriage," not a civil union.

Even this method of achieving legal equality would not necessarily generate social fairness, however. Disentangling the legal status from a religious ritual would still not be fair to same-sex couples, since they are not likely to be allowed to marry by most religious communities, at least at this time. Since legal "civil unions" would still likely map onto the cultural idea of "marriage" for different-sex couples, same-sex couples would remain locked outside the gates of the cultural institution of marriage, looking on at the privileged group.

At this point, we're already rolling down the equity slope, with at least three different options for trying to equalize the status of different-sex married couples and same-sex couples. From here we start picking up speed.

Married Couples—Unmarried Couples

We could instead look at how different-sex couples who do not marry fare in comparison to their married counterparts. We could also ask the same question of same-sex couples if we split them into two groups in Figure 8.1: same-sex couples who would marry if they could (group B1 on line 2) and same-sex couples who would choose not to marry (group B2 on line 3). Expanding the right to marry to include same-sex couples would not resolve all inequities, since unmarried same-sex couples would be left out, just as unmarried different-sex couples (group C1) do not get the same rights and benefits as married couples.

In crafting the PACS to be open to all unmarried couples, same-sex and different-sex alike, French politicians reframed the equity comparison group for gay couples in just this way.[18] The lawmakers wanted to avoid both the appearance and the reality that the law would treat gay couples like married couples. Instead, French gay and lesbian couples got what heterosexual cohabiting couples already had—rights of "concubinage," or cohabitation—along with a new option that politicians claimed all unmarried couples need—the registered contract called a PACS.

Some observers and activists in the United States also argue that unmarried different-sex couples have legitimate reasons for choosing to be unmarried, such as a concern about state involvement in the relationship or other ideological objections to marriage. But, according to this view, unmarried couples are otherwise similar to married couples in terms of needs and at least some characteristics, arguing for equal treatment.[19]

Or, are we comparing apples and oranges? Marriage is different in at least two big ways. First, couples must actively choose to marry. Second, the partners in a marriage take on responsibilities for each other, in addition to being recognized for certain rights and benefits. Those responsibilities are sometimes onerous, as when a husband has to pay off his wife's gambling debts or when a wife has to use her own income and assets to provide for her husband who might otherwise qualify for public assistance. Sometimes married couples pay more in taxes than they would owe as two single taxpayers.[20]

Highlighting the active choice and the responsibilities of marriage complicates the comparisons of couples who are or would be married (A and B1) with couples who do not choose to marry (B2 and C1). If same-sex couples had the right to marry and we could distinguish B1 from B2, then we might conclude that we were comparing apples and oranges when looking at married and unmarried couples. When same-sex couples do not have the right to marry, we can't separate the two groups, so comparing them to unmarried heterosexual couples makes more sense. In other words, not allowing same-sex couples to marry heightens the need to compare married couples to unmarried couples and to consider addressing a whole new set of differences in treatment.

Some of the differences in treatment and outcomes between these groups of couples (and between couples and single people) seem glaringly unfair. For example, a married person has two chances to get health insurance: through his or her own job and through a spouse's job. So it is alarming but not surprising that far more unmarried same-sex and different-sex couples lack insurance than do married people.[21] Equity and equality are both served by removing some of the external material benefits to marriage and rooting them in something else, as in programs providing universal health coverage. Many European countries have such social policies, which reduce the benefits of marriage considerably in those countries compared with the United States. With this equity strategy in the context of health policy, individuals in group A get the same rights to certain material protections as individuals in groups B1, B2, and C1, and people who are not in couples (all of the other lines in Table 1) also get those rights, too.

Most pieces of the seemingly "privileged" status of marriage are not so easily reduced to benefits that can be or should be dismantled, however. Many of the rights of marriage relate to the couple itself, including practical rules for the division of property, inheritance rights, or survivorship rights. These rights recognize the long-term nature of relationships and the intertwining of individuals' material belongings and financial assets. Figuring out what is "yours, mine, and ours" in the case of death or divorce requires either a prior agreement or some default rules. Marriage is a default package of rules and standards to guide couples and judges.

Unmarried couples might want rules, too. (Presumably these rules are not an issue for truly single people in most situations, other than for inheritance purposes.) Different-sex couples have the option of marrying, of course, but if they choose not to marry, they can write cohabitation agreements and wills that define some of these divisions and customize an agreement. But many more unmarried couples are probably left uncovered by either private or public (marital) agreements about what happens at death or dissolution. Unfortunately, we have little data about what happens when cohabiting couples split up or when one partner dies.

Two positive strategies for narrowing the gap between the rights of married and unmarried couples have been proposed and used in different countries. The first strategy recognizes the relationships of unmarried cohabiting couples on the basis of certain criteria, usually related to the length of time a couple has lived together and whether they have children. Some scholars call this process "ascription," since the government ascribes or assigns a relationship even if the couple does not declare one. If a couple meets those criteria, then that relationship is treated in ways similar to those available to married couples for certain purposes, such as taxation, pensions, public assistance eligibility, and survivorship rights. In other words, governments assign both rights and responsibilities to these couples. The Netherlands, Belgium, France, Germany, Denmark, Norway, Sweden, Iceland, and Finland all provide a degree of recognition for the relationships of cohabiting couples. The legal scholar Kees Waaldijk and colleagues have calculated that informal cohabitation gives cohabiting couples in those countries anywhere from 23% to 75% of the legal consequences of marriage.[22]

Common-law marriage in the United States might seem similar to these laws on first glance, but in fact recognition of common-law marriages is rare, and they actually become legal marriages once that relationship is recognized. Otherwise, U.S. law offers far less recognition of the rights and responsibilities of unmarried cohabiting couples than does Europe. Some courts recognize a contractual obligation or a status-based obligation for two people who live together if the relationship ends or one party dies.[23] But only under some circumstances and in some parts of the United States do cohabiting different-sex partners who break up have any legal obligation to provide postrelationship support or to divvy up joint property in a particular way. Note that the kind of recognition appears to vary across continents: European countries typically recognize cohabiting couples' relationships more fully while the relationship persists; the United States tends to focus on what happens when the unmarried relationship ends.

The second strategy to give rights to unmarried couples is to create a new legal status with a set of rights and obligations that falls in between marriage and cohabitation. Such statuses are open to both different-sex couples and same-sex couples in the Netherlands (registered partnership, although little difference remains with marriage) and France (PACS). In the United States, domestic partnerships in California, New Jersey, and Maine are open to same-sex couples and to different-sex couples, although different-sex couples must sometimes include one (California) or two (New Jersey) partners age 62 or older. Note that this policy option differs from the civil unions discussed earlier and from registered partnership laws that are limited to same-sex couples, as in the Nordic countries and Germany.

At this point, we can draw two important conclusions that show the limits to the broader equity comparison for same-sex couples that incorporates unmarried couples (line 2 and 3 of Figure 8.1). First, cohabiting couples and couples with alternative statuses are not exactly equal to married couples in terms of rights and responsibilities. Something is always left out, usually legally and always culturally, since these statuses are not marriage. Second, same-sex couples end up with fewer options than different-sex couples. In each of the countries or states that have created an alternative status, the goal was to provide a compromise position for same-sex couples to avoid opening up marriage. In all but three of those situations, the Netherlands, Belgium, and Norway, the compromise alternative-to-marriage status has been the stopping point for same-sex couples, at least to date.[24]

Married Couples—Nonromantic Relationships

But our slide down the equity slope is not over. What about nonromantic relationships? Some participants in family policy debates have questioned the need for placing sexual relationships at the center of state recognition. James Dobson made this very point in Colorado, in fact.

Both opponents and proponents of giving marriage or partnership rights to same-sex couples have argued that many other kinds of cohabiting relationships, such as that between an aunt and a niece or nephew or between two adult siblings, should be recognized and given similar rights. Instead of romance or sex, interdependency and caretaking might be alternative markers of relationships that the state should recognize and facilitate.[25] Although one obvious criterion for being recognized might be cohabitation, in practice it is hard to justify why multihousehold families should be excluded if other characteristics of interdependency and caretaking are present. Conceivably, groups larger than two adults might also be included in such policies, although I know of no such policy examples. We might compare the legal treatment of these other groups (groups C2-C4 in Figure 8.1) to married couples, thus expanding the kinds of couples and family configurations that would receive treatment similar or equal to that granted married couples with respect to rights and obligations.

While I do not know of any formal policies that recognize related couples, unrelated couples, and larger family forms, two states, Hawaii and Vermont, have enacted a policy that allows most pairs of people who cannot marry because they are related or cannot marry for another reason to register with the state and to receive some limited benefits. Belgium is the only European country to allow siblings or other relatives to register as "legal cohabitants," the Belgian form of registered partnership that preceded the opening of marriage to same-sex couples.[26]

Hawaiian legislators created "reciprocal beneficiaries" to allow any two individuals who could not marry (including but not limited to same-sex couples) to register and receive certain statutory benefits with respect to inheritance rights, state pension benefits, and taxes. The legislative findings in the bill clearly demonstrate the legislature's own equity comparisons:

> [Hawaii Revised Statutes §572C-2] However, the legislature concurrently acknowledges that there are many individuals who have significant personal, emotional, and economic relationships with another individual yet are prohibited by such legal restrictions from marrying. For example, two individuals who are related to one another, such as a widowed mother and her unmarried son, or two individuals who are of the same gender. Therefore, the legislature believes that certain rights and benefits presently available only to married couples should be made available to couples comprised of two individuals who are legally prohibited from marrying one another. [L 1997, c 383, pt of §1]

In 2000, Vermont actually created both the civil union status mentioned earlier and a reciprocal beneficiary status. Two unmarried individuals who are over eighteen and are too closely related to marry (or to enter a civil union) may file a notarized declaration to become reciprocal beneficiaries. The rights that go with the status are much more limited than those available in Hawaii but include hospital visitation and health care decision-making rights that are the same as those for a spouse, as well as some other rights related to nursing homes and anatomical gifts.

At this end of the equity slope, we might again be comparing apples and oranges. Do other kinds of couples (or even larger families) take on the mutual obligations and responsibilities of support that are imposed on married couples? What are those other couple relationships like? Our ability to infer similarity or to impose uniformity is limited when it comes to other kinds of couples. Legal marriage is mapped onto a social and cultural institution. The legal and cultural aspects mutually create an institution called marriage that is reinforced by both aspects and enforced by a larger society when the law is silent. Other kinds of relationships cannot draw on the same power. There's nothing close to a common understanding of mutual obligation to support or care for a sibling, uncle, ex-lover, or best friend. Defining a useful "default contract," as marriage does, for many different needs and expectations would likely be impossible.

After this quick slide down the equity slope, we are left with many— probably too many—new family policy possibilities to consider all at once. Most will not solve the problem of unfair treatment of same-sex couples, as I noted earlier. In the context of family relationships, the goal of "equity" is too blunt an instrument to be a sufficient guide for those who want to be fair. In a world ruled by principle, we might decide that some of the benefits of marriage should belong to all people, regardless of their family relationships. In those cases, an equity perspective calls on policymakers to pull those out of the marriage package and deal with them separately, as some Canadian policymakers have done.[27] When it comes to rights that go to couples or responsibilities that might be imposed on couples, though, fairness alone cannot determine the best way to deal with family structures that look very different from one another. We might want to match the level of rights to the level of responsibility taken on by the couples, for instance, or we might want to ensure that an individual agrees to the responsibilities that they are taking on for another person.

In the real world, the actual policies and marriage alternatives that have emerged in the debate over marriage equality probably reflect less an altruistic, high-minded search for fairness than something closer to raw political power. As the policy analyst Deborah Stone argues, political advocates will choose "equity frames," or ways of presenting choices, that are in the advocates' strategic interest and that promote a particular political goal.[28] As the next section shows, the most skillful users of strategic equity frames have been opponents of marriage equality for gay couples.

The Political Equity Trap

In the introduction to this chapter, I showed how powerful actors make arguments based on equity that appear to be supportive of rights for same-sex couples. James Dobson and Focus on the Family publicly endorsed Colorado's reciprocal beneficiary bill, lauding the fact that the bill treated same-sex couples without discrimination. In communications with their members, though, Focus on the Family spokespeople emphasized that their support was strategic.

Recall that the reciprocal beneficiary bill was introduced as an alternative to a more expansive domestic partnership relationship for same-sex couples. A newsletter for Focus supporters quoted Dale Schowengerdt from the Alliance Defense Fund (an organization co-founded by James Dobson)[29] on the strategic value of the less ambitious bill: "It really eviscerates any arguments for civil unions, or domestic partnership. . . . The bill does not create a status, and does not give benefits based on a status, and that's what civil unions and domestic partnerships do."[30]

The history of the debate about same-sex couples in the United States and Europe is filled with examples of the Colorado dynamic. The reciprocal beneficiary, domestic partnership, registered partnership, and civil union statuses all emerged as political compromises to give same-sex couples benefits and rights without opening up marriage. The discussion of other family forms often originated with opponents of same-sex marriage, either because they recognized the needs of same-sex couples but wanted to avoid formally equating same-sex couples with married couples or because they wanted to sabotage the efforts to extend rights for same-sex couples. In this context, alternatives to marriage become a weapon in the effort to slow or even stop the political progress that same-sex couples make in moving toward marriage.

In the United States, Hawaii was the first to go down this road. "Reciprocal beneficiaries" were born in 1997 in the wake of a court decision that was leading toward marriage rights for same-sex couples in Hawaii. A referendum created a constitutional amendment that gave state legislators the power to limit access to marriage to different-sex couples.[31] As part of the legislative compromise to reserve marriage for different-sex couples, lawmakers also created the reciprocal beneficiary status to give inheritance rights, tax rights, and some other benefits to same-sex couples and to other couples who could not marry.

The strategy was exported to other states. Tellingly, Focus on the Family bragged about its involvement in the Hawaiian efforts, using Hawaii as an example of why Colorado should use the same strategy.[32] In Vermont, the reciprocal beneficiary option constituted a political halfway house for Republicans who were squeamish about giving full recognition to same-sex partners but who also did not want to align themselves with the extreme no-rights-for-same-sex-couples position.[33]

In New Jersey, in contrast, a gay political organization promoted a bill to define domestic partnerships that raised the question of whether lots of kinds of families should be included.[34] The initial draft of the bill included a sweeping set of possible relationships that could be included as domestic partners. Political leaders who supported rights for same-sex couples objected to the breadth, arguing that such a bill was not politically feasible because of its potential expense and competition with marriage. The organization's initial proposal was based on a principled concern for equity, as well as a political desire to create a larger coalition of directly interested parties, but that coalition did not materialize. Eventually, the bill was amended so that only same-sex couples and older different-sex couples were eligible to register as domestic partners.

In Europe, as in the United States, alternative registration statuses like registered partnerships were simply compromise positions in the same-sex marriage debate.[35] The inclusion of couples other than same-sex romantic couples was considered but quickly rejected in some countries. Many policymakers wanted to reserve marriage for heterosexual couples and wanted to discourage them from a further retreat from the institution.

In France, Belgium, and the Netherlands, however, the eventual alternative was opened to different-sex couples as well as same-sex couples. The more inclusive approach represented the political context of the debate.

- In France, early versions of the legislation that eventually created the PACS strategically included more expansive coverage for other types of couples, such as siblings or friends, to avoid a focus on homosexuality.[36] In the end, only romantic couples were allowed to form a PACS, with different-sex couples included as a way of reducing homophobia-based opposition to the legislation, not because of demands for inclusion by those couples.[37] Daniel Borillo and others have noted that limiting the PACS to same-sex couples would have clashed with the French tradition that "preclude[s] special laws applying only to minority groups."[38]

- In the Netherlands, the possibility of a policy that would cover many family forms was dismissed as a distraction in the absence of a vocal interest group.[39] Interestingly, but perhaps not surprisingly, the inclusion of different-sex couples generated more right-wing opposition to registered partnerships than did the inclusion of same-sex couples, since partnership would compete with marriage.[40]

While the alternatives to marriage created for same-sex couples in different countries might seem to be politically equivalent compromises, differing only in some legal details, the cross-national experience to date suggests otherwise. These new statuses are certainly political compromises. New statuses also have the potential to be transitional and transformational, changing attitudes about marriage equality for same-sex couples over time, as William Eskridge has argued.[41] But some new statuses can also be political traps, blocking further political progress toward marriage for same-sex couples.

Certain key differences between marriage and an alternative status appear to distinguish a dead-end status from a transitional compromise. When a status comes with a package of rights and responsibilities that is very different from the package that accompanies marriage, it might seem that marriage equality advocates have farther to go to achieve equality, increasing the possibility that an alternative is a political dead end. However, the bigger block toward convergence with marriage seems to occur when many kinds of families or couples are allowed to register for the alternative status (which often coincides with a relatively meager package of rights and responsibilities). Since the status is designed for at least some couples whose expectations and needs will not be those of married couples, it seems to be more difficult for policymakers to consider adding on to the rights and responsibilities for that status to make it more marriage-like. For instance, siblings or an aunt and niece might not want to be potentially liable for alimony should their relationship end; close friends might not want to assume financial responsibility for each other's needs or debts.

In practice, the new statuses that include nonromantic couples have not been expanded, while those that are similar to marriage have become closer to marriage or have contributed to the process of opening up marriage in some way. The Dutch example is a case in point. The legal scholar Kees Waaldijk outlines a "law of small change" to explain how the Netherlands moved from nonrecognition of same-sex couples to full marriage rights. Once sodomy laws were gone and antidiscrimination laws covered sexual orientation, family law began to equalize. The process began when same-sex couples were accorded the same treatment as different-sex cohabiting couples in the law. Registered partnership was the compromise in 1998 and came with almost all of the rights and responsibilities of marriage. Only different-sex and same-sex couples who met the requirements of marriage could register, and siblings and other close relatives were excluded. Over the next couple of years, the Dutch parliament closed the remaining obvious differences in pension rights and residency requirements that distinguished registered partnerships from marriage.[42] Waaldijk argues that the tiny gap left was so small that opening up marriage to gay couples was not seen as a socially or politically risky step by 2000. I would only add to Waaldijk's account the point that the Dutch registered partnership model stuck very closely to marriage, making the convergence between registered partnership and marriage possible.

Other countries have seen a similar dynamic. The original registered partnerships in the Nordic countries had most of the same entrance requirements as marriage and most of the rights and responsibilities of marriage. While partnerships were limited in some ways that marriages were not, over time that gap has narrowed. The Danish registered partnership law originally limited partnerships to couples with at least one Danish citizen, but ten years later Danish lawmakers made it easier for noncitizen partners to register, and state church priests can now bless same-sex unions.[43] Iceland also loosened the nationality requirements and made it easier for a partner to adopt the other partner's child.[44] Sweden equalized adoption and custody rights for registered partners in 2003, and lesbian couples now have the right to alternative insemination.[45] The original 2001 German "life partnership" extended a limited set of rights, including inheritance, wrongful death compensation, public health insurance coverage, name changes, residence permits for foreign partners, and a few others. In 2004, the Bundestag, the lower house of Germany's parliament, added the right to adopt a partner's child and extended laws of divorce, property division, and alimony to life partners.[46]

Two states in the United States, California and New Jersey, have also experienced the convergence dynamic, first passing a simple domestic partnership law that granted fewer rights and obligations than marriage, followed by some closing of the gap. California almost completely closed the gap legislatively, starting with a 1999 partnership registry law that gave partners sixteen rights, including hospital visitation rights and the right of public employers to offer partner benefits. A 2002 law added rights related to parenting, unemployment insurance, and medical decision making. A year later, a new law extended almost all of the remaining state rights and responsibilities of marriage to partners as of 2005. In 2005, the state legislature passed a law giving gay couples the right to marry, but the governor vetoed the bill. The gap between the state-granted rights of domestic partnership and marriage closed with a final step in 2006, when the California legislature agreed to allow domestic partners to file state taxes jointly like married couples. (And, as noted earlier, from June to November 2008, same-sex couples could marry in California, until voters overturned a California Supreme Court decision.)

New Jersey's domestic partner law was passed in 2004. A year later, the legislature added inheritance rights for domestic partners that are equivalent to those of a spouse and the authority to make funeral arrangements.[47] In late 2006, a New Jersey Supreme Court ruling, in *Lewis v. Harris*, required New Jersey's legislature to grant all of the rights and responsibilities of marriage to same-sex couples. The legislature chose to do so by creating a third status, civil unions, instead of adding onto domestic partnerships, perhaps because that status was open to older different-sex couples (age 62 or older), as well, who would not have wanted all of the rights and responsibilities of marriage. Since the creation of civil unions, only individuals age 62 or older can enter a domestic partnership.[48] Over time, I suspect, domestic partnership will be a dead end with respect to rights and responsibilities.

Belgium, France, and Hawaii are clearer models of the political equity trap. As noted earlier, these three jurisdictions deviated significantly from the marriage model in constructing alternative relationships. And, in all three cases, the new kind of partnership did not progress toward marriage. Foreshadowing events in New Jersey, Belgian lawmakers opted to open marriage to same-sex couples rather than to add onto the country's legal cohabitation status.[49] In France, the package of rights that goes to couples with a PACS have not changed measurably since that status was created, in 1999. Reciprocal beneficiaries in Hawaii actually now get *fewer* rights than they did when that status was created. Provisions that granted health insurance benefits to reciprocal beneficiaries of state employees have expired. While the battle to give same-sex couples access to marriage continues in

France and succeeded in Belgium, the alternative statuses have remained static, suggesting that the possibility of a political trap that creates dead ends is real.

As noted earlier, another alternative to marriage prominent in Europe is recognition of cohabiting couples, but this strategy comes with its own set of political limits that prevents full equality between couples who cohabit and those who marry. In many European countries, unmarried cohabiting couples receive some rights, benefits, and obligations of marriage. Such rights sometimes are written into law, but they are also often granted through policy guidelines, regulations, or court decisions about property division, wrongful death suits, inheritance, and alimony.[50] Demand for these rights was apparently inferred by European policymakers from the existence of large numbers of cohabiting couples, related court cases, and (only rarely) more direct lobbying.

As progressive as these equalizing laws have been, though, these countries have been reluctant to make cohabitation the full equivalent of marriage. Rights for cohabitors appear to extend only rarely to community property rights, inheritance rights, or alimony rights, for instance.[51] Furthermore, as I mentioned earlier, in some cases cohabitors are viewed as having *obligations* to each other, as well as rights. The demographer Turid Noack points out the four most common justifications for Norway's recognition of cohabitors: "the need to protect the weak; to make necessary adjustments to changing family behaviour; to prevent strategic behavior [e.g., not marrying to avoid losing social benefits]; and to avoid unjust differences in rights and benefits between married and cohabitants."[52] Note that only one of the four justifications is rooted in equity. Partners' implicit obligations to each other may be an important reason for formally recognizing cohabiting couples' relationships in Europe.

Since recognition of cohabiting couples involves imposing obligations, extension of the range of rights and responsibilities that come with cohabitation is controversial. Equalizing the status of cohabitation and marriage would, in effect, eliminate couples' ability to choose how they wish to be treated by the state. European and Canadian policymakers are sensitive to this tradeoff between equity and autonomy.[53] Noack describes a Norwegian commission on cohabiting couples and its decision to oppose both voluntary and compulsory registration systems for cohabiting different-sex couples.[54] For couples who reject marriage because they do not want the state involved in their private relationships, as do some same-sex couples discussed in chapter 2, the state's intervention in an unmarried relationship might seem particularly intrusive or objectionable.

In the end, the use of equity as a guide for recognizing relationships runs into some big challenges, and those challenges require policymakers to balance fairness with other concerns. I would characterize this set of challenges faced by policymakers as an *opt-in/opt-out dilemma*:

- *Opt-in strategies* for granting rights and obligations, such as marriage or even some alternative registration processes, are underinclusive. Some couples (or other family configurations) will always be left out if they do not marry or register, and the number of such couples could be large, as the next section demonstrates.
- *Opt-out strategies*, such as giving rights to *de facto* or cohabiting couples who have opted out of marriage, run the risk of overinclusiveness—some of those couples will have rights and obligations imposed that they might have consciously wished to avoid by not marrying. In other words, they lose the ability to truly opt out.

I believe that framing the dilemma in this way helps to clarify the role of alternatives to marriage in the debate over marriage equality for same-sex couples. Policymakers cannot pursue equity as a goal without running into potentially serious conflicts with other values of autonomy, choice, and privacy, in particular. Combining this tradeoff with the political pitfalls of alternatives to marriage that stop far short of equality for gay couples suggests that no alternative can be a satisfying substitute. While advocates of alternatives might (or might not) be well meaning in considering the needs of same-sex couples, in the realm of politics these alternatives will be strategically crafted or politically limited in ways that create barriers to full equality for same-sex couples over the longer term.

Is There a Demand for Alternatives to Marriage?

One important way to assess the meaning and value of alternatives to marriage is to look at what people say and do on a broader scale. In chapter 3, Dutch couples argued that registered partnership was a helpful step on the way to marriage equality, but once marriage was available, the importance of registered partnership shrank to a "bit of nothing" for many Dutch gay and lesbian couples.

Unfortunately, we rarely have such direct evidence of how couples and other family forms view alternative statuses. In the political debate, most of the equity arguments come from a fairly small number of gay, lesbian, and bisexual activists or from antigay activists. Many of those GLB activists, at least, are motivated by altruism and genuine concern for other family structures, but they speak for people in those family structures who are notably absent in these debates. The danger is that the vocal activists are not capturing the true needs and wishes of the people for whom they speak.

If activists are tapping into a serious unmet need, we would expect to see people taking advantage of their new options. In chapter 3, however, we saw that romantic couples usually choose marriage when they have formal options, even in Europe. The evidence to date suggests a very low demand for an alternative status among nonromantic couples, too.

Vermont and Hawaii provide a reciprocal beneficiary status for nonromantic couples, but in practice it is not very popular. Exactly zero reciprocal beneficiaries have registered in Vermont seven years after the law was passed.[55] In fact, the Vermont Civil Union Review Commission invited lobbying groups for seniors to talk about whether reciprocal beneficiaries should be expanded to include seniors, but no group even wanted to testify.[56]

The State of Hawaii does not track how many reciprocal beneficiaries are same-sex couples and how many are other family configurations. However, the small number—823 over six years—and the lack of other options for same-sex couples strongly suggests that the majority of the 823 are same-sex couples. Furthermore, there were 2,389 same-sex couples recorded in Hawaii in Census 2000, so it is plausible that all 823 reciprocal beneficiaries are same-sex couples, implying a 34% take-up rate, at best, even for same-sex couples.

Why might the demand be so low for statuses other than marriage and among couples other than same-sex couples? There are several possibilities. Maybe people don't realize these options are available, although in Hawaii and Vermont they have been available for several years now and were created during a highly visible debate about same-sex marriage. Some evidence suggests that people know about these other options but choose not to register. Vermont's Department of Health tracks the number of visits to the department's reciprocal beneficiary Web page, as well as downloads of the brochure describing that status. In 2006, a thousand people reviewed and downloaded this information but decided that, for whatever reason, the reciprocal beneficiary status was not something they would sign up for.[57]

As a result, I suspect the more likely possibility is that the principled alternatives are not very attractive on either a practical level or a symbolic level, as discussed in chapter 3. Some practical reasons are simple: people who are legally related already have certain inheritance rights and rights to make medical decisions about legally related family members, perhaps reducing demand for reciprocal beneficiary-type registration. So the gains to reciprocal beneficiary status may be seen as small and the possible downsides unknown for many couples.

Full Freedom to Choose Marriage

On one level, even if lots of other kinds of couples and families were to lobby for and take advantage of formal alternatives to marriage, same-sex couples would still be treated unfairly from one crucial angle. Without the right to choose marriage, same-sex couples face options different from those available to heterosexual couples and remain in a second-class position. As I argued in this chapter, the claims that alternatives might be the way to "enough" equality for same-sex couples fail when viewing the reality of alternatives. They are designed to be different from marriage, and those differences are deliberate—they are intended to placate heterosexuals and to keep same-sex couples unequal. The strategic design of alternatives might also set back the hopes of same-sex couples if the alternatives are further limited by a tradeoff with autonomy or by the needs of very different kinds of couples who share the same status.

But it is just as clear that these alternatives do not suit any kind of couple particularly well. We need to know more about what these other couples need from a legal perspective before we will be able to better design a useful one. More research and more political involvement from other kinds of families will be necessary before policymakers figure out the right mix of rights and responsibilities.

However, the European experience suggests a somewhat different and potentially more interesting family policy agenda. The official goal of the marriage equality movement is to give same-sex couples the same right— the freedom to choose—to marry that heterosexual couples have. But some have asked whether this "choice" is an unadulterated preference for whatever social and personal value marriage offers.[58] Instead, maybe this choice is guided or even coerced, on some level, by the need for the legal and financial benefits that go to married couples. From this perspective, the benefits that act as a carrot to reward some couples for marrying are the stick that drives other couples to make a choice that they would otherwise not make.

If policymakers wanted to encourage couples to marry freely and without coercion, then surely one of the first items of business would be to open up marriage to same-sex couples. Beyond marriage, couples who simply want to ensure that they have some legal protection in case of dissolution could write a cohabitation contract or draw on laws guiding the division of property and alimony for cohabiting couples, perhaps laws constructed along the lines of the principles suggested by the American Law Institute. (And, of course, those possibilities would be applied to same-sex couples as well as different-sex couples, too.) In the U.S. policy context, full freedom to marry would also require that health care benefits be provided without respect to marriage—and almost certainly without respect to employment.

The pieces of a policy agenda that support a full freedom to marry would not have to happen all at once in order to further the principle of freedom of choice, as well as the principle of fairness. While the same-sex marriage debate has opened up the discussion of family recognition in the United States in a healthy way, the principle of fairness should not require same-sex couples to forgo a fight for equality until all other family forms are recognized, especially if some people in those other family forms do not want formal recognition. Just as the claim that gay people destroyed marriage in Scandinavia unfairly and erroneously scapegoats same-sex couples, the demand that same-sex couples must defer the right to marry until a new set of alternatives to marriage exists seems equally unfair.

In Europe, rights for same-sex couples and an expanded recognition of the needs of other kinds of families and individuals happened for the most part over time without an obvious sense of a necessary order. That approach makes sense given the different needs and desires of people in these different family configurations. Politics shaped some of the European proposals related to gay and lesbian couples and carved out new statuses for gay couples to avoid opening marriage in most countries. The United States can learn from the experience of these countries and the experiments with new statuses in a handful of states. Alternatives to marriage don't necessarily lead to equality for same-sex couples, and concerns about equity can lead policymakers down a dead end road, especially when guided by those eager to avoid equality.

9

The Pace of Change

Are We Moving Too Fast?

Given the longevity and adaptability of marriage as a social and legal institution, the rapid inclusion of same-sex couples that began in Europe in 1989 can seem both remarkable and natural at the same time. Earlier chapters showed how changes in the institution of marriage and the emergence of same-sex couples who wanted to marry brought the two together. As of 2007, 62% of European Union residents live in a country that grants formal legal recognition (either marriage or something legally similar) to same-sex couples. The gradual but steady spread of the principle of equality in marriage rights suggests that the time was ripe in Europe for opening marriage to same-sex couples.

In contrast, only 21% of the U.S. population lives in a state that gave most or all marriage rights to gay couples as of August 2008. The slower pace of change and the rapidly mobilized resistance to the idea of marriage for same-sex couples in the United States suggests to some observers that it is just not ready yet. The political advice to go slow also comes from many directions, including some allies who support the principle of gay equality. As Rabbi Michael Lerner points out, "The fact is, there are millions of Americans who believe in equal rights for gays and lesbians . . . but who draw the line at marriage."[1]

A more incremental approach to equality that starts by introducing alternatives to marriage in stages might give time for people to get used to the idea and might someday lead to opening up marriage itself. Some have pointed to the creation of registered partnership in Europe as the kind of compromise needed in the United States, where a different name—"civil unions"—has become popular. The communitarian thinker Amitai Etzioni sees civil unions as a useful compromise given the incompatible worldviews of opposing advocates. "Such a compromise is not the best of all worlds," he admits. "But it is the best that one can achieve in our society at this stage in history."[2] In chapter 8 I looked in detail at whether the United

States should seek the answer to the demands of gay couples by pursuing alternatives to marriage. As we will see in this chapter, even the alternative approaches in Europe went farther and faster than the proposed alternatives in the United States.

In addition to the pressure to slow down and compromise, we also see concerns about the pace of change in the outrage expressed by President George W. Bush and others about "activist judges" who are supposedly out of step with popular opinion. The judicial process appears to have abruptly shifted the gradually evolving movement toward recognizing the civil rights of lesbian, gay, and bisexual people to a dramatically new "punctuated equilibrium" when decisions by Vermont's highest court led to the creation of civil unions in 2000 and the Massachusetts Supreme Judicial Court allowed gay couples to marry beginning in 2004. (The 2008 marriage decision by the California Supreme Court was still called judicial activism by opponents, even though that decision came after eight years of legislatively enacted registered domestic partnerships and the passage of marriage equality legislation not once but twice.)

Obviously, Americans disagree about the pace of change related to legal rights for gay couples. Depending on whom you ask, things are moving too slowly, too fast, or just about right. What if we calibrated changes in the United States on the European scale, where change seems to have taken place more gradually over the past eighteen years? A closer look at Europe suggests both how and why the laws changed there. In this chapter, I identify the key factors that predicted changes in laws for the pioneering countries that recognized gay couples in the 1990s and in a second wave of change since 2000. With those factors, we can ask a more local question: Is the United States really that different from Europe in the pace and progress of granting legal status to same-sex couples? Perhaps surprisingly, applying the same factors that predict change in Europe to the fifty United States suggests that change is moving at pretty much the same moderate pace in both places.

How and Why Change Occurred in Europe

A few years ago, the Dutch gay newspaper *De Gay Krant* published a booklet outlining the long road to the "opening up of civil marriage"[3] for gay couples in the Netherlands beginning in the 1980s.[4] This "how-to" guide for activists in other countries highlighted several crucial factors related to success in the Dutch struggle:

- A group of dedicated gay leaders formed around the newspaper (rather than the gay and lesbian activist organizations, which were not enthusiastic about marriage).
- Progressive and openly gay members of the Dutch parliament strategized and supported the activist efforts.
- Grassroots activists pushed local municipalities to create partner registries that raised public consciousness of the issues for gay couples.
- Public support for gay couples was strong and became stronger: a majority of Dutch people supported equal rights for gay couples as early as 1990, and by 1995 73% of the public agreed that gay couples should be allowed to marry.
- Finally, the founding of a national governing coalition without Christian Democratic parties helped to pave the way to registered partnership and, eventually, marriage equality, although bureaucratic inertia led to years of waiting for the final change.

As noted in chapter 8, the legal scholar Kees Waaldijk organizes the historical process in the Netherlands into a tidy "law of small change" to account for the passage of same-sex partner recognition laws.[5] With each step, gay people come closer to equality, undermining the idea that gay men and lesbians should be treated unequally by the law. But the remaining gap also provides a temporary practical and symbolic "condemnation of homosexuality" that mollifies opponents.[6] After Dutch lawmakers enacted registered partnership in 1998, he concludes, there was no remaining reason to exclude same-sex couples from marriage.

While the Dutch example might not be a precise road map for activists in other countries, Waaldijk's approach looks like a simple way to explain *how* countries might gain rights for gay couples—incrementally. Another legal scholar, Yuval Merin, claims that these incremental legal changes are even *necessary* for countries to get to the point of passing laws related to partnership.[7] Behind the tactical question of *how* looms the larger strategic consideration of *why* eight pioneering countries broke through the barrier for same-sex couples by the end of the twentieth century, while others did not. And what about the eleven second-wave countries that have granted gay couples rights since 2001? Will other countries—and states—inevitably follow the innovators?

Different images spring to mind when we think about the kind of legal and social change implied by giving gay and lesbian couples marital rights. The seemingly ordered and rational deliberations of legislatures contrast sharply with boisterous, impassioned demonstrations by gay rights organizations or conservative churches. We might imagine heated discussions in churches or pictures of earnest gay couples on television. Or perhaps some relatively quiet cultural process has undermined old prejudices about homosexuality and created an opening for new ideas and policies. In fact, the many factors that contribute to policy change are tough to disentangle and remain somewhat mysterious, even to people who study change.

Practical Pressure for Change

Some economists, for instance, argue that a country's formal legal institutions, such as marriage, reflect ways of promoting the efficient use of resources.[8] In this context, marriage can be interpreted as a highly practical contract that allows families and societies to organize their lives more productively. The commitment to a long-term relationship and the rules for dividing up assets and income if the relationship ends underlie most of the economic and practical advantages of marriage, as I have noted in other chapters. Marriage promotes efficient families—and therefore efficient societies—in many ways, according to this view:

- *Promoting specialization of labor.* The Nobel Prize-winning economist Gary Becker argues that marriage increases household efficiency by promoting the division of labor, which for heterosexual couples means that men primarily work for pay outside the home, and women have primary responsibility for working inside the home.[9] This kind of specialization allows the family to more efficiently meet its needs for meals, happiness, entertainment, learning, and other aspects of life than if both partners did all kinds of work. Specialization is risky for each individual, though, since the household might break up. In Becker's theory, a long-term commitment sealed by a marriage contract is important for providing security for both spouses and making specialization more likely.
- *Reducing "transaction costs."* Robert Pollak argues that marriage has practical value by reducing transaction costs for couples, which are the costs in time and money involved in negotiating a legal relationship.[10] In a sense, marriage is a standard contract that defines what will happen if the marriage ends by death or divorce, specifying who gets marital property and control of children. The long-term nature of marriage removes the need to renegotiate the terms of the legal relationship as couples experience changed circumstances.[11] Families

can grow in size and wealth, for example, but the underlying marital contract does not need to change to accommodate growth.

- *Providing social insurance.* Pollak also notes that wealth and income pooling by married couples and families provide insurance against bad times, such as the failure of a harvest or the loss of a job. An employed person has a legal obligation to support his or her spouse financially if necessary, an obligation and expectation built into many countries' social welfare systems.
- *Signaling commitment.* Eskridge argues that the willingness to marry is an important signal of commitment to a relationship.[12] By agreeing to marry, each partner signals greater effort to maintain the relationship, a greater likelihood that the relationship will endure, and perhaps an agreement to make a fair settlement if, despite the good intentions of both individuals, the relationship should end.
- *Taking advantage of economies of scale.* By encouraging larger household sizes (more than one adult), marriage helps families take advantage of "economies of scale."[13] Economies of scale mean that doubling the inputs of time and other resources in some task results in more than double the output of family-related goods and services. For example, living alone, a person might require a half-hour to prepare a meal for herself, but it might only take forty-five minutes for one person to prepare a meal for two people who live together, a savings of fifteen minutes for the couple.
- *Promoting the provision of caring labor.* The long-term nature of the marital commitment promotes reciprocity and altruism, as partners take care of each other and any children they might be raising together. The unpaid work done in families is essential for the survival of healthy human beings.[14] From this perspective, "reproduction" does not end when a baby is born; families are places where human beings are continually reproduced.

Since more efficient families make for more efficient societies, policymakers have a practical incentive to pay attention to the needs of families. As families and their needs change, and here we could include same-sex couples, the law should adapt. The actual mechanism of translating needs into institutional change is a bit fuzzy in economists' theories, however. One possibility draws on a theory of the evolution of societies that win out in economic competition. Policymakers might believe that the failure to legally recognize same-sex couples will put their country at a competitive disadvantage by reducing economic efficiency.[15] In my view, a more plausible story is that the tension between the kind of families created by law and the kinds of families that actually exist leads to political mobilization to create legal changes to bring law and social practice into line.[16]

Either way, at a minimum, the first step toward change would require an awareness of the existence of same-sex couples and the needs of such couples for marriage or marriage-like rights and responsibilities. As Connecticut state senator Leonard Fasano, a Republican who voted in favor of civil unions, recently put it, "There is an error, there is a problem that has been brought to our attention. What is before us is what are we going to do about all of the problems that exist because of it."[17] This view gives us one prediction about which countries will be likely to recognize same-sex couples, if the efficiency goal is a driving force: *countries with highly visible gay and lesbian populations are likely to give marriage rights to same-sex couples in order to promote individual—and therefore social—well-being and economic productivity.*

Another practical set of concerns related to the value of marriage in promoting efficiency also exists, however: the contribution of marriage to an individual's or group's economic well-being varies from country to country. In some countries the state has actually taken over some of the traditional economic responsibilities of the family. Gosta Esping-Andersen uses the term "de-familialization" to describe state provision of social insurance, pensions, child care, and other such family needs.[18] Also, as I have mentioned in previous chapters, some countries treat cohabiting couples and married couples similarly for some purposes, such as taxation or distribution of pension benefits. In such places, marriage may have a smaller economic impact for couples and individuals.

When marriage is less economically important to couples, a country's practical incentives to give marriage rights to same-sex couples might be lessened to some degree. On one hand, if marriage has less practical value for creating economically efficient family outcomes, then the demand for change by same-sex couples is likely to be reduced. Similarly, from the state's perspective, de-familializing policies reduce the need to include same-sex couples in marriage in order to reap the practical gains associated with improving the well-being of couples and their children, as long as same-sex couples are treated like other unmarried couples.

On the other hand, marriage will still improve couples' well-being as long as the state continues to favor married couples in some ways (as when states waive taxes on inheritances from spouses) and as long as other contractual elements of marriage have meaning for the couple (such as rules for the division of property when a marriage ends). Dutch couples recognized and valued those practical aspects of marriage, as I discussed in chapter 2. The implication that emerges from this perspective is, therefore, ambiguous: *Countries that provide valuable social welfare benefits to individuals may be more or less likely to recognize same-sex couples than countries that rely more heavily on families to provide for individual needs.*

Political Pressure for Change

In contrast to those who argue that a focus on practical concerns might drive changes in who can marry, some scholars have noted that legal institutions are closely linked to how resources are divided up. A focus on the distribution of the economic and social "pie"—as opposed to the size of the pie, as in the practical efficiency concern—means that power and political competition are more important than practicalities and efficiency in shaping laws and other social institutions.

Economists, political scientists, and sociologists note that laws often benefit one group more than other social groups.[19] Changes in laws, including marriage laws, could be motivated by a desire to change an existing institution that favors one group over another—in this case, a law that favors heterosexual couples over gay and lesbian couples. From this perspective, changes in the attitudes of powerful groups or changes in the holders of political power might matter more than economic efficiency in understanding changes in laws. Studies of gay-related legislation across the United States suggest that markers of relative political power and attitudes toward homosexuality are important predictors of how debates will play out.[20]

What are opponents fighting over in this case? It's hard to identify the concrete economic interest at stake. Giving same-sex couples access to marriage appears to me to be a classic example of what economists call a "Pareto-improving" policy: no one loses economically by opening up marriage to same-sex couples, while some will gain economically.[21] Although marriage comes with rights that give financial benefits to some married couples, marriage also comes with responsibilities that involve financial obligations, as I noted in earlier chapters. Not surprisingly, studies in the United States have found that giving same-sex couples marriage rights would boost the federal budget by nearly $1 billion per year and many millions more at the state level.[22]

However, some groups might gain in a cultural or political sense by forbidding same-sex couples from marrying. For instance, the Catholic

Church has taken a strong stand worldwide against extending any recognition to same-sex couples.[23] In the United States, conservative interest groups have long used political battles on gay rights issues, including the battle over same-sex marriage, as fundraising opportunities.[24] On an individual level, people who subscribe to traditional religious beliefs about the sinfulness of homosexuality may be uncomfortable with states' sanctioning of those relationships and would therefore oppose attempts to give same-sex couples marital rights.

William Eskridge suggests that the process for changing laws related to same-sex couples might be a complex combination of political and cultural change.[25] He argues that the decline in homophobic attitudes creates a more liberal social environment for gay and lesbian people. These environmental changes then encourage gay people to be more open about their existence and to mobilize politically. Openness and mobilization provide more information that falsifies the stereotypes and misinformation that perpetuate homophobia, thus contributing to less homophobia and more progressive legal change leading to equality for gay people and same-sex couples in some legal realms. These new progressive laws then perpetuate the cycle of change.

From various political and cultural perspectives, then, we would expect to see governments open up the rights and responsibilities of marriage to same-sex couples when two different kinds of political shifts occur. First, groups that favor allowing same-sex couples to marry might gain in political strength or social bargaining power. *The rising power of left-leaning political parties, the increasing influence of gay social movement organizations, or the declining influence of religious organizations would all make laws recognizing same-sex couples more likely.* Second, the interests and goals of those who maintain political power might change. *If social norms regarding homosexuality or marriage became less restrictive over time, both among elites and the larger public, then laws affirming same-sex relationships will be more likely to emerge.*

Comparing Countries: First Impressions

The main way to tease out the underlying causes of change from real world observations is to make comparisons.[26] Scholars sometimes compare cultural, social, or economic changes at different points in time *within* a single country to investigate the links between those changes and the passage of a new law.[27] Another approach is to compare countries using somewhat broader ways of tracking or measuring differences and contrasting the experiences of those with the partnership or marriage equality law to those without such laws. If countries with similar laws have certain factors in common, those characteristics are likely candidates for actual *causes* of change, especially if countries that have different laws do not share those factors.

Here I will set the experiences of different countries alongside one another and look for commonalities and contrasts that will help us understand why some countries give legal rights to same-sex couples while other countries do not. A comparison between the eight countries in the first wave and other countries sharpens the set of factors that seem to explain change. Recent changes allow me to compare a larger group of countries chosen from the nineteen with partnership laws in 2007 to other European and North American countries (plus Australia) that do not allow same-sex couples to choose a public legal status. The comparisons use quantitative and qualitative tools developed by social scientists that make it possible to assess the role of religion, political ideology, political parties, the lesbian and gay social movement, gay visibility, and family dynamics in giving rights to same-sex couples.

The first four countries to create registered partnerships for same-sex couples were Scandinavian countries: Denmark, the pioneer in 1989, followed by Norway (1993), Sweden (1994), and Iceland (1996). The Netherlands was the first non-Nordic country to let same-sex couples (and, in this case, different-sex couples) register their partnerships in 1998. Just three years later, the Dutch were the first to allow same-sex couples to marry. Belgium took the same road as the Netherlands, first giving same-sex and different-sex couples registered partnership in 1998 and then opening marriage to same-sex couples, in 2003. France enacted its PACS in 1999 for same-sex and different-sex couples, and Germany allowed same-sex couples to register as "life partners" (*Lebenspartnerschaft*) beginning in 2001.

Just a glance at that list of countries hints at some common factors and some unique ones underlying the recognition of gay couples. Each of the eight countries has a parliamentary democracy and sets family policy at the national level. The debates about providing marriage rights to same-sex couples also reveal some possible common underlying rationales and conditions for changing policy.[28]

Cultural and historical differences provide a unique quality to a political debate or policy design in any given country, however. These broad cultural differences are hard to capture in quantitative terms that allow easy comparisons. For instance, the Nordic countries are known for their egalitarian approach to their citizens' social welfare, although within that region, each country is known for a different set of national characteristics.[29] The Dutch are celebrated for their history of tolerance toward unpopular groups in general and gay people in particular, placing same-sex marriage on a logical historical continuum. Even seemingly common factors across countries might have different meanings in different national contexts. Leftist political parties might be homophobic in one country, as some have said about the Socialists in France,[30] while highly supportive of rights for gay couples in another, as in the Green Party in Germany.[31]

Organized National Gay and Lesbian Movement

In each country, an organized national gay and lesbian movement planted and cultivated the seeds of the idea that same-sex couples should be given the right to marry or, failing that, that they at least should have some of the same rights that married and unmarried different-sex couples have. In some countries, those organizations have long histories: the modern groups in Norway and Denmark have roots that date back to 1948,[32] and the Dutch COC dates back to 1946.[33] The Danish National Association for Gays and Lesbians proposed a law giving rights to couples as early as 1984.[34]

In some countries, no consensus existed within the organized gay and lesbian political movement that gaining access to marriage rights was an important or even desirable goal. In the Netherlands, for instance, the COC did not immediately join the political efforts of the *Gay Krant*, the newspaper at the center of marriage organizing and lobbying, because COC leaders prioritized issues of individuals' rights, rather than couples' rights.[35] Some gay activists in Norway and Denmark also expressed ambivalence about the adoption of an institution at the heart of heterosexual life.[36]

Existence of Important Precursors

By the time most of the eight first-wave countries passed partnership laws, they had already passed laws giving gay men and lesbians some important rights. These precursors fit with Yuval Merin's ideas and Kees Waaldijk's "law of small change," mentioned earlier. However, Waaldijk (and Merin) also notes that the pattern of small changes is not completely consistent.[37] Some countries (Germany and Belgium) recognized partners without national legislation forbidding discrimination, and some countries that had the precursors did not enact partnership laws until much later in the second wave (Luxembourg, Slovenia, Switzerland, and the Czech Republic). It's also important to remember that these common precursors might not tell us much about *why* each country enacted partnership laws, since some of the same factors might influence passage of nondiscrimination laws *and* partnership laws.

Common Practical Roots

The political impetus for pursuing rights for couples had some common roots in different countries, too, particularly in the acknowledgment that same-sex couples needed legal recognition in order to gain access to the rights and benefits that strengthen and support families. Not surprisingly, the AIDS epidemic revealed the concrete disadvantages of an unequal status for gay male couples in some places.[38]

In several countries, government commissions were appointed to investigate the need for the recognition of partnerships and appropriate policies, providing both an analytical basis for the laws and a tool for achieving agreement on an eventual law. Indeed, Denmark's law came after a commission report in 1984.[39] Sweden set up several commissions to investigate policy with respect to gay people, with the first convening in 1977[40] and another recommending a partnership law in 1993.[41] A Dutch commission recommended a registered partnership law similar to the Danish model in 1992, and a later commission produced a 1997 report on opening up marriage.[42] The French Hauser commission recommended a form of recognition of couples that was somewhat different from the eventual PACS.[43]

Importance of Left Governments

In most cases, the partnership laws were passed by parliaments when leftist parties were in the majority. The connection between left-leaning parties and partnership bills is striking in both first-wave and second-wave countries. In many cases, the debate over partnership laws began while a conservative government was in power, but positive action came only once the government had changed:

- Norway began discussions under a center-right coalition in 1989, but the bill ultimately passed with the support of the labor minority government in 1993.[44]

- The French Socialist Party initially introduced a partnership bill in 1990 but could not pass it until 1999, after the party came to power.[45] The debate over the PACS became a classic left-right issue, according to Borillo.[46]
- In the Netherlands, the registered partnership bill progressed only once the Christian Democratic Party was no longer in the government, after 1994.[47] The parliament voted to open up marriage with the support of the leftist government and with leadership from Boris Dittrich, an openly gay member of parliament whose party pushed for inclusion of marriage equality in the coalition agreement that created the 1998 government.[48]
- Members of Germany's parliament from leftist parties introduced bills giving couples rights beginning in 1982, but the bills went nowhere until the Social Democrat-Green coalition gained power in 1998.[49] In fact, in these countries, pro-gay parties often campaigned on their plans to give rights to same-sex couples.
- After winning the March 2004 elections, Spain's new socialist prime minister, José Luis Rodríguez Zapatero, announced that he would support giving same-sex couples marriage rights, a goal accomplished in 2005.

Even the apparent exceptions to this pattern are consistent with the expectation that conservative governments generally do not favor such laws. One important exception to the leftist government pattern was the pioneer. In 1989, Denmark was governed by a coalition headed by the Conservative Party, but the coalition included parties that had long favored a registered partnership law, and the parties took no official stand on the registered partnership bill.[50] The importance of parties was somewhat diminished, however, by the fact that sometimes parties released their members to vote their conscience in a "free vote," as in Denmark.[51]

Iceland's situation also diverged from the ideological pattern. The rightwing Independence Party led the center-right coalition government in 1996 when Iceland's partnership bill passed, but all parties officially supported ending discrimination against gays and lesbians.[52]

Common Issues in the Debate

At least until 2000, when the Dutch parliament voted to allow samesex couples to marry, all nine countries wanted to clearly separate the statuses of marriage and registered partnership. The Germans did so because they believed that their constitution required them to maintain marriage as the most privileged status for couples. In other cases, some members of parliament worried that they might weaken marriage if they allowed same-sex couples access to that status. The issue of parenthood loomed large in these debates, leading all nine countries to take out any semblance of equal rights with respect to adoption or parenthood for gay couples.

Common Opponents

Much of the opposition to giving rights to same-sex couples came from religiously motivated activists. In some cases, outright opposition emerged from official church bodies, as in the state churches of Sweden and Norway or the Catholic Church in France.[53] In the Nordic countries, such opposition did not become a serious political impediment to change.[54] However, French religious traditionalists in the Catholic Church and other churches mounted a strenuous opposition to the passage of the PACS, including a January 1999 demonstration in Paris attended by 100,000 opponents.[55] As a more recent example, the Catholic Church mobilized tens of thousands of opponents to protest the Italian civil partner bill in May 2007.[56]

Importance of National Cultural Traditions

Some unique factors emerged as being important in the debates about partnership laws within countries. As Henning Bech predicted after the Danish law came into being, other countries would need to "mobilize supplementary support for their cause, in the form of powerful national cultural traditions and symbols."[57] Those cultural traditions are difficult to define, and it is hard to evaluate their relative importance in the debate, but local observers have noted certain patterns that appear to me to be relevant although hard to measure precisely:

- The concept of *"frisind,"* or "broad-mindedness, tolerance and social responsibility in securing real equal opportunity for everyone," played an important role in Danes' willingness to take the lead in creating a new legal relationship for same-sex couples.[58]
- In the Netherlands, the politics of accommodation of different groups in society contributed to the increasing acceptance and integration of gays and lesbians. As Schuyf and Krouwel put it, "This political culture and its institutions are geared toward achieving *consensus* between the various social groups, all of which are minorities."[59]

- The Swedish emphasis on consensus and universal social welfare underlay its recognition of same-sex partners. Rydström notes, "In Scandinavia, everybody should be included in society, but everybody should also adhere to quite specific norms of behaviour."[60]
- In France, a universalist model of citizenship that was deeply embedded in the French concept of republicanism spurred the creation of a new status that would be available to both same-sex and different-sex couples, rather than a special status just for gay men and lesbians.[61] Such an approach contrasts with an American-style identity politics model, in which gay interests are reflected in legislation specifically focused on same-sex couples.[62]

Expanding the Comparisons

The existence of similarities among different countries that give partnership or marriage rights to same-sex partners does not prove that those factors are major contributors to legal change. Other countries that did not give rights to gay couples might display similar characteristics, dynamics, and traditions. Furthermore, other important background characteristics that have not been highlighted by the local analysts reviewed here might also turn out to be important.

Comparisons of countries with and without partner recognition laws should provide additional insights into crucial determinants of same-sex partnership laws. Broadening the scope of comparisons permits increased breadth but imposes a loss of detail and cultural nuance. The advantage of the broader approach is the inclusion of more countries and the ability to capture some broad differences that might not be apparent from a more detailed comparison. The broader approach also adds the potential to generalize the findings to more countries.

To get a better sense of the role of practical and political factors that various social sciences suggest are important, I compared countries with and without partnership recognition for gay couples. More specifically, I limited the countries "with recognition" to those that provide gay couples with a way to publicly register their partnerships that is similar to or equivalent to marriage.[63] In addition to the European countries I've discussed so far, I added other European and North American countries, plus Australia, when data were available for comparison. I used two academic approaches, one that compares statistics about the countries and one that is more qualitative and translates the statistics into broader characteristics. Appendix 1 describes the data and statistical procedures in more detail, but the important points to know are that the approaches draw on the theoretical and country-specific first impressions already discussed and that the findings from the two procedures complement each other.

From a statistical perspective, I looked at which practical and political characteristics are associated with (or are correlated with) giving registration or marriage rights to gay couples. The practical possibilities include:

- A gay visibility index that measures the number of gay businesses in 1990 per million residents of a country
- Divorce rates and cohabitation rates (the proportion of heterosexual couples who are not married), which measure the actual choices of couples to end or avoid marriage and at least partly reflect the perceived need to be married
- Social expenditures by a country as a proportion of the country's GDP, which reflects the existence of social support programs that might make marriage less necessary as a source of social insurance and support
- The proportion of residents who believe that marriage is an outdated institution.

The political measures capture both the potential power of allies or opponents of gay issues and the degree of tolerance of homosexuality in general:

- The proportion of residents who would not like to have a homosexual as a neighbor
- The proportion of residents who are highly religious, as measured by attending religious services at least once a month
- The proportion of workers who are union members (or "union density"), which is often related to support of more liberal social programs
- Gay political power, measured both by a gay organization index that measures the number of gay civic and political organizations per million residents and by the existence of a long-term national gay organization from the mid-1980s through the mid-1990s.

Figure 9.1 compares the average values of those variables for the countries in the first wave of recognition (eight countries by 2000) and in the second wave of post-2000 recognition. The first-wave countries had higher values of the practical characteristics and of the more liberal values of the political characteristics. Gay businesses were more common, marriage was less common, and the state picked up more responsibility for welfare in the first-wave countries. Also, first-wave countries had more gay organizations, more gay-tolerant residents, and a less religious population than the other countries that did not recognize gay relationships. However, all countries were similar on average in terms of fertility rates. (All of the variable values for each country are presented in Figure A.1.)

The statistical regressions allow me to hold the values of some factors constant to see if the other factors are related to the probability of recognizing gay couples. Several characteristics pop out as important for predicting the first wave of eight countries by 2000. (The detailed regressions

Figure 9.1

Comparisons of Measures Across Country Types

	Efficiency-related variables								
Country Type	Business Index	% Cohab. Couples		Public social expenditures (% GDP)		Divorce Rate		Marriage outdated inst.	
	1990	1990	2000	1990	2000	1990	2000	1990	2000
1st wave	16.8	15.8%	27.0%	23.8%	23.5%	40.0%	44.6%	16.5%	20.6%
2nd wave	11.7	7.4%	14.0%	17.0%	18.9%	32.0%	38.6%	13.5%	20.2%
No recognition	7.8	3.9%	8.9%	16.0%	18.9%	22.3%	31.1%	12.6%	16.2%

	Conflict-related variables							
Country Type	No homosexual neighbor		Attend religious services at least monthly		Gay Org. Index	National gay org.	Union density	Catholic history
	1990	2000	1990	2000	1990	1985–1995	1995	
1st wave	21.0%	12.1%	17.5%	16.4%	10.0	88.9%	47.0%	22.2%
2nd wave	36.6%	19.2%	32.0%	25.4%	5.5	60.0%	25.0%	40.0%
No recognition	52.1%	39.4%	50.8%	48.9%	3.0	44.4%	29.4%	66.7%

	Gender-related variables			
Country Type	Women's labor force participation rate		Fertility rate	
	1990	2000	1990	2000
1st wave	67.1%	70.8%	1.8	1.7
2nd wave	63.1%	66.3%	1.7	1.4
No recognition	55.1%	55.1%	1.9	1.6

are reported in Figures A.2 and A.3.) From the practical side, greater visibility of gay people (as measured by the gay business index), a high heterosexual cohabitation rate, and higher social spending increased the likelihood of recognizing gay partnerships. From the political side, less religious countries, more tolerant countries, countries with high union density, and those with higher gay organization index values were more likely to recognize partners in that first wave.

When I grouped the second-wave countries with the first-wave countries, the same factors were still important. One exception was that the social expenditures of the countries in the combined waves were not different from those in countries that did not recognize same-sex couples. Tolerance of homosexuals was much higher among the first-wave countries, however, as Figure 9.1 shows.

Since it seems likely that these different characteristics cluster together, I used a second technique designed to capture that clustering. Here I recategorized the main variables into two possibilities, such as "tolerant" or not, according to the average values of those variables. These new categories captured each country's characteristics in a simpler way. Appendix 1 describes the method for identifying which countries share recognition policies and the clusters of possible characteristics.

Certain characteristics clearly go together to define the first-wave countries. They shared all three characteristics of low religiousness, high tolerance, and high levels of cohabitation. In addition to those three characteristics, all first-wave countries also had either a high gay business index or a high gay organization index, and most had high levels of social expenditures.

Only two countries with a similar set of characteristics did *not* recognize gay couples by 2000. Finland shared all of the characteristics of the first-wave countries: low religiosity but high tolerance, social expenditures, cohabitation, gay business, and gay organization indices. Not surprisingly, Finland just missed being part of the first wave; it passed its partner registration law in 2001.

Australia had low social expenditures but otherwise shared the key characteristics with Iceland. In sharp contrast with Iceland, though, Australia adopted a federal constitutional amendment in 2004 that banned both marriages by same-sex couples in Australia and the recognition of same-sex marriages contracted in other countries. Perhaps the conservatives' long-term hold on national politics in Australia prevented the expected movement, or perhaps some other unique factor in Australian culture has blocked the changes we would expect to see.[64] Even the election of a more gay-friendly Labor government has not yet led to major changes, although the government announced in April 2008 that it would amend one hundred laws related to pensions and hospital visitation to give same-sex couples the same rights that unmarried different-sex couples have in those areas.[65]

Looking at the second wave countries, those that passed registration or marriage laws since 2001, we find that they are more diverse. Tolerance of homosexuality and relatively high levels of cohabitation continue to be characteristic of gay marriage/partnership countries. Along with high tolerance and cohabitation rates, the recognition countries also have one of three configurations of other characteristics:

1. High social expenditures and low religiosity
2. High social expenditures, a high gay business index, and a low gay organization index
3. Low social expenditures, high religiosity, a low gay business index, and a high gay organization index.

Clearly, the presence of a religious population no longer rules out rights for gay couples. Spain and Canada depart from the first-wave mold, with relatively high religiosity and different patterns for social expenditures (Spain high, Canada low). While cohabitation in Spain was quite low in the 1990s, it was catching up with its neighbors by 2000. The United Kingdom joins Iceland's configuration as a tolerant country with low religiosity and social expenditures, as well as active and visible gay populations.

The Czech Republic originally stood out as something of an oddity among the second-wave countries. Although low in religiosity, the Czech Republic had low cohabitation rates, tolerance, social expenditures, and gay community organization in the 1990s, all factors that made it look very different from the first-wave countries. By 2000, however, Czech people looked more like their counterparts in other gay-friendly countries, with high levels of cohabitation, tolerance, and social expenditures. The fact that Czech society changed in the direction predicted by the first-wave countries before passing a partnership law adds plausibility to my interpretation that these are very likely to be characteristics that lead to change in laws.

Expanding to distinguish between the first-wave and second-wave countries suggests that new paths to change are emerging. One difference in the Canadian case (and the South African case) is that the legislative opening up of marriage came only after high courts directed the government to allow same-sex couples to marry. This route clearly diverges from that of the first-wave countries, each of which made changes legislatively. The startling rapidity of Spain's decision to be the third country to let gay couples marry partly reflects unexpected political turns that brought leftist parties to power. But several Spanish provinces had already created a partnership status for same-sex couples, suggesting that gay advocates had already been at work planting the seeds that bore fruit when the national political tide turned.

One lesson to draw from these experiences is that both the practical and the political appear to matter in considerations of gay marriage and partnership laws, as social science theories suggest. Gay visibility and organizing increase the chances of change. Countries that are less religious and more tolerant of gay people are likely to have lower barriers to change. In fact, high levels of tolerance and cohabitation appear to be *necessary conditions* for country-level change, with low levels of religiousness and a national level commitment to social spending (on housing, old age, survivors, health, families, employment, unemployment, and income support) adding greatly to the movement toward change.

The most surprising finding is the apparent link between cohabitation by heterosexual couples and the legal recognition of gay couples. Perhaps those new heterosexual families constitute a political bloc pushing for change, although such a mobilization does not show up in accounts of family law change that I have read. Those accounts of the rise of cohabitation point to court decisions and legislative changes that respond to specific cases or to heterosexuals' demographic trends. Or perhaps policymakers have already dealt with the needs of those families and are ready and willing to address the needs of gay families, as the histories of some of the countries suggest. In some (but far from all) cases, as in Sweden, the Netherlands, and Canada, the extension of rights and responsibilities placed on unmarried heterosexual couples to gay couples preceded the enactment of marriage or registered partnership.[66] Time will tell if explicit acknowledgment of de facto same-sex couples (as they're sometimes called) in Portugal will lead to more formal recognition of the right of same-sex couples to actually *choose* public recognition through marriage or registration.

Another possible reason for the link between cohabitation and recognition of gay couples is that, as marriage is less necessary for economic survival or to meet a cultural obligation, it becomes less common and less popular, so policymakers and the public are more willing to open up the institution to new families who seek it. That dynamic lines up with more conservative advocates of marriage equality in the United States, such as Jonathan Rauch and Andrew Sullivan, who suggest that policymakers should see the marriage equality movement as help for shoring up the institution. However, connecting gay partnership rights to the decline of interest in marriage is also consistent with the views of opponents like Stanley Kurtz who argue that gay marriage is a step in the general unraveling of marriage, although my argument from chapter 5 is that the unraveling is overstated and is clearly not caused by giving rights to gay couples. More likely, I suspect, policymakers now see change in families and marriage as inescapable, which might make them more open to additional change, such as allowing gay couples to participate in the institution.

Calibrating the Pace of Change in the United States

In my rough dating scheme, Europe is in the middle of its second wave of passage, with the barriers to change slowly lowering. But what about the United States? By identifying the conditions for change that worked in Europe and similar countries, we can understand how the various United States compare.

Ten states provide (or will soon provide) at least some legal rights to same-sex couples who register their relationship with the state as of August 2008. Only Massachusetts and Connecticut allow same-sex couples to marry as this book goes to press. Vermont, Connecticut, New Jersey, California, New Hampshire, and Oregon all offer a civil union or domestic partnership status to same-sex couples, and these statuses comes with virtually all of the state-granted rights and responsibilities of marriage. Three other states offer more limited packages of rights for same-sex couples who register with the state as "reciprocal beneficiaries" (Hawaii) or domestic partners (Washington and Maine).[67] The District of Columbia also offers domestic partners almost all of the rights of marriage.[68] Taken as a whole, states that hold one-quarter (24%) of the American population give same-sex couples at least some rights.

One way to assess whether this first wave of states is moving too fast is to compare them to the first-wave of European countries that recognized gay couples. To perform this comparison, I used state-level measures of the three key necessary conditions for change identified for the first wave of countries: high heterosexual cohabitation rates, low religiosity, and high tolerance of homosexuality.[69] While the American measures are somewhat different from those used in the international context, the relative uniformity of data collected in the United States presents the opportunity to use variables more closely related to the concepts identified in the theoretical framework:

- Heterosexual cohabitation rates come from Census 2000, calculated as the proportion of different-sex couples who classify themselves as "unmarried partners."[70]
- As a state-level measure of tolerance, I used state-level tolerance measures calculated by Gregory Lewis from several surveys that asked about the morality of homosexual behavior or whether homosexual acts should be legal or not.[71]
- For the religiosity measure, I calculated the proportion of the state's population that are adherents (i.e., members, their children, and other nonmember participants) of evangelical churches from the 2000 Religious Congregations and Membership survey of religious bodies, conducted by the Association of Statisticians of Religious Bodies.[72]

For each measure, I calculated the average value across states and gave individual states a score of one for each of the following conditions: above-average cohabitation rates, above-average tolerance measures, and below-average proportions of evangelical residents.[73] Figure 9.2 presents the actual values of the main measures for each state and the total scores.

Figure 9.3 shows the twenty states that have a score of three, indicating that they have measures of cohabitation, tolerance, and religiosity that make them most like the first wave of European countries to recognize rights for same-sex partners. States that recognize same-sex couples are marked with an asterisk. Nine out of the ten first-wave states have all three characteristics. New Jersey is the lone exception, left off the list because of its relatively low rate of heterosexual cohabitation.

As noted earlier, some legal scholars have argued for an incrementalist view in which states and countries considering rights for couples build on past legislative successes on other gay issues, such as outlawing employment discrimination based on sexual orientation. It's true that all ten of the states that give rights to gay couples have a nondiscrimination law, too. However, the civil rights law was enacted *after* the domestic partnership

Figure 9.2
Key U.S. Factors Related to Change

State	% Cohabiting Diff.-Sex Couples	% Evangelical Adherents	% Expected to Support Legal Gay Sex	Overall Score
Alabama	5.3%	40.6%	39.6	0
Alaska	11.7%	12.5%	69.0	3
Arizona	9.7%	9.5%	69.6	3
Arkansas	6.0%	43.1%	47.6	0
California	9.1%	7.2%	73.2	3
Colorado	8.6%	10.6%	73.6	3
Connecticut	8.3%	2.4%	78.8	3
Delaware	9.7%	5.2%	63.1	3
Florida	9.3%	14.0%	63.1	3
Georgia	7.5%	27.8%	54.7	0
Hawaii	8.9%	8.1%	84.1	3
Idaho	7.0%	9.0%	57.0	1
Illinois	7.7%	10.3%	66.8	2
Indiana	8.4%	16.0%	57.0	1
Iowa	7.7%	11.7%	66.0	2
Kansas	6.3%	15.6%	64.2	1
Kentucky	7.0%	33.7%	43.6	0
Louisiana	8.5%	21.5%	55.3	1
Maine	11.2%	3.3%	65.7	3
Maryland	9.1%	7.7%	70.4	3
Massachusetts	8.7%	2.4%	76.6	3
Michigan	8.8%	10.8%	63.6	3
Minnesota	8.2%	11.1%	67.3	2
Mississippi	7.5%	39.7%	42.8	0
Missouri	8.2%	24.7%	60.1	0
Montana	8.0%	11.2%	67.7	2
Nebraska	7.0%	14.6%	64.7	1
Nevada	11.6%	5.4%	76.2	3
New Hampshire	10.2%	2.4%	74.6	3
New Jersey	7.6%	2.4%	72.3	2
New Mexico	10.3%	13.1%	54.8	2
New York	9.1%	2.9%	72.9	3
North Carolina	7.2%	25.6%	51.0	0
North Dakota	7.2%	9.7%	57.5	1
Ohio	8.4%	10.0%	60.0	2
Oklahoma	6.2%	41.5%	50.4	0
Oregon	9.9%	11.4%	73.2	3
Pennsylvania	8.1%	5.7%	64.6	2

Figure 9.2 (*continued*)

State	% Cohabiting Diff.-Sex Couples	% Evangelical Adherents	% Expected to Support Legal Gay Sex	Overall Score
Rhode Island	9.5%	1.6%	72.9	3
South Carolina	7.4%	29.4%	55.1	0
South Dakota	7.7%	13.8%	59.7	1
Tennessee	6.7%	37.0%	45.2	0
Texas	6.7%	24.4%	55.4	0
Utah	4.5%	1.9%	55.7	1
Vermont	11.3%	2.4%	77.9	3
Virginia	7.3%	17.1%	62.0	0
Washington	9.5%	9.8%	68.1	3
West Virginia	7.4%	11.1%	46.8	1
Wisconsin	9.0%	12.7%	65.4	3
Wyoming	8.3%	11.4%	65.7	2
Average	8.3%	14.5%	62.9	

Figure 9.3

Predictions of State-Level Partnership Rights for Same-Sex Couples

Alaska
Arizona
California*
Colorado
Connecticut*
Delaware
Florida
Hawaii*
Maine*
Maryland
Massachusetts*
Michigan
Nevada
New Hampshire*
New York
Oregon*
Rhode Island
Vermont*
Washington*
Wisconsin

* States with formal recognition of same-sex couples.

in Maine, and the two laws were enacted at the same time in Oregon. The gap in time between the two legal changes also varies considerably among the countries and states that recognize gay couples. Overall, these patterns suggest to me that civil rights laws are neither absolutely essential nor enough on their own to generate further movement toward marriage equality. The close link in the timing of nondiscrimination laws and the granting of partnership status probably reflects the fact that passage of civil rights laws stems from many of the same kinds of social and political changes that produce laws related to gay couples.

More important, though, the similarities in the path to change in European countries and in the United States suggest that both practical and political factors are driving the policies that grant marriage or partnership rights to gay couples. From this broad perspective, the movement to give legal recognition to same-sex couples is not racing ahead of social values or being foisted on an unprepared public by activist judges. The comparisons in this chapter suggest that changes in the United States have also been orderly and responsive to the differences in the needs and political characteristics of the different states.

These comparisons also give us a sense of what to expect in the near future. Of the remaining eleven states on the list, four (Colorado, Maryland, New York, and Rhode Island) have had active and, in some cases, nearly successful efforts to create rights for registered gay couples in the last year or two. New York's governor, David Paterson, supports marriage equality and directed the state to recognize same-sex marriages entered into in other states or countries. Maryland's highest court narrowly ruled against a gay marriage challenge, and the legislature passed two bills in 2008 that give domestic partners some rights with respect to hospital visitation and to the transfer of property to each other without paying certain state taxes, but neither bill created a domestic partner registry.[74] Rhode Island couples and New York couples are allowed to marry in Massachusetts, and pressure is mounting to open marriage up in Rhode Island, too. In chapter 8, I told the story of Colorado's near win on domestic partnership, in which opponents deployed the alternatives-to-marriage strategy.

At some point, the United States is likely to shift into its own second wave. A look at the states with two of the three conditions for change suggests some serious candidates. New Jersey has already added civil unions and domestic partnership options, and demands for marriage equality have not diminished. New Mexico's House passed a civil union-style domestic partnership bill in 2007, but the Senate's amendments stopped the bill from being approved before the legislative session ended.[75] A gay marriage court challenge is already under way in Iowa. Illinois is seriously considering a civil unions bill as I write.

Studying a moving target is difficult, and, no doubt, by the time this book appears in print, new countries and states will have decided to legally recognize gay couples through marriage or some other status. The United States is unlikely to catch up with Europe any time soon, but so far the two continents are moving with the pace of the societies therein. The states and countries that seemed most prepared to recognize a new form of family—the more tolerant, less religious, and more diverse entities in terms of families—are the ones granting recognition to gay and lesbian couples.

10

Conclusion

Marriage Under Renovation?

The old parts of Amsterdam are crammed with charming canal houses tilting toward soggy spots in the moist Dutch soil. Fortunately, over the centuries the houses have been propped up and maintained by loving attention and increasing engineering knowledge. During my sabbatical year, we lived on the top floor of such a house built on the Prinsengracht in the mid-1700s, one of the newer houses in the semicircles radiating outward from Central Station to the Singelgracht.

Our Dutch friends told us stories of the decline of the old houses in the postwar period, which eventually led to threats of demolition and redevelopment. Artists, squatters, and other young Dutch people refused to let the city planners and developers have their way, even mounting blockades and protests to preserve the beautiful buildings.[1] As a result of their efforts, many streets have retained their timeless quality, and I can easily match up existing buildings to century-old photos taken by the Dutch painter George Hendrik Breitner.

A walk along the canals at night literally gives outsiders a window into modern Dutch life in the old houses. The practice of having open curtains on big picture windows is said to come either from the passion for light in a northern climate or from the Dutch Calvinist tradition of showing that the residents have nothing to hide. A glance into most of those windows now reveals not the dark, historically accurate furnishings of an earlier era, though, but innovative interior designs, modern art, and the latest technology. Sneaking into little alleys and courtyards allows a glimpse behind the buildings, where modern additions of rooms and skylights meld into the brick and sky to infuse new life into the old structures. The blending of old and new gives Amsterdam a sense of history *and* modernity, preservation and transformation, respect for the past and an acknowledgment of change.

These architectural images are my hopeful metaphor for marriage at the start of the twenty-first century. Marriage itself is an ancient institution that has weathered many changes. For centuries, marriage has linked men with women, linked families with each other, and linked the past to the future. Historians tell us that the details of what marriage means and does have varied over time and culture, though. Most obvious from our current historical vantage point are the dramatic changes in marriage over the past century as the old institution has been reshaped to accommodate the changing position of women, economic pressures that increase demands on the family, and even medical advances that prolong the life of married couples long past important milestones.[2] Changes in divorce law, the elimination of most restrictions on who may marry whom, the move toward gender neutrality, the changes in when people marry (if they marry)–all of these changes reflect some addition or renovation to the underlying structure and meaning of marriage in Europe and the United States. Those changes have been essential to maintain the relevance and usefulness of the institution in modern life.

The latest new consideration for marriage is whether to let same-sex couples in. In the historical context, maybe the biggest surprise in the culture war over same-sex marriage is that the debate itself demonstrates the continuing relevance of marriage. This point is different from claiming that gay and lesbian couples will destroy marriage, or revitalize marriage, or inspire more marriages. While some see the issue as a political struggle over the social position and moral worth of gay, lesbian, and bisexual people–and it is also that, especially for many LGB activists and allies—the other, equally important practical side is that many same-sex couples want to marry. That fairly recent turn of events arises from a historical process of increasing visibility and acceptance of the gay community, a process that has intersected with a concept of marriage that is more open and appealing to gay people.[3] In the context of changing family configurations, marriage will retain its relevance only by evolving, including being open to those family newcomers, like same-sex couples who want to marry.

Not everyone sees change as a good thing. Is marriage an adaptable, resilient institution, able to meet the challenges of a market-driven, secularizing world? Or is marriage brittle, already weakened so that the entrance of gay couples would be the final insult leading to total collapse? History suggests the former—that marriage has adapted when necessary. But those who do not like the changing patterns of married couples' lives, or higher divorce rates, or delays in marriage, worry that marriage by gay couples will "lock in and reinforce" the troublesome trends, in the words of Stanley Kurtz and David Blankenhorn. While I side with the historians in seeing change as necessary adaptability, this book is not really arguing that point. Instead, I have argued here that even a less adaptable, more fragile sort of marriage would not be significantly rocked by the entrance of same-sex couples. Marriage poses more of a challenge to gay people than gay people do to marriage.

Will Gay People Change Marriage?

We can answer the key questions raised in the American debate over gay marriage by looking to the experience of the Netherlands and other European countries that have given gay couples the right to marry or access to a parallel institution like registered partnership. My answer to the big question guiding this book is "No"—gay people will not change marriage in any significant way on their own. I come to this conclusion from four directions: gay and lesbian couples' decisions to marry (the verb), the ideas about marriage (the noun) held by gay and lesbian people, the marriage choices made by heterosexual couples, and heterosexuals' opinions about gay couples' marriages.

The actions of same-sex couples in the Netherlands suggest that gay people are interested in marriage for the same reasons that heterosexual couples marry. Gay couples chose *to marry* because they wanted to have a child, because they had some practical needs, or because they wanted to affirm and express their commitment to each other and to the world. Whether and how gay couples get to be married depends on the complex interplay of life conditions, the cultural and practical value of marriage, the barriers to marriage, and the processes of accepting or overcoming the barriers.

The marriage and registration rates for gay couples are still low in comparison with those of heterosexual couples, though, which remains a source of concern for some people in the debate. Almost one-quarter (and counting) of Dutch same-sex couples have either registered their partnerships or married, whereas more than 80% of different-sex couples have done so. Greater proportions of same-sex couples have sought a legal status in the United States, with 51% of Vermont's same-sex couples entering civil unions and 44% of Massachusetts's gay couples marrying so far, although in both cases the rate will take time to catch up with the 90% of American different-sex couples who are married.

Obviously, it is far too early to conclude that gay people have voted with their feet *against* marriage, since it will take time for couples to get through the decision-making process. Furthermore, gay couples have absorbed some of the same concerns about marriage that stop heterosexual couples from marrying: some believe that marriage would add nothing to their relationship on a practical or emotional level or that marriage is old-fashioned and conservative, and some couples simply cannot agree. Gay culture was built on a foundation of legal inequality, and defensive critiques of marriage by some lesbians and gay men at least partly reflect their exclusion from the institution. Those critiques remain a barrier for some people who might otherwise contemplate marriage. However, the Dutch experience suggests that ideological opposition to marriage is likely to fade in importance as new couples form and younger GLB people grow up in a time when marriage is possible and encouraged. Add to the ideological concerns the fact that it takes only one partner who adamantly opposes marriage to keep a couple from entering into that status, and I would argue that the rate of gay marriage should probably be seen as remarkably high rather than low under the circumstances.

The many options for couples in the Netherlands provide clear evidence that marriage stills occupies the preferred status for committed couples. Like heterosexual people, gay people choose marriage over other legal statuses. In the Netherlands, marriage is far more popular than registered partnership for gay and straight couples alike. Dutch couples got the political point of registered partnerships—to make a statement about the inferiority of gay people generally—and have reacted with disdain for that new status now that marriage is an option, calling registered partnership "a bit of nothing." The rejection of registered partnership is the true referendum that we see in the Netherlands, in my view, as same-sex couples reject the dry, accounting-like connotation of "registered partnership" and opt instead for the rich cultural meaning and emotional value of marriage. As Martha described the unique advantage of marriage over registered partnership, "Two-year-olds understand [marriage]. It's a social context, and everyone knows what it means." Registered partnerships may offer a useful political compromise, but they will never be seen as more than a consolation prize, not a valuable alternative to marriage and marriage equality in either the Netherlands or the United States.

We can see the relative value of marriage and its alternatives only when couples have both options. For same-sex couples, marriage is also more popular in the Netherlands than registered partnership is in other countries. Gay couples in other European countries appear to be registering at lower rates than Dutch couples. In the United States, gay couples in

Massachusetts (and probably California) are marrying at rates far greater than the rates at which same-sex couples in Connecticut and New Jersey are entering civil unions, the compromise status that has been more acceptable to state legislatures. When Vermont became the first state to give same-sex couples civil unions, in 2000, civil unions were the only game in town and drew in most of Vermont's gay couples and thousands of same-sex couples from other states. Now that gay men and lesbians in the United States see their Massachusetts and Connecticut gay friends marrying, civil unions will never be greeted as warmly as they were in 2000.

Contrary to the fears expressed by opponents of marriage equality, the marriage patterns of heterosexuals have not been knocked off course once gay couples have the same or similar rights. In Europe, the timing of events makes it fairly easy to distinguish cause and effect. Giving gay couples rights did not lead the sky to fall on marriage. The only reason that some countries had high rates of unmarried cohabitation and nonmarital births after gay couples won rights is that those countries had high rates long *before* gay marriage or registered partnership was a politically viable prospect. In fact, the same marriage trends are evident in countries without legal recognition of same-sex couples, kicking gay marriage off the list of possible causes for changing heterosexual marriage and fertility patterns. However, cultural comfort with family diversity and political changes in the treatment of unmarried couples probably made it more likely that same-sex couples would win marriage equality in the Netherlands, as well as in the other European pioneers in giving gay couples rights, as I showed in chapter 9.

If we turn from choices to marry to ideas about marriage, we find additional evidence that same-sex couples will not significantly change marriage. For the most part, lesbians and gay men share ideas about the meaning of marriage with their heterosexual peers, as my interviews and survey data show in the Netherlands and the United States. Of course, on another level, gay people are just as critical of the old-fashioned ideas about marriage as younger heterosexual people are. Children do not alone define a successful marriage. Mutual respect and understanding, as well as a willingness to cooperate and share family labor, define the new roles for married men and women. We can see gay couples putting ideas about marriage into practice in their decision making about whether to marry, as well as in their wedding ceremonies and their own views of marriage.

One important outcome of gay couples' decision-making process is sometimes a reconsideration of what marriage means to one or both partners. I saw people in same-sex couples identify the aspects of marriage that they did not like and then peel away the objectionable parts of the cultural idea of "marriage" to accommodate a partner's desire to marry or to reconcile ideas with more pressing needs or feelings. In particular, feminists were hesitant to enter an institution that had long treated women as subordinate to their husbands. Even though the legal institution of marriage has stripped out the formal inequality, lingering doubts about the social meaning of marriage continue to trouble lesbian feminists. And yet, some feminists overcame those doubts by reframing what it means to marry as a political act that counters the assumption that spouses will take on traditional roles assigned to men and women. For Miriyam, a Dutch lesbian feminist, the way to change marriage was for women to marry other women. Dutch couples sometimes incorporated such explicit feminist messages in their wedding ceremonies.

However, I do not think that this kind of individual rethinking of the meaning of marriage will lead to widespread cultural change. For one thing, the number of same-sex couples is relatively small to begin with, and the number who marry is even smaller. More important, same-sex couples are largely reflecting the same doubts about the organization of marriage and married lives that heterosexual couples have expressed over the past decades. In the Netherlands, the rising labor force participation rates of married women and more gender egalitarian views about marriage among heterosexuals suggest that it's gay people who have the anachronistic view of marriage if they equate marriage with a rigid traditional division of labor between men and women.

Gay couples' other unfamiliar ideas about marriage reflect gay people's unique vantage point on the institution. Clearly, for gay couples, marriage is political, and that awareness might make some heterosexuals nervous. Seeing marriage as a political institution clashes with the view of some gay marriage opponents that marriage is an unchanging social and religious institution that was always and everywhere designed solely to bring a man and a woman together to produce children.

Gay people didn't make marriage political, though. Throughout history, governments and other authorities have made decisions about who could marry whom and what marriage legally entailed. Those were political decisions influenced by, in some cases, religious beliefs and dogma (which also change), as well as by culturally defined roles for husbands and wives. But there have been differing opinions and interests that led to political struggle over those decisions, such as the treatment of women's property, marital rape, child custody issues, and decisions about who may marry whom. Certainly, the issue of marriage equality for gay couples is one of the hottest political issues of the twenty-first century in the United States and elsewhere, but marriage is no stranger to controversy.

Heterosexual reactions in the Netherlands also reveal how easily gay people have been integrated into marriage as an institution. Just as gay people recognize marriage as a desirable and useful option, gay couples report that heterosexual families and peers recognize them as marriageable and married. Heterosexual friends and family members encourage gay and lesbian couples to marry and offer unsolicited words and deeds that acknowledge the importance of a gay couple's wedding. Heterosexuals even police the cultural markers of marriage, making sure that gay couples use the proper terms like "husband" and "wife" and that they mark anniversaries. The reactions remind married gay couples that they have entered into an institution that has a public meaning, as well as a personal one.

But heterosexual reactions in the Netherlands also reveal that tensions and even discomfort with change exist among some Dutch people, just as we see in the United States debate. Not all family members react with joy at the news of an impending wedding by a gay son or lesbian daughter. Whether this discomfort reflects a lack of acceptance by a mother, in particular, with the relationship or her embarrassment at having to "come out" as a parent of a gay child in announcing a same-sex marriage, a negative reaction signals the need for some negotiation and adaptation. Parents' eventual reconciliation with the idea of marriage probably reflects a shift more in how they view their gay child's relationship than in how the parents view marriage, although more research will be necessary to fully explore this dynamic.

Overall, marriage appears to fit the lives of gay and lesbian couples, and others in the couple's larger social world appear to agree. The fact that same-sex couples are willing to take on the social status and obligations of being married is not surprising, given the similar ideas about marriage that gay couples share with their heterosexual peers. Heterosexual people are already moving in the same direction of change that gay and lesbian people seem to want to take marriage. Both behavior and ideas suggest that gay couples will not change marriage in any negative way.

Will Marriage Change Gay People?

At least some of the debate about marriage equality focuses on what gay men and lesbians lose by not having access to marriage, or conversely, what they might gain if allowed to marry. Gay relationships have gained cultural recognition from families and communities through a process of negotiation, confrontation, and time. In a sense, gay couples built their own relationships by "being together" and demonstrating commitment in real time rather than through a cultural and legal ritual.

Will marriage improve or transform these relationships? Research on heterosexual marriage suggests that married people are healthier, live longer, and are wealthier than single people, among other advantages. While some social scientists have argued that same-sex couples might reap similar gains, others imply that the declining institutional force of marriage might diminish the opportunity for gain among same-sex couples. From that perspective, letting same-sex couples marry would provide a natural experiment by which to assess the continuing power of marriage as a social institution.

The evidence from Dutch couples suggests that couples clearly gain in several ways. At an individual level, some of the advantages stem from reducing the social exclusion of gay men and lesbians. Exclusion makes LGB people angry and alienated, regardless of their desires or intentions related to marriage. Equal access to marriage made everyone I spoke with feel more accepted by society. Gains from inclusion could include improvements in the mental and physical health of gay people by reducing "minority stress" and increasing social support for gay couples.

Other positive effects of marriage per se found in the social science literature will take more time to emerge, but the immediate effects are moving in the right direction. Many individuals who married reported feeling different, more responsible, or more special with regard to their relationships as a result of marriage, and those effects might well translate into healthier, longer-lasting relationships. No one I spoke with reported any other major changes in labor force participation or the distribution of household chores as a result of marriage, which at least partly reflects differences in the expectations of what a husband or wife should do in the context of a marriage of a same-sex couple.

Some gay critics of marriage argue that any gains experienced by gay couples will come at the expense of giving in to state regulation of relationships and giving up individual autonomy. However, the potential for tradeoffs is limited in at least a couple of ways. Marriage creates new zones of privacy for couples, and marriage no longer means trading in one's individuality for a wedding ring. Today's marriage means a partnership of individuals, rather than accepting older models that subsume a wife's identity into her husband's.

Other worries about the effects of marriage focus on the costs to the GLB community as a whole. Removing the bonds of inequality that helped create and hold together a diverse gay community could mean big changes ahead for gay people and gay culture. Any large-scale change will take many years to play out, but, in the short run, Dutch gay people have not abandoned their identities. If anything, marriage has made gay people more visible, as they have new opportunities and reasons to come out as gay when discussing their marriages. The example of the Netherlands also shows that formal marriage equality does not immediately guarantee fully equal treatment. The most obvious issue is the fact that gay couples' marriages are accepted as valid in only the handful of countries that recognize them, as well as other evidence that antigay bias persists in Dutch culture.

The GLB activists who have dissented from the movement for marriage rights worry most about losing distinctive and positive aspects of gay culture, though. The specter of assimilation looms large for the dissidents, who do not want gay people to adopt wholesale what they see as the flawed institutions of heterosexuality. As noted earlier, feminists have the biggest issues with marriage, but the Dutch couples suggest that there is little reason to expect same-sex couples to adhere to rigid expectations about spousal roles.

From the perspective of some American marriage dissidents, the most troubling political aspect of the campaign for marriage is that it diverts resources—time and money—from causes or issues that they consider more important. The political fallout of the marriage movement, with its political compromises and the resulting political backlash, might also limit options for expanding support for all kinds of family structures, not just the two-person couple or nuclear family.

On the basis of my reading of the evidence, though, I believe that the marriage movement resources are dwarfed by the resources being poured into health care reform and other social justice issues. An instant redirection of the marriage resources would barely be noticed at the political level. More important, political activism is not necessarily a zero-sum game. States that allow same-sex couples to marry or register as partners or enter into civil unions, including Massachusetts, California, Vermont, and Connecticut, are among the states that have made the most progress toward realizing liberal goals, such as expanding health insurance coverage to all residents.

One very likely impact of eliminating political effort to recognize same-sex couples, however, would be the end of progress toward marriage equality. The European countries that have enacted policies of equality have done so as the direct result of enormous effort by the gay political movement in each country. As I showed in chapter 9, activists in those countries did not simply ride a demographic wave to legislative victory. Abandoning the efforts to win equal rights for gay couples would also hurt unmarried heterosexual couples in the United States, far more of whom have gained from gay efforts to encourage the provision of domestic partners health benefits.

Dissidents' opposition to the marriage equality movement might well be related less to these more rational claims (as suspect as I think the claims are on an empirical level) and more to a fundamentally emotional concern about the effect of marriage on the gay community. If marriage pulls the two spouses deeper into their relationship and farther from relationships with friends and other family members—in other words, if marriage is "greedy," as some have called it—then that inward pull could devastate relationships built up over the years within the community and lead to isolation and stigmatization of single GLB people and others who do not want to marry.

It's hard to counter an emotional point with facts, especially when the fear has at least some foundation. One constructive response might be for same-sex couples to do as some of the Dutch couples did when they consciously involved their friends and family members in their weddings, symbolizing a wider notion of family than a limited focus on the nuclear family. In the end, maybe the best antidote to these fears and concerns will be time, as same-sex married couples find themselves facing the same challenges faced by GLB single people and heterosexual married people alike and responding in ways that expand rather than contract their social possibilities.

Do We Need Alternatives to Marriage?

The civil union or registered partnership option for same-sex couples has become a convenient compromise position for policymakers who want to give same-sex couples the same rights and responsibilities as married couples without calling that relationship "marriage." This desire to reserve the famous label for heterosexual couples has led some to argue that maybe a substitute is sufficient and that we might even want to consider a fuller range of legal options beyond marriage for couples and other family structures. Looking for alternatives has also been a major task for the gay marriage dissidents, many of whom would prefer to get rid of marriage entirely.

The case for alternatives gets trickier in the political context. Strategic opponents of gay rights reframe the debate to move away from a comparison between married different-sex couples and committed same-sex couples and instead compare same-sex couples with just about any other kind of family *except* married couples. As they roll down this "slippery equity slope," as I called it in chapter 8, the conservatives offer new alternatives to deflect legislative attention from proposals that move same-sex couples closer to marriage. They use these alternatives, such as creating a limited "reciprocal beneficiary" status, to counteract comprehensive domestic partnership bills or civil unions that give all of the state-granted rights of marriage to gay couples. The alternatives to civil unions would broaden the group covered by moving farther away from marriage, usually by including other twosomes who are not allowed to marry (like a brother and a sister or an aunt and a nephew). In the end, such alternatives seem more likely to be a dead end than a short-term compromise, since adding significant new rights and responsibilities could be unattractive to people in any nonmarriage-like relationships that are included.

The bottom line, in my view, is that wanting to do right by all family forms and actually pulling that goal off is very hard for policymakers. Equity is not a clear enough guide, since applying that principle can block the path to marriage equality for same-sex couples. For many same-sex couples, civil unions alone will never be enough, since that new invention does not come with the rich social and cultural meaning of marriage. We see a clear preference for marriage in the higher rates of marriage than of registered partnership or civil union in the countries and states that offer both. And, for the other kinds of families, the needs and desires are not so clear. Very few have used the limited opportunities that have emerged out of the gay marriage debate, suggesting that policymakers need to craft a status that is better tailored to the specific needs of those families rather than grafting them onto the effort of same-sex couples to win the right to marry.

Are We Moving Too Fast?

In practice, alternatives serve primarily one important purpose: slowing down the pace of change. Opponents of marriage equality who blame "activist judges" who pushed the issue before the public was ready for those developments are (at least partly) expressing anxiety about the pace of change. Although some gay people have advocated for the right to marry for decades, the goal of marriage equality did not seem particularly realistic until Hawaii came close to allowing gay couples to marry, in the 1990s, or less than twenty years ago. Vermont gave same-sex couples something very close to marriage in 2000, and, four years later, gay couples began to marry in Massachusetts. It took four more years for Connecticut and (briefly) California to open up marriage to gay couples.

Assessing the appropriate speed for changes in policy is a tricky proposition. Change can't come fast enough for same-sex couples who are ready to head to city hall for a marriage license at a moment's notice. (In 2004, thousands of same-sex couples from forty-six states and several countries flocked to San Francisco during the brief one-month window during which the mayor allowed gay couples to marry.) On the other side, any change is too much, too fast for opponents of gay marriage. That leaves us needing another perspective on the time issue.

Using the European timeline to measure the pace of change in the United States might help us understand why things happened here when they did. In 1989, Denmark created registered partnerships for gay couples, and a steady stream of countries has adopted similar policies or even full marriage equality. Was what happened in these countries so different from what has happened here at roughly the same rate?

Looking at the factors that characterize the first-wave policy innovators of the 1990s, we see several key similarities: low religiousness, high tolerance of homosexuality, and high levels of cohabitation. In addition to those three characteristics, all first-wave countries also had either a high gay business index or a high gay organization index, and most had high levels of social expenditures. These common factors imply that policymakers were responding both to the practical needs of visible gay populations and to the relative political strength of gay people and their political allies.

Over time, the expanding set of countries that recognize gay couples has started to look a little different. Tolerance of homosexuality and relatively high levels of cohabitation continue to be important, but more religious countries like Canada and Spain have just opened up marriage to same-sex couples. As more countries offer equality to gay couples, the barriers to other countries appear to be falling faster.

The same necessary conditions for change are present in nine of the ten states that have given gay couples rights in the United States so far. We see similar characteristics in several other states that may soon act. So my answer to this section's question is, "No, we're moving at the rate predicted by the experiences of other countries." The liberal states are moving faster than the conservative ones, the ones with more diverse families are changing faster, and the states where there is more religious opposition are moving more slowly.

In my view, another implication of this perspective on the timing of change is that the United States cannot hide behind the "American exceptionalism" banner to separate itself from policy developments in other parts of the world. Yes, its "marriage culture" is different from that in some parts of Europe. On average, Americans are more religious and more likely to marry (both gay and straight couples alike), but that marriage culture is probably also a response to the very different set of economic and social incentives to marry. Instead of saying, "We're different, so we don't have to pay attention to the rest of the world," Americans should be saying, "Let's look to the rest of the world to help us understand what will happen if we give gay couples the right to marry."

Structural Renovation or Cosmetic Redecoration?

The evidence from the Netherlands, as well as comparisons with other European countries and the United States, demonstrates that same-sex marriage is more of a cosmetic makeover of the old institution of marriage than a structural reconstruction. Even so, anyone who's lived through a renovation of a home knows that redecorating is messy and stressful, displacing families and disrupting lives. Planning carefully can sometimes help, but even the best imagination and planning can't completely relieve the stress of seeing a familiar and beloved home's wiring ripped out or its kitchen stripped bare. In the end, not everyone is satisfied with the outcome, but the hope is that an old structure has been made more usable, up to date, and appealing in the process.

Like many people, I've gone through home renovations and lived to tell about it. While writing this book, I've also lived through most of the changes discussed here: deciding whether to marry, responding to positive and negative reactions, planning a wedding, creating a meaningful ceremony, coming out as a woman who has a female wife, and addressing the social and legal implications of a new status. My relatives treat my wife differently, my employer extends benefits to her, and we feel more committed to each other—all outcomes that help me easily overlook the fact that my taxes have risen. I've seen firsthand that we're all living through a time of great cultural, social, and economic change, and so much change can feel threatening and stressful. Is it reasonable to add to that stress by questioning the restrictions on gay couples' ability to marry?

Here a little perspective can be particularly helpful for interpreting the findings in this book. From the perspective of same-sex couples, the potential gains to marriage equality are large in terms of stronger families and the benefits of greater inclusion in society. The social debate and the lived experiences of gay men and lesbians who can finally marry their partners all suggest that the institution of marriage retains the power to shelter, shape, and serve the lives of couples who marry. From the perspective of heterosexuals, the changing composition of couples lining up for marriage licenses will barely be noticeable directly. What marriage means to heterosexuals has already changed, and its current form is a good fit for the interests of gay men and lesbians. From the perspective of the social institution of marriage, all the evidence shows no sign of damage. Opening up marriage to same-sex couples is just the latest step toward renewing marriage's continuing relevance in the twenty-first century.

Appendix 1

Constructing Measures and Making Comparisons

Using various international data sources, I created measures related to the efficiency and conflict theoretical stories for each country. To get a clearer sense of which factors were most important in potentially *causing* the change in laws, I focused on measures from the time before the laws were passed. With the exception of Denmark, all of the nine countries with laws enacted them after 1990, and Denmark's law was passed in 1989. Therefore, the measures used here for looking at the first wave of countries come from 1990 or the early 1990s, and those for looking at the first and second waves together come from 1999 or 2000.

The appendix tables show the actual values of these measures for each country (Fig. A.1). Figure 9.1 in the text of the chapter compares average values for the countries with and without partnership laws.

Calculations from the World Values Survey provide several important variables.[1] The WVS collects cross-sectional, individual-level data on values and norms for many different topics, including sexuality, gender, and homosexuality, in fifty different countries. Survey language and concepts were translated for each country and were administered by professional survey organizations in Western countries and elsewhere, mostly by local survey researchers.[2] I have used only data from the second and fourth waves of the survey, conducted from 1990 to 1993 and from 1999 to 2000. Not all questions were asked in each country's survey. Sample sizes ranged generally from 1,000 to almost 3,000 in the countries reported on in this book. All but a few countries have representative national samples of adults over 18 years old, selected through stratified multistage random sampling. Some countries oversampled particular subpopulations, such as younger age groups or racial groups, and the WVS provides individual sampling weights used here to account for oversampling within countries. Because the unit of analysis here is the country, I aggregated individual responses up to the country level. All of the attitude measures come from the WVS, as do the cohabitation rates per country.

Other data on demographic and economic measures come from the Organization for Economic Cooperation and Development (OECD), the European Union, and the International Labor Organization. My own counts of gay businesses and organizations come from the listings in the *Spartacus Guide for Gay Men* in 1990, a travel guide published annually. The data on national gay and lesbian political organizations come from the "Pink Book" summaries of the worldwide gay social movement published by the International Gay and Lesbian Association (ILGA) in 1985, 1988, and 1993.[3]

Multivariate Regression Method

This method, using ordinary least squares estimation, calculates the impact of one independent or explanatory variable while holding the other variables constant. The dependent variable is one if a country has a same-sex partner recognition (SSPR) law and zero if it does not. Figure A.2 compares the first-wave of countries to all others; Figure A.3 compares the first- and second-waves countries to all other countries. Each column in Figures A.2 and A3 is a separate regression using just the variables with reported coefficients. Each coefficient shows the impact of a change in the independent variable on the probability of a country's having an SSPR law, holding the other variables in the equation constant. For instance, in the first column of Figure A.2, the coefficient of –0.015 for "homosexual neighbor not OK" means that a country in which 40% of respondents say that they would not like a homosexual neighbor is 15% less likely to have an SSPR than is a country in which 30% of respondents do not want a homosexual neighbor. Rather than using a stepwise regression method, which is sensitive to the order in which variables are entered, I experimented with different specifications to retain variables that seemed to be important in different combinations. The small sample size limits the power of these tests and the number of variables that can be included, but the regressions demonstrate, first, that some explanatory factors are correlated with each other and, second, that some explanatory factors appear to be closely related to having an SSPR.[4]

Figure A.1 Country Values on Practical and Political Variables

	Women's labor force partic. 1990	Women's labor force partic. 2000	Social expend. as share of GDP 1990	Social expend. as share of GDP 2000	Fertility 1990	Fertility 2000	Divorce 1990	Divorce 2000	Do not like homosexual neighbor 1990	Do not like homosexual neighbor 2000	Believe marriage outdated 1990	Believe marriage outdated 2000	Attend religious services regularly 1990	Attend religious services regularly 2000	Cohab. Rate 1990	Cohab. Rate 2000	Gay business index	Gay organization index	Gay national organization	Catholic history	Union density
Australia	62.3	66.1	14.1	17.9	1.9	1.8	35.3	46		24.7		18.5		25.1	6.0	11.8	13	8.8	1	0	28.6
Austria	55.4	62.2	23.7	25.3	1.5	1.3	36	49.8	43.3	25.4	12.0	20.1	43.9	42.5	10.2	18.2	7.3	3.6	0	1	36.6
Belgium	46.3	56.9	25	25.3	1.6	1.6	31.5	59.8	23.5	17.4	22.5	30.6	30.6	27.3		19.3	28.5	6.4	1	1	38.1
Canada	69	71	18.4	16.7	1.8	1.6	41.8	45.1	29.7	16.9	12.5	22.3	40.0	35.9	11.6	16.4	10.8	5.9	1	0	31
Czech Republic	64.8	64.2	16	20.3	1.9	1.1	35.2	53.7	53.2	19.7	10.6	11.4	10.8	11.7	5.1	11.7	1.6	1.2	0	1	36.3
Denmark	78.6	76.3	25.5	25.8	1.7	1.8	43.6	37.5	11.7	8.0	18.0	15.0	10.8	11.9	23.6	25.8	10.5	9.1	1	0	68.2
Finland	74	72.2	24.5	21.3	1.8	1.7	52.6	53.2	25.2	21.2	12.5	17.9	11.0	14.0	12.4	34.9	11.0	7.2	1	0	59.7
France	57.6	61.9	25.3	27.6	1.8	1.9	36.9	40.9	24.4	15.6	29.1	36.3	16.9	11.9	15.5	32.1	13.2	5.3	1	1	6.1
Germany	57.5	63.7	22.5	26.3	1.5	1.4	30	46.4	35.2	12.6	15.0	18.1	25.3	23.3	10.6	14.6	11.9	6.1	0	0	29.6
Hungary	58.2	52.9	20.6	20.6	1.9	1.3	37.5	49.9	75.3	53.4	11.1	14.9	23.0	17.6	4.3	8.9	2.2	1.5	0	1	52.5
Iceland	80.4	85.7	14	15.3	2.3	2.1	41.5	30.7	20.1	7.9	6.2	8.3	9.4	12.0	24.4	31.4	27.5	23.5	1	0	70.7
Ireland	43.3	56.2	15.5	13.6	2.1	1.9	0	13.7	33.2	27.3	9.9	22.4	87.7	69.0	1.0	6.6	9.1	6.9	1	1	36
Italy	44.6	46.8	19.9	23.2	1.3	1.2	8.7	13.2	39.2	28.7	13.5	17.0	53.4	53.7	2.8	5.3	9.4	1.9	1	1	30.6
Netherlands	53.1	65.7	24.4	19.3	1.6	1.7	29.7	39.3	12.0	6.1	21.2	25.0	30.4	25.1	11.0	31.9	27.6	9.6	1	0	21.8
Norway	72.6	77.5	22.6	22.2	2.0	1.9	46.4	39.6	19.5	14.3	10.1	13.5	12.7	12.5	13.8	23.2	13.7	17.0	1	0	51.7
Poland	64.8	61.1	15.1	21.2	2.1	1.3	16.6	20.3	70.5	55.2	6.4	9.3	83.6	78.2	1.8	6.6	1.9	0.4	0	1	27
Portugal	61.3	63.3	13.7	20.2	1.6	1.5	12.9	30	49.6	25.9	23.2	24.8	41.2	54.0	2.7	8.6	15.6	1.4	0	1	18.8
Spain	42.6	53.2	20	20.4	1.3	1.2	10.5	17.4	32.4	16.4	13.7	17.5	43.1	35.9	2.2	12.8	14.6	1.4	0	1	11.4
Sweden	83.4	77.3	30.5	28.8	2.1	1.5	47.8	53.9	17.4	6.1	13.9	20.4	10.5	9.4	20.5	30.2	7.7	5.7	1	0	77.2
Switzerland	71.1	73.2	13.5	18	1.6	1.5	28.3	26.4		18.5	13.1	24.1	42.5	24.5	10.0	12.2	18.9	11.9	1	0	20
Turkey	36.7	29	7.6	13.2	3.1	2.2	5.6	6.6	91.7	90.3	11.3	8.5	38.1	39.5	0.3	0.6	0.5	0.1	0	0	22
U.K. (Britain)	68.2	69.8	17.2	19.1	1.8	1.7	44.1	50.5	31.1	24.3	17.6	25.9	23.4	18.9	7.9	16.8	12.3	7.2	1	0	26.2
United States	69.7	72.7	13.4	14.6	2.1	2.1	48.4	50.6	41.0	23.3	7.5	10.1	61.2	60.3	4.7	13.2	11.2	2.4	1	0	12.7

217

The regressions in Figures A.2 and A.3 test first for the importance of tolerant attitudes about homosexuality. The negative coefficients on the attitudes toward homosexuality variables in the initial specifications (i.e., columns) show that SSPRs are more likely when fewer residents of a country would *not* like to have homosexuals as neighbors. In other words, greater tolerance of homosexuality is associated with a higher likelihood of having an SSPR.

Notably, however, that effect diminishes and becomes statistically insignificant when other variables are entered into the equation, since many of the variables measured here are correlated with tolerance.[5] Depending on the specific model, several other variables are associated with a statistically significant higher probability of an SSPR:

- Cohabitation often has a statistically significant and positive impact.
- The public social expenditures variable is positively related and significant in many specifications.
- In some regressions, the church attendance measure of religiosity is statistically significant and negatively related to having an SSPR.

Most other variables are not statistically significant in the bulk of the regressions, with a few exceptions. The business index is positively correlated with SSPRs, as predicted, but the value is small and never statistically significant except where it appears as the sole variable (not shown here). The only political power variable that is significant is the organization index, which is also positively correlated with SSPRs (both waves) but is only sometimes statistically significant.

Running regressions on just the SSPR countries to predict which would be first-wave innovators reveals few differences between the first and second waves when looking at 1990 values of variables. Greater tolerance of homosexual neighbors and higher social expenditures predicted passage in the first wave but were not always statistically significant. Using 2000 variable values, however, I found that higher cohabitation rates in 2000 and higher organizational index values were also associated with first-wave passage. In other words, the first-wave countries were the most tolerant of homosexuality and may have experienced greater political activism by gay organizations. The first-wave countries may have also been more tolerant of family diversity than the second-wave countries, as evidenced by higher cohabitation rates.

Figure A.2

Regression Coefficients for Being in First-Wave of Same-Sex Partnership/Marriage

Variable	(1)	(2)	(3)	(4)	(5)	(6)	(7)	(8)
Constant	0.973** (0.17)	-0.81 (0.62)	-0.26 (0.40)	0.08 (0.43)	-1.44** (0.50)	-1.14** (0.51)	0.88** (0.30)	-1.03 (0.64)
Business index		0.024* (0.014)	0.017 (0.012)	0.021 (0.014)	0.026** (0.010)			
Public social expenditures (% GDP)		0.050** (0.018)				0.043** (0.014)	0.049** (0.017)	0.048** (0.018)
Marriage outdated								
Cohabitation rate			0.048** (0.014)			0.043** (0.012)	0.024 (0.016)	0.021 (0.020)
Union density				0.010** (0.004)				
Church attendance							-0.008** (0.004)	-0.001 (0.004)
Organization index						0.035* (0.02)	0.020 (0.019)	0.035 (0.021)
Homosexual neighbor not OK	-0.015** (0.004)	-0.001 (0.006)	0.001 (0.006)	-0.007 (0.006)	0.008 (0.005)	0.004 (0.005)	-0.008* (0.005)	0.004 (0.006)
Adjusted R2	0.38	0.54	0.60	0.48	0.73	0.69	0.51	0.67
N	22	22	22	22	22	22	22	22

Notes:

** statistically significant at 5% level

* statistically significant at 10% level

Qualitative Comparisons

Qualitative Comparative Analysis (QCA) takes a set of dichotomous qualitative features of countries, including both outcomes and causal factors, and uses Boolean logic to identify more parsimonious sets of factors that characterize all countries with SSPRs. The first step is to characterize the possible causal factors and to assign values to those factors for each country. Here I used the quantitative values of the independent variables discussed earlier to define the presence or absence of a characteristic. For each variable, I calculated the mean for all countries. Countries whose values were above the 1990 variable mean were assigned a value of one;

Figure A.3
Regression Coefficients for Being in First or
Second Waves of Same-Sex Partnership/Marriage

Variable	(1)	(2)	(3)	(4)	(5)	(6)	(7)	(8)
Constant	1.02** (0.13)	0.45 (0.65)	0.40 (0.35)	1.15** (0.23)	1.1* (0.60)	1.29** (0.21)		
Business index		0.011 (0.014)	0.003 (0.013)	0.008 (0.010)	0.007 (0.012)			
Public social expenditures (% GDP)		0.017 (0.022)			-0.002 (0.019)			
Marriage outdated								
Cohabitation rate			0.022* (0.011)		0.005 (0.012)			
Union density								
Church attendance				-0.014** (0.004)	-0.013** (0.005)	-0.014** (0.004)		
Organization index						0.001 (0.015)		
Homosexual neighbor not OK	-0.017** (0.004)	-0.013* (0.006)	-0.009 (0.006)	-0.009* (0.005)	-0.008 (0.006)	-0.011** (0.004)		
Adjusted R2	0.39	0.36	0.46	0.63	0.59	0.62		
N	23	23	23	23	23	23	23	23

Notes:
** statistically significant at 5% level
* statistically significant at 10% level

those below the mean got a value of zero. For instance, for all countries, the average percentage of inhabitants who reported that they would not like to have a homosexual neighbor was 36.5 in 1990.[6] Countries below that average were coded as one for tolerant; countries above the average received a zero. Figures A.4 and A.5, "Boolean truth tables," show the main variables and their codes for the twenty-three countries with sufficient data.[7] Countries in brackets have the same variable values but do not have an SSPR law.

First I considered a set of the basic variables from all of the theory categories. For comparison with the regressions, the baseline model considers

Figure A.4
Truth Table of Combinations of Variables—Wave 1

Countries	Number of Cases	Has SSPR	Religiosity	Tolerant	High Cohab.	High Soc. Exp.	G/L Bus. Index	G/L Org. Index
Belgium, Germany, Netherlands, Norway [Finland]	4	1	0	1	1	1	1	1
Denmark, Sweden	2	1	0	1	1	1	0	1
France	1	1	0	1	1	1	1	0
Iceland [Australia]	1	1	0	1	1	0	1	1
Czech Republic	1	0	0	0	0	0	0	0
Hungary	1	0	0	0	0	1	0	0
U.K.	1	0	0	1	0	1	1	1
Austria	1	0	1	0	0	1	0	0
Ireland	1	0	1	1	0	0	0	1
Italy, Poland, Turkey	3	0	1	0	0	0	0	0
U.S, Portugal	2	0	1	0	0	0	1	0
Spain	1	0	1	1	0	1	1	0
Canada	1	0	1	1	1	0	0	1

cohabitation, tolerance of homosexuality, state social expenditures, religiosity, gay business visibility, and gay organizational density. Those six variables define 64 (2^6) possible combinations of factors. As can be seen in the truth table in Figure A.4, I analyzed countries that represent 13 different combinations for the first wave; Figure A.5 presents 15 actual combinations for the second wave.

The next step is to minimize the truth table to reduce the conditions describing the countries with an SSPR to the smallest combinations that are logically possible. Ragin describes the simple rule for reducing the conditions: "[C]ombine rows that differ on only one causal condition but produce the same outcome." In Figure A.4, for example, the first two lines of the truth table differ only in that the first line has a 1 value for a high G/L Business Index value, but the second has a 0 value. Therefore, one combination of the five other characteristics is sufficient

Figure A.5
Truth Table of Combinations of Variables—Wave 1 & 2

Countries	Number of Cases	Has SSPR	Religiosity	Tolerant	High Cohab.	High Soc. Exp.	G/L Bus. Index	G/L Org. Index
Belgium, Germany, Norway Finland	4	1	0	1	1	1	1	1
Denmark, Sweden	2	1	0	1	1	1	0	1
France	1	1	0	1	1	1	1	0
Iceland, Netherlands, U.K., Switzerland [Australia]	4	1	0	1	1	0	1	1
Czech Republic	1	1	0	1	1	1	0	0
Spain	1	1	1	1	1	1	1	0
Canada	1	1	1	1	1	0	0	1
Austria	1	0	1	1	1	1	0	0
Ireland	1	0	1	1	0	0	0	1
Italy	1	0	1	1	0	1	0	0
Poland	1	0	1	0	0	1	0	0
U.S	1	0	1	1	1	0	1	0
Hungary	1	0	0	0	0	1	0	0
Turkey	1	0	1	0	0	0	0	0
Portugal	1	0	1	1	0	1	1	0

to describe those seven countries more simply that the two separate combinations of six characteristics: low religiosity, high tolerance, high cohabitation, high social expenditure, and a high G/L organization index. In this initial step of the reduction process, the G/L Business Index value does not aid in describing countries with SSPR laws, since countries with those five characteristics have an SSPR law regardless of the G/L Business Index value. The main chapter text describes the findings in more detail.

Appendix 2

Methods in the Dutch Couples Study

To understand the decisions and experiences of Dutch same-sex couples, I collected qualitative data from interviews with same-sex couples in the Netherlands in the first half of 2004. I interviewed one or both members of six male couples and thirteen female couples for sixty to ninety minutes about their decision to marry, to register, or to remain legally single. I interviewed a total of thirty-four people out of the thirty-eight included in the nineteen couples.

The sample came mainly from the social networks and email networks of Dutch friends and colleagues, along with some couples from the friendship networks of interviewees (a snowball sampling method). I asked colleagues in the Netherlands to circulate by e-mail the following announcement seeking participants in the study:

> I am looking for people in same-sex couples who are willing to be interviewed for a research study. My main question is this: How and why did you decide whether to get married or to register as partners—or to remain unmarried and unregistered?
>
> All answers will be confidential. The interview would last from one hour to 90 minutes. I can conduct the interview at your convenience, either in your home or my office at the University of Amsterdam. The interview would be in English.
>
> About the researcher: I am an economist and professor at the University of Massachusetts, and now I am a visiting researcher at the University of Amsterdam. I have written a book and many articles on economic and political issues for lesbian, gay, and bisexual people in the U.S. I'm also a lesbian (with a partner) who has been active in the U.S. lesbian community for 20 years. While I am living in the Netherlands, I am working on a book about same-sex marriage and registered

partnership laws in Europe. The interview research will be part of the book.

If you would be willing to be interviewed, please contact:

Lee Badgett

My sampling was driven by the need to recruit as diverse a sample as possible with respect to the marital status of couples. Toward the end of the study, I did not follow up on participants' suggestions for additional married couples to interview, but instead I recruited additional unmarried and unregistered couples to provide a broader range of experiences of such couples for the study.

Characteristics of the Sample

Overall, the sample was heavily female, urban (fourteen lived in Amsterdam or its suburbs), binational, well educated, politically left, not religious, with most between thirty-five and fifty years of age. Almost all of the couples had been formed well before 2001, the year that marriage was opened to same-sex couples, and most had been together since at least 1998, the year that registered partnership became available. All of the couples (with the exception of one male couple) saw their relationship as characterized by an intention to stay together indefinitely. Only five couples out of nineteen had neither married nor registered as partners, so this sample of couples overrepresents married or registered couples compared with the estimated 25% of Dutch same-sex couples that have married or registered.

To my knowledge, no detailed demographic data have been published on the race, age, or ethnic composition of married or registered same-sex couples in the Netherlands. Therefore, it difficult to know what kind of biases my sample has, other than a likely bias toward middle-aged and highly educated Dutch people. Given that all but two participants had postsecondary education, my sample is skewed toward middle- or even upper-middle class couples. As a result, my study might leave out different experiences of working-class Dutch couples or those from younger or older age cohorts.

However, the survey by Katharina Boele-Woelki suggests that my sample is not dissimilar from a random sample of Dutch married couples.[1] In that survey, the average age of same-sex registered partners and married couples was in the early forties when the couples formalized their relationships, which was significantly older than the ages of marriage or registration for different-sex couples. Likewise, the average education level and income level were quite similar for all registered or married couples, whether same-sex or different-sex, and the education level was on the high end, while average couple incomes were roughly in the middle of the Dutch income range.

However, my sample appears fairly homogeneous along the lines of race or ethnicity used in the United States. (The Boele-Woelki et al. survey did not gather ethnicity data.) From the perspective of the Netherlands, however, the diversity of this sample is not terribly different from that of the Dutch population. A key social concept that the Dutch use is "allochtone," a term that refers to people with at least one foreign parent, thus capturing both immigrants and children of immigrants. Out of 16.4 million residents of the Netherlands in 2007, 3.2 million people could be classified as allochtone, or 19.4% of the population.[2] About 55% of the allochtone Dutch residents are considered to be from non-Western countries, including Turkey and Asian, Latin American, and African countries. (Although the public controversies surrounding immigration to the Netherlands from Muslim countries have highlighted the visibility of that group, in fact only 5% of the population is Muslim, mostly Turkish and Moroccan immigrants, constituting a minority even of the allochtone.)[3]

My sample of Dutch couples is reasonably diverse in terms of being allochtone. At least two people out of thirty-eight members of couples in the study (5%) had parental or their own roots in a former Dutch colony. Nine other members of couples (24%) were nonnative Dutch: six were from the United States (one of whom was a U.S. resident), two were from Australia, and one was from a Latin American country. One of those from the United States was born in a South American country. Overall, even in this small nonrandom sample, the proportion of allochtone persons is roughly comparable to that in the Dutch population, both in overall proportion (eleven out of thirty-eight, or 29%) and in the non-Western proportion of the allochtone (four out of eleven, or 36%).

I would argue that concerns about bias in this sample are reasonable, given the sampling method, but that the overall effect of any bias on my findings may be small for several reasons. First, the sample is varied with respect to important characteristics. Within these couples are one or more young people, Western and non-Western allochtone people, rural residents, and nonuniversity-educated people. Therefore, I have access to at least some experiences of people in all of those groups, which are otherwise relatively underrepresented. The respondents from underrepresented groups usually expressed motivations, concerns, and experiences with marriage similar to those of people from the more heavily represented groups. Some respondents had unique experiences related to their parents' ethnicity, not surprisingly, which I was able to capture and discuss because of the variation in the sample. Of course, there are other dimensions of variation that I might have missed, a problem inherent in qualitative research and one that pushed me to draw on survey data from probability samples of the Netherlands (and the United States) that covered similar topics wherever possible.

Second, I make no claims about how common the experiences of these couples are because it would be inappropriate to do so given my nonrandom sampling. In my analysis of the data, I attempted to capture the full range of responses that I heard. I simply noted situations in which a response or experience was common to more than one individual or couple without drawing conclusions about the population frequency of those responses or experiences.

Finally, in some ways, the sample might well cut against the bias when considering motives for marriage. My sample is an economically privileged group of couples who have many legal options, including those involving expensive consultations with attorneys and financial planners. It is not clear how this economic bias affects my findings about how same-sex couples understand marriage and decide whether to marry.

There are reasons to believe that lower-income couples need marriage both more and less than more economically advantaged couples. Having less wealth might reduce concerns about the need for property division upon dissolution or about inheritance issues, reducing the demand for marriage. But, as several respondents in the study pointed out, marriage achieves many organizational needs for families much more cheaply than the creation of documents with a lawyer, perhaps increasing demand for marriage among lower-income couples. One respondent even argued that the right to marry is more important for lower-income same-sex couples because they have a smaller range of economically feasible or attractive choices. However, it is also possible that low-income people feel economically insecure and might therefore conceal their gay identity to avoid discrimination, including avoiding public acts such as marriage. In this case, the conceptual framework developed in chapter 2 would need to be expanded, at the very least to add a new barrier related to a generalized stigma related to homosexuality. While I had no such cases among the couples I studied, I did find couples who concealed their marital status, although their rationale for doing so was rooted not in a wish to conceal their sexual orientation but instead in the belief that the legal status had no social relevance.

Overall, while this sample is unlikely to be representative of all same-sex couples in the Netherlands, the kind of detailed qualitative data that I collected will be valuable in understanding the complex process of decision-making within a particular political and cultural context and in documenting most of the range of factors that influence couples' decisions about marriage.

Interview Protocol

I asked an initial battery of questions about the birthplace, education, religion, age, and political beliefs of each individual in a couple, including those who were not present. The main part of the interview consisted of a semistructured set of questions about the relationship, the decision-making process, and the effects of the couple's legal status. I sought answers from both members of the couple for these questions, and when one partner was not present, I asked the respondent what answers he or she thought the absent partner would give to most of questions. (In the analysis of the data, I gave the reports of absent partners' likely responses less weight than actual own responses to questions.)

The main topics were usually asked in roughly this order:

1. Can you tell me how you met? (To get history of relationship up until present time)
2. Why did you decide to marry (or register as partners)? Or, (if not married) have you ever thought about marrying, and, if so, why have you not married?
3. Why did you decide to marry rather than register as partners? (Or the other way around)
4. Please tell me about the day you married. (Follow-up questions on ceremony, what they wore, who was invited, who attended, their reactions)
5. Did you feel different after you married? Did anything change for you as a result of being married? (Follow-up questions on the reactions of family, friends, and others)
6. How did others react to your marriage (or to your remaining unmarried)?
7. Has the right to marry a same-sex partner had an impact on Dutch society more broadly, like on opinions about gay and lesbian people, or political changes, or social changes?

At the end of the interview I asked the respondents if they had questions about my research project. Up to that point, I did not provide any opinions about the answers to my interview questions, and I did not offer any personal information (other than what was in my initial query). In many cases, couples asked me about the political situation with respect to same-sex marriage in the United States, about why I was interested in the Dutch situation, and about my own marriage intentions and opinions about marriage.

As I wrote drafts of the chapters using the interview data, I recontacted as many couples as I could reach to offer them the chance to read and make comments or suggestions about my interpretations. Several did respond with suggestions and comments that I incorporated.

In my discussion of the results, I use pseudonyms for all but one couple, who insisted that I use their real names. Because of the complications and potential confusion of using Dutch surnames, I gave each participant in the study only a first name as a pseudonym.

Method of Analysis

After the interviews were transcribed and I had corrected the transcripts, I analyzed the data using the grounded theory approach to analysis of qualitative data as developed by (among others) Anselm L. Strauss.[4] Initially, two assistants and I conducted detailed line-by-line readings of more than half of the transcripts in an open coding process designed to identify concepts that fit the data.[5] Following Strauss, our analysis "included word-by-word inspection, the generating of theoretical questions and possible answers to them (hypotheses), the use of stimulating internal and external comparisons, and the exploration of similarities and differences."[6] We used these close readings to discover and categorize meaningful conditions, interactions, consequences, strategies, and tactics that the individuals and couples used in the context of marriage, linking many of these concepts and categories.

My assistants and I wrote frequent theoretical memos during the entire analytical process to capture the insights that emerged during the coding process. Over time, we identified core categories that were central to ideas about marriage and to making decisions about marriage, using the frequency of observation as well as the connections to other categories as criteria for identifying which categories were central. Eventually, we developed a set of codes—the core categories, related categories, and their respective dimensions—that provided adequate conceptual density and explanatory power for the main questions driving the study.

I then used the basic set of codes to code each interview transcript in HyperResearch. As my analysis progressed, this electronic coding and data organization allowed me to expand the web of theoretical relationships among the various categories as I used the fully coded data to verify or reject hypotheses about connections between categories.

The couples:

Women:

Pauline & Liz (married)
Margriet & Miriyam (married)
Martha & Lin (married)
Rachel & Marianne (married)
Andrea & Katherine (married)
Hester & Julia (married)
Marta & Tineke (married)
Nancy & Joan
Anna & Joke
Anneke & Isabelle
Laura & Ria (registered partners, about to convert to marriage)
Ineke & Diana (registered partners)
Ellen & Saskia (about to be married at the time of the interview)

Men:

Otto & Bram (married)
Jan & Paul (married)
Erik & James
Rob & Piet
Paul & Javier (registered partners)
Gert & Willem (registered partners)

Notes

NOTES TO CHAPTER 1

1. Tony Perkins, "Here comes the groom," Washington Update, Family Research Council (June 16, 2008), http://www.frc.org/get.cfm?i=WU08F10&f=P G07J01(accessed August 16, 2008).

2. Janet Folger, "How same-sex marriage points to end of the world," World-NetDaily (May 20, 2008), http://www.frc.org/get.cfm?i=WU08F10&f=PG07J01 (accessed August 16, 2008).

3. Maggie Gallagher, "The stakes: Why we need marriage," National Review Online (July 14, 2003), http://www.nationalreview.com/comment/comment-gallagher071403.asp.

4. See, e.g. Nan Hunter, "Marriage, law and gender: A feminist inquiry," in Sex Wars: Sexual Dissent and Political Culture, ed. Lisa Duggan and Nan D. Hunter (New York: Routledge, 1995).

5. William N. Eskridge, Jr., The Case for Same-Sex Marriage: From Sexual Liberty to Civilized Commitment (New York: Free Press, 1996); Andrew Sullivan, "Unveiled: The case against gay marriage crumbles," The New Republic (August 13, 2001).

6. David Brooks, "The power of marriage," New York Times (November 22, 2003), http://Query.nytimes.com/gst/fullpage.html?res=9B06EED133BF931A 15762C1A9659C8B63(accessed May 24, 2008); Jonathan Rauch, Gay marriage: Why It Is Good for Gays, Good for Straights, and Good for America (New York: Times Books, 2004).

7. Douglas W. Allen, "An economic assessment of same-sex marriage laws," Harvard Journal of Law & Public Policy 29 (June 2006): 949–980.

8. Michael Warner, The Trouble With Normal: Sex Politics, and the Ethics of Queer Life (Cambridge, MA: Harvard University Press, 1999); Nancy D. Polikoff, "We will get what we ask for: Why legalizing gay and lesbian marriage will not 'Dismantle the legal structure of gender in every marriage," Virginia Law Review 79 (October 1993): 1535–1550.

9. Amitai Etzioni, "A communitarian position for civil unions," in Just Marriage, ed. Mary Lyndon Shanley (Oxford: Oxford University Press, 1999); William Galston, Comments on "Can gay marriage strengthen the American family?" (2004), www.brookings.edu/~/media/Files/events/2004/0401children%20%20 %20families/20040401.pdf (accessed January 8, 2008).

10. Angela Shah, "Frank calls for order in gay-rights effort; lawmaker tells UT crowd that political discipline is best way to get results," *Austin American-Statesman* (Texas) (April 3, 1999).

11. Elizabeth Birch, "Wedded States," Online Newshour (May 23, 1996), www.pbs.org/newshour/bb/law/may96/gay.marriage.5=23.html (accessed October 28, 2008).

12. Robert Mankoff, "There's nothing wrong with our marriage, but the spectre of gay marriage has hopelessly eroded the institution" (cartoon), *The New Yorker* (July 26, 2004).

13. For instance, Kathleen Hull finds that opponents of gay marriage focus on moral and cultural issues, while proponents of gay marriage focus on individual rights. My approach is related to hers but focuses more on reconciling the culture-individual distinction. See Kathleen E. Hull, *Same-Sex Marriage: The Cultural Politics of Love and Law* (Cambridge: Cambridge University Press, 2006).

14. An exception is the recent insightful book by William Eskridge and Darren Spedale, *Gay Marriage: For Better or for Worse? What We've Learned From the Evidence* (New York: Oxford University Press, 2006), which explores the experience of Denmark and the other Scandinavian countries.

15. William N. Eskridge, Jr., *Equality Practice: Civil Unions and the Future of Gay Rights* (New York: Routledge, 2001); Robert Wintemute, "Introduction," in *The Legal Recognition of Same-Sex Partnerships: A Study of National, European and International Law*, ed. Robert Wintemute and Mads Andenaes (Oxford: Hart, 2001); Kees Waaldijk, "Major legal consequences of marriage, cohabitation and registered partnership for different-sex and same-sex partners in the Netherlands," in Waaldijk, *More or Less Together: Levels of Legal Consequences of Marriage, Cohabitation and Registered Partnership for Different-Sex and Same-Sex Partners* (Paris: Institut National d'Etudes Demographiques, 2004).

16. See Barry D. Adam, Jan Willem Duyvendak, and Andre Krouwel, eds., *The Global Emergence of Gay and Lesbian Politics: National Imprints of a Worldwide Movement* (Philadelphia: Temple University Press, 1999).

17. Joanna Radbord, "Lesbian love stories: How we won equal marriage in Canada," *Yale Journal of Law and Feminism* 17 (2005): 99–131.

18. Anthony M. Kennedy, *Lawrence et al. v. Texas* (opinion), Vol. 02-102, Supreme Court of the United States (2003).

19. Antonin Scalia, *Lawrence et al. v. Texas* (dissent), Vol. 02-102, Supreme Court of the United States (2003).

20. Stanley Kurtz, "The end of marriage in Scandinavia: The "conservative case" for same-sex marriage collapses," *The Weekly Standard* 9(February 2, 2004): 26–33.

21. Stanley Kurtz, "Deathblow to marriage," *National Review Online* (February 5, 2004).

22. U.S. Supreme Court cases have established that marriage is a "fundamental right", so the U.S. Constitution limits states' ability to limit access to marriage.

So far, federal courts have not found that denying marriage to same-sex couples is a violation of that fundamental right. However, the Supreme Court has said that states cannot outlaw interracial marriages (*Loving v. Virginia*), for example.

23. M. V. Lee Badgett, Gary J. Gates, and Natalya C. Maisel, "Registered domestic partnerships among gay men and lesbians: The role of economic factors," *Review of Economics of the Household* 6 (2008): 327–346.

NOTES TO CHAPTER 2

1. Liesbeth Steenhof, "Over 50 thousand lesbian and gay couples," *Statistics Netherlands Web Magazine* (November 15, 2005) (accessed March 13, 2006).

2. See Kees Waaldijk, "Small change: How the road to same-sex marriage got paved in the Netherlands," in *The Legal Recognition of Same-Sex Partnerships: A Study of National, European and International Law*, ed. Robert Wintemute and Mads Andenaes (Oxford: Hart, 2001); Eskridge and Spedale, *Gay Marriage*; Maggie Gallagher and Joshua K. Baker, "Demand for same-sex marriage: Evidence from the United States, Canada, and Europe" (Manassas, VA: Institute for Marriage and Public Policy, 2006), 3.

3. Caleb H. Price, "Do gays really want 'marriage'?" *Citizen* (June 2006) (accessed June 1, 2006); Stanley Kurtz, "Why so few? Looking at what we know about same-sex marriage," *National Review Online* (June 5, 2006) (accessed January 14, 2007).

4. Conducting interviews with a relatively small group of individuals is a common research approach in the social sciences for exploring complex new topics that are hard to capture in surveys.

5. Appendix 2 contains additional details on my interview methods and respondents.

6. Waaldijk, "Major legal consequences of marriage, cohabitation and registered partnership for different-sex and same-sex partners in the Netherlands."

7. Waaldijk, "Small change," 437–464; Hans van Velde, *No Gay Marriage in the Netherlands* (Netherlands: Gay Krant, 2003).

8. All but one of those couples had registered as partners before marriage became a legal option.

9. Larry L. Bumpass, James A. Sweet, and Andrew Cherlin, "The role of cohabitation in declining rates of marriage," *Journal of Marriage and the Family* 53 (November 1991): 913–927; Marin Clarkberg, Ross M. Stolzenberg, and Linda J. Waite. "Attitudes, values, and entrance into cohabitational versus marital unions," *Social Forces* 74 (December 1995): 609–632; Ronald R. Rindfuss and Audrey VandenHeuvel, "Cohabitation: A precursor to marriage or an alternative to being single," *Population and Development Review* 16 (December 1990): 703-726; Pamela J. Smock, "Cohabitation in the United States: An appraisal of research themes, findings, and implications," *Annual Review of Sociology* 26 (2000): 1–20.

10. Kathleen Kiernan, "Unmarried cohabitation and parenthood: Here to stay? European perspectives," in *The Future of the Family*, ed. Daniel P. Moynihan, Timothy M. Smeeding, and Lee Rainwater (New York: Russell Sage Foundation, 2004), 65–95.

11. See Appendix 2 for more details.

12. However, these characteristics are common to those observed in a survey of a sample of Dutch same-sex couples by Katharina Boele-Woelki, Ian Curry-Sumner, Miranda Jansen, and Wendy Schrama, *Huwelijk of geregistreerd partnerschap? Evaluatie van de wet openstelling huwelijk en de wet geregistreerd partnerschap* (Utrecht: Ministerie van Justitie and Universiteit Utrecht, 2006). In that study, the average age of same-sex registered partners and married couples was in the early forties, significantly older than the ages of marriage or registration for different-sex couples. Likewise, the average education level and income level was quite similar for all registered or married couples, whether same-sex or different-sex.

13. See Appendix 2 for a longer discussion of this issue.

14. As of 2002, registered partners of birth mothers also get automatic parental authority to children born after the partners register, so the conversion to marriage was not necessary to achieve that status. Waaldijk, "Major legal consequences of marriage, cohabitation and registered partnership for different-sex and same-sex partners in the Netherlands," 140.

15. This finding varies from that of Eskridge and Spedale, whose interviewees did not feel pressure from family to register as partners. Perhaps this difference in findings reflects a cultural interpretation of the difference between marriage and registered partnership.

16. Boele-Woelki et al., *Huwelijk of geregistreerd partnerschap?*

17. Ibid.; these authors also find more romantic and commitment-related reasons for marrying among the same-sex and different-sex couples who married than they did for registered partners.

18. Matthijs Kalmijn, "Marriage rituals as reinforcers of role transitions: An analysis of weddings in the Netherlands," *Journal of Marriage and the Family* 66, (August 2004): 582–594.

19. Rose M. Kreider and Jason M. Fields, *Number, Timing, and Duration of Marriages and Divorces: Fall 1996* (Washington, DC: U.S. Census Bureau, 2001); see Eurostat for Western Europe.

20. Rosemary Auchmuty, "Same-sex marriage revived: Feminist critique and legal strategy," *Feminism & Psychology* 14 (February 2004): 101–26; Eskridge and Spedale, *Gay marriage.*

21. Nancy F. Cott, *Public Vows: A History of Marriage and the Nation* (Cambridge, MA: Harvard University Press, 2000); Stephanie Coontz, *Marriage: A History* (New York: Viking, 2005).

22. Anna C. Korteweg, "It won't change a thing: The meanings of marriage in the Netherlands," *Qualitative Sociology* 24 (Winter 2001): 507–525.

23. Boele-Woelki et al. *Huwelijk of geregistreerd partnerschap?*

24. Jan Latten, *Trends in samenwonen en trouwen: De schone schijn van burgerlijke staat* (Netherlands: Centraal Bureau voor de Statistiek, 2004) (accessed May 25, 2008), Charts 5 & 6.

25. Ibid.

26. Ibid.

27. For the United States, see Ellen Lewin, *Recognizing Ourselves: Ceremonies of Lesbian and Gay Commitment* (New York: Columbia University Press, 1998); Gretchen Stiers, *From This Day Forward: Commitment, Marriage, and Family in Lesbian and Gay Relationships* (New York: St. Martin's Griffin, 1999); Kathleen E. Hull, "The cultural power of law and the cultural enactment of legality: The case of same-sex marriage," *Law and Social Inquiry* 28 (July 2003): 629–657; Michelle V. Porche, Diane M. Purvin, and Jasmine M. Waddell, "Tying the knot: The context of social change in Massachusetts," paper presented at the panel "What I Did for Love, or Benefits, or . . .: Same-Sex Marriage in Massachusetts," American Psychological Association, Washington, DC (2005); Ellen Schechter, Allison J. Tracy, Konjit V. Page, and Gloria Luong, "'Doing marriage': Same-sex relationship dynamics in the post-legalization period," paper presented at "What I Did for Love, or Benefits, or . . .: Same-Sex Marriage in Massachusetts" (Washington, DC, 2005); Pamela Lannutti, "The influence of same-sex marriage on the understanding of same-sex relationships," *Journal of Homosexuality* 53(2007): 135–151; Michelle V. Porche and Diane M. Purvin, "'Never in our lifetime': Legal marriage for same-sex couples in long-term relationships," *Family Relations* 57 (April 2008): 144–159. For Denmark, see Eskridge and Spedale, *Gay Marriage.* For the United Kingdom, see Beccy Shipman and Carol Smart, "'It's made a huge difference': Recognition, rights and the personal significance of civil partnership," *Sociological Research Online* 12 (2007), http://www.socresonline.org.uk/12/1/shipman.html.

28. See Schecter et al., "Doing marriage," on couples in Massachusetts; Stiers, *From This Day Forward*; and Hull, "The cultural power of law and the cultural enactment of legality," asked couples about their intentions to marry or prioritization of marriage as an issue.

29. For Denmark, see Eskridge and Spedale, *Gay Marriage*, 102. Gunnar Andersson, Turid Noack, Ane Seierstad, and Harald Weedon-Fekjaer, "The demographics of same-sex 'marriages' in Norway and Sweden," *Demography* 43 (February 2006): 79–98, find that many male same-sex couples who have registered as partners in Norway and Sweden are binational couples.

30. Couples in Denmark and in the U.K. also resisted the idea that they were "selling out" their feminist or other political values by registering as partners. See Eskridge and Spedale, *Gay Marriage*, 97; Shipman and Smart, "'It's made a huge difference.'"

31. Schechter et al., "'Doing marriage'"; Hull, "The cultural power of law and the cultural enactment of legality"; Stiers, *From This Day Forward*; Lewin, *Recognizing Ourselves.*

32. Sharon S. Rostosky, Ellen D. B. Riggle, Michael G. Dudley, and Margaret Laurie Comer Wright, "Commitment in same-sex relationships: A qualitative analysis of couples' conversations," *Journal of Homosexuality* 51.0 (October 11, 2006): 199–223; Stiers, *From This Day Forward.*

33. Rostosky et al., "Commitment in same-sex relationships"; Hull, "The cultural power of law and the cultural enactment of legality"; Stiers, *From This Day Forward.*

34. Boele-Woelki et al., *Huwelijk of geregistreerd partnerschap?*

NOTES TO CHAPTER 3

1. Eskridge and Spedale, *Gay Marriage.*

2. Available at http://statline.cbs.nl/StatWeb/publication/DM=SLEN&PA=37772eng&D1=0-47&D2=0,50-57&LA=EN&VW=T.

3. Steenhof, "Over 50 thousand lesbian and gay couples."

4. The number of civil partnerships is from http://www.statistics.gov.uk/cci/nugget.asp?id=1685 (accessed 5/25/08), and the number of couples is an unpublished estimate from the Labour Force Survey tabulated by Jonathan Wadsworth, personal communication, March 31, 2008.

5. Gallagher and Baker, "Demand for same-sex marriage," 7.

6. Price, "Do gays really want 'marriage'?"

7. U.S. Bureau of the Census, *America's Families and Living Arrangements: 2006,* Table A1, "Marital status of people 15 years and over, by age, sex, personal earnings, race, and hispanic origin, 2006," www.census.gov/population/www/socdemo/hh-fam/cps2006.html (accessed March 28, 2008).

8. Dale Carpenter, "The Volokh Conspiracy: Why so few gay marriages?," (April 28, 2006) http://volokh.com/archives/archive_2006_04_23-2006_04_29.shtml#1146256206 (accessed July 28, 2008); Paul Varnell, "Do gays want to marry?," (May 10, 2006) http://www.indegayforum.org/news/show/30943.html (accessed July 28, 2008); Eskridge and Spedale, *Gay Marriage.*

9. While some convenience samples of gay and lesbian people have found higher rates of partnering, studies of random samples suggest a range from 25% to 50%. See Christopher Carpenter and Gary J. Gates, "Gay and lesbian partnership: Evidence from California," *Demography* 45 (August 2008): 573–590; Dan Black, Gary J. Gates, Seth G. Sanders, and Lowell Taylor, "Demographics of the gay and lesbian population in the United States: Evidence from available systematic data sources," *Demography* 37 (2000): 139–154; Henry J. Kaiser Family Foundation, *Inside-out: A report on the experiences of lesbians, gays and bisexuals in America and the Public's views on issues and policies related to sexual orientation* (2001), http://www.kff.org/kaiserpolls/3193-index.cfm (accessed February 18, 2007).

10. Carpenter, "The Volokh Conspiracy: Why so few gay marriages?"; Varnell, "Do gays want to marry?"

11. Carpenter, "The Volokh Conspiracy: Why so few gay marriages?"

12. Ibid.; Eskridge and Spedale, *Gay Marriage*.

13. See Waaldijk, *More or Less Together*. The measures compare the rights for same-sex couples to those of married different-sex couples, creating a measure of the percentage of rights that same-sex couples receive for a given legal status. I calculated the difference between the rights available through partnership or marriage and the next-best status.

14. I calculated this rate using the 1999 World Values Survey for all countries except Norway, for which I use the 1996 rate.

15. Patrick J. Egan and Kenneth Sherrill, "Marriage and the shifting priorities of a new generation of lesbians and gays," *PS: Political Science and Politics* 38 (April 2005): 231.

16. Henry J. Kaiser Family Foundation, *Inside-out.*

17. A. R. D'Augelli, H. J. Rendina, A. J. Grossman, and K. O. Sinclair, "Lesbian and gay youths' aspirations for marriage and raising children," *Journal of LGBT Issues in Counseling* 1(4): 77-98.

18. Alternative calculations that adjust same-sex partnership rates by the number of years in effect and the number of unmarried people in the state also give much higher rates than those for the European countries.

19. Figures in this paragraph and the next are available in Gary J. Gates, M. V. Lee Badgett, and Deborah Ho, "Marriage, registration and dissolution by same-sex couples in the U.S.," Williams Institute, UCLA School of Law, July 2008, http://ssrn.com/abstract=1264106.

20. Steenhof, "Over 50 thousand lesbian and gay couples."

21. Boele-Woelki et al., *Huwelijk of geregistreerd partnerschap?* also find that 30% of married same-sex couples report that recognition by others was an important factor in their choice of marriage, while different-sex couples and registered partner same-sex couples were less than half as likely to report that rationale for their choices.

22. For studies of commitment ceremonies in the United States, see Lewin, *Recognizing Ourselves,* or Stiers, *From This Day Forward.*

23. This description of the contrast between marriage and the PACS comes from Wilfried Rault, "The best way to court. The French mode of registration and its impact on the social significance of partnerships," paper presented at the conference "Same-sex couples, same-sex partnerships & homosexual marriages: A focus on cross-national differentials," Institut National d'Etudes Demographiques, Paris (2004).

24. Jens Rydström, "From outlaw to in-law: On registered partnerships for homosexuals in Scandinavia, its history and cultural implications," paper presented at the conference "Same-sex couples, same-sex partnerships, and homosexual marriages: A Focus on cross-national differentials," Institut National d'Etudes Demographiques, Paris (2004), 179.

25. See Majority Decision, *In re Marriage Cases*, California Supreme Court, S147999 (2008), especially pages 81, 101-106, and 117-118.

26. Steenhof, "Over 50 thousand lesbian and gay couples."

27. Statistics Netherlands, *Key figures marriages and partnership registrations* (2004); Arie de Graaf, "Half of unmarried couples have a partnership contract," *Central Bureau of Statistics Web Magazine* (March 22 2004), http://www.cbs.nl/ en-GB/menu/themas/bevolking/publicaties/artikelen/archief/2004/2004- 1418-sm.htm (accessed March 30, 2006).

28. Ian Sumner, "Happily ever after? The problem of terminating registered partnerships," paper presented at the conference "Same-sex couples, same-sex partnerships, and homosexual marriages: A focus on cross-national differentials," Institut National d'Etudes Demographiques, Paris (2004), 35–46; Mila van Huis, "Flash annulments remain popular," *Central Bureau of Statistics Web Magazine* (May 24 2005).

29. Van Huis, "Flash annulments remain popular."

30. Claude Martin and Irène Théry, "The PACS and marriage and cohabitation in France," *International Journal of Law, Policy, and the Family* 15.0 (April 2001): 135–158.

31. Figures in this paragraph are from Gates, Badgett, and Ho, "Marriage, registration and dissolution by same-sex couples in the U.S."

32. The rationale behind limiting domestic partnerships for different-sex couples to older couples appears to have been a reluctance to reduce the probability of marriage while recognizing that older couples might prefer not to marry to avoid problems with inheritances or pensions.

33. Personal communication from Susan Cochran, Department of Epidemiology, UCLA, 2005.

34. See M. V. Lee Badgett, R. Bradley Sears, and Deborah Ho, "Supporting families, saving funds: An economic analysis of equality for same-sex couples in New Jersey," *Rutgers Journal of Law & Public Policy* 4 (2006): 37-38.

35. Marion C. Willetts, "An exploratory investigation of heterosexual licensed domestic partners," *Journal of Marriage and Family* 65(2003): 939-952.

36. Michael Ash and M. V. Lee Badgett, "Separate and unequal: The effect of unequal access to employment-based health insurance on same-sex and unmarried different-sex couples," *Contemporary Economic Policy* 24 (October 2006): 582-599.

NOTES TO CHAPTER 4

1. Kurtz, "The end of marriage in Scandinavia."

2. Stanley Kurtz, "Death of marriage in Scandinavia," *Boston Globe* (March 10, 2004); Kurtz, "The end of marriage in Scandinavia"; Stanley Kurtz, Testimony before the Subcommittee on the Constitution, Committee on the

Judiciary, U.S. House of Representatives (2004), http://frwebgate.access.gpo.
gov/cgi-bin/getdoc.cgi?dbname=108_house_hearings&docud=f:93225.pdf.

3. Jonathan Rauch, Andrew Sullivan, William Eskridge, and Darren Spedale
have also taken on Kurtz online and in print.

4. U.S. Senate, Congressional Record: Proceedings and Debate of the 109th
Congress, Second Session (2006), Vol. 152, S5415–S5424, S5450–S5473.

5. This report looks only at trends in demographic measures during the
1990s. Patrick F. Fagan and Grace Smith, "The transatlantic divide on marriage:
Dutch data and the U.S. debate on same-sex unions," *The Heritage Foundation,*
Web Memo #577 (2004), http://www.heritage.org/research/Family/wm577.
cfm (accessed October 4, 2004).

6. M. Van Mourick, A. Nuytinck, R. Kuiper, J. Van Loon, and H. Wels,
"Good for gays, bad for marriage," *National Post* (August 11, 2004). Van Mourik
and Nuytinck are law professors. Joost Van Loon is a social theorist whose self-
described areas of expertise are risk, technology, and media, http://www.ntu.
ac.uk/research/school_research/hum/staff/7120.htm (accessed January 18,
2007).

7. Kurtz, "The end of marriage in Scandinavia."

8. Coontz, *Marriage: A History.*

9. Tavia Simmons and Martin O'Connell, *Married couples and unmarried
partner households: 2000.* Available at Census 2000 Special Reports, www.census.
gov/prod/2003pubs/censr-5.pdf.

10. Liesbeth Steenhof and Carel Harmsen, *Same-sex couples in the Netherlands,*
paper presented at the conference "Same-sex couples, same-sex partnerships, and
homosexual marriages: A Focus on cross-national differentials," Institut National
d'Etudes Demographiques, Paris (2004); Eskridge and Spedale, *Gay Marriage.*

11. Donna K. Ginther, Marianne Sundström, and Anders Björklund, "Selection
or specialization? The impact of legal marriage on adult earnings in Sweden," paper
presented at the Population Association of America meeting, Los Angeles (2006).

12. Eskridge, *Equality Practice.*

13. *Statistics Norway, Statistics Yearbook 2007,* Table 93, "Asylum applications,
by country and the seeker's citizenship. Nordic countries." Oslo, Norway: Statistics Norway, www.ssb.no/en/yearbook/tab/tab-093.html.

14. Jan Latten, personal communication, March 12, 2004. See also Latten,
Trends in samenwonen en trouwen; Joop Garssen, personal communication, June
18, 2004.

15. All statistics are from national statistical agencies.

16. Statistics Denmark, *Statistical Yearbook 2003,* p. 5, www.dst.dk/asp2xml/
puk/udgivelser/get_file.asp?id=3985&sid=entire2003.

17. Ryan T. Anderson, "Beyond gay marriage: The stated goal of these prominent gay activists is no longer merely the freedom to live as they want," *Weekly
Standard* (August 17, 2006).

18. Michael Svarer, "Is your love in vain? Another look at premarital cohabitation and divorce," *Journal of Human Resources* 39 (Spring 2004): 523–535.

19. Kurtz, "Death of marriage in Scandinavia."

20. Nonmarital birth rates in the next few paragraphs are primarily from Eurostat for the 1990s (Eurostat, 2004), epp.eurostat.ec.europa.eu.

21. Statistics Denmark, *HISB3 Summary Vital Statistics,* www.statbank.dk/Statbank5a/SelectVarVal/define.asp?MainTable=H1583&Planguage=1&PXSIde=0.

22. Statistics Norway, "Live births and late fetal deaths: 1951–2007," www.ssb.no/fodte_en/tab-2008-04-09-01-en.html.

23. Statistics Netherlands, "Size and composition of household, position in the household" (January 1, 2004), http://www.statline.cbs.nl/StatWeb/publication/?VW=T&DM=SLEN&PA=37312eng&D1=31-50&D2=(I-11)-I&HD=081108-2206&LA=EN.

24. Stanley Kurtz, "Unhealthy half truths: Scandinavian marriage is dying," *National Review Online* (May 25, 2004).

25. David Coleman and Joop Garssen, "The Netherlands: Paradigm or exception in western Europe's demography?" *Demographic Research* 7 (September 10, 2002): 433-468; Arno Sprangers and Joop Garssen, *Non-marital-fertility in the European economic area* (The Hague: Centraal Bureau voor de Statistiek, 2003).

26. Stanley Kurtz, "Going Dutch: Lessons of the same-sex marriage debate in the Netherlands," *Weekly Standard* 9 (May 31, 2004): 26–29.

27. Stanley Kurtz, "Dutch debate," *National Review Online* (July 21, 2004).

28. Finland did not pass its partner registration law until 2001, so it is included in the nonpartnership countries for this comparison.

29. Kathleen Kiernan, "The rise of cohabitation and childbearing outside marriage in Western Europe," *International Journal of Law, Policy, and the Family* 15 (April 2001): 1–21.

30. Joop Garssen, personal communication (June 18, 2004).

31. Statistics Denmark, *FAM4: Families by region, type of family, size, and number of children* (2004), http://www.statbank.dk/FAM4.

32. Statistics Norway, *Statistics Yearbook 2003,* "Population statistics, Marriages and registered partnerships (2002)"; Statistics Norway, *Statistics Yearbook 2004,* Table 2, "Families, by type of family. Children under 18 years of age, 1974–2004."

33. Joop Garssen and M. V. Lee Badgett, "Equality doesn't harm 'family values,'" *National Post (Canada)* (August 11, 2004); Statistics Netherlands, "Size and composition of household, position in the household" (January 1, 2004), http://www.statline.cbs.nl/StatWeb/publication/?VW=T&DM=SLEN&PA=37312eng&D1=31-50&D2=(I-11)-I&HD=081108-2206&LA=EN.

34. U.S. Bureau of the Census, "Households and families: 2000" (2001).

35. Kiernan, "The rise of cohabitation and childbearing outside marriage in Western Europe."

36. Data for the Netherlands are not available for these measures.

37. Gunnar Andersson, "Children's experience of family disruption and family formation: Evidence from 16 FFS countries," *Demographic Research* 7 (August 14, 2002): 343–364.

38. These Family and Fertility Studies that Andersson analyzes are also used by Kiernan in the work cited earlier.

39. The comparisons come from data available at The Clearinghouse on International Developments in Child, Youth, and Family Policies at Columbia University, http://www.childpolicyintl.org/ (accessed April 2006).

40. See the 2006 debate between Jonathan Rauch, Stanley Kurtz, and the author on Maggie Gallagher's blog, http://www.marriagedebate.com/md-blog/2006_02_26_mdblog_archive.htm.

41. Eskridge and Spedale, *Gay Marriage,* 181.

42. Ibid., 184–185.

43. In these calculations I have left out respondents who answer "don't know," since the data for certain years do not include these responses.

44. To test for the statistical significance of these changes within countries, I regressed country dummy variables and interaction terms with the 1999 survey. The changes from 1990 to 1999 were statistically significant at the 10% or lower level for France, the United Kingdom, Denmark, Ireland, the United States, Canada, Poland, the Czech Republic, Slovenia, and Turkey.

NOTES TO CHAPTER 5

1. From Merriam-Webster online dictionary, www.m-w.com (accessed July 28, 2008).

2. In developing this analysis of potential cultural changes, I drew on papers written in 2006 as part of a project called "New Approaches to Explaining Family Change and Variation": Naomi Quinn, "An Anthropological Perspective on Marriage" and Jennifer Johnson-Hanks, S. Philip Morgan, Christine Bachrach, and Hans-Peter Kohler, "The American Family in a Theory of Conjunctural Action," http:.//www.soc.duke.edu/~efc/.

3. At an individual level, though, some individuals felt that the existence of an explicit social role for spouses was still strong enough that they rejected the individual option to marry for that reason, even though they approved of same-sex couples having that choice as a whole.

4. See also, for example, Andrew J. Cherlin, "The deinstitutionalization of American marriage," *Journal of Marriage and the Family* 66 (November 2004): 848–861; P. Van den Akker, L. Halman, and R. de Moor, "Primary relations in Western societies," in *The Individualizing Society. Value Change in Europe and North America.,* ed. P. Ester, L. Halman and R. de Moor (Tilburg, The Netherlands: Tilburg University Press, 2004): 97–127; Coontz, *Marriage: A History*; E. J. Graff, *What Is Marriage For?* (Boston: Beacon Press, 1999).

5. However, I argue in chapter 6 that the passage of time might well alter the degree of choice experienced by same-sex couples, placing gay men and lesbians in a position much more similar to that of heterosexual people who still face some social expectations and pressure to marry.

6. Ramona Faith Oswald's analysis of the experiences of GLBT people at heterosexual weddings shows that GLBT people often felt excluded or marginalized in the context of the wedding ritual and the accompanying events. See R. F. Oswald, "A member of the wedding? Heterosexism and family ritual," *Journal of Social and Personal Relationships* 12 (2005): 349–368.

7. Kathleen Hull points out that distinguishing between legal and cultural elements in the gay marriage issue makes it harder to argue that "marriage has a single, natural, God-given essence." See Kathleen E. Hull, *Same-Sex Marriage: The Cultural Politics of Love and Law* (Cambridge: Cambridge University Press, 2006), p. 202.

8. Coontz, *Marriage: A History*; Cott, *Public Vows*; Mary Ann Glendon, "For better or for worse?" *Wall Street Journal (Eastern Edition)* (February 25, 2004); Graff, *What Is Marriage For?*

9. Lawrence Kurdek, "The allocation of household labor in gay, lesbian, and heterosexual married couples," *Journal of Social Issues* 49 (Fall 1993): 127–139; Lawrence Kurdek, "Lesbian and gay couples," in *Lesbian, Gay, and Bisexual Identities Over the Lifespan: Psychological Perspectives*, ed. Anthony R. D'Augelli and Charlotte J. Patterson (New York: Oxford University Press, 1995); Philip Blumstein and Pepper Schwartz, *American Couples: Money, Work, Sex* (New York: Morrow, 1983); Raymond W. Chan, Risa C. Brooks, Barbara Raboy, and Charlotte J. Patterson, "Division of labor among lesbian and heterosexual parents: Association with children's adjustment," *Journal of Family Psychology* 12 (September 1998): 402–419; Charlotte J. Patterson, Erin L. Sutfin, and Megan Fulcher, "Division of labor among lesbian and heterosexual parenting couples: Correlates of specialized versus shared patterns," *Journal of Adult Development* 11 (July 2004): 179–189; see also Sondra E. Solomon, Esther D. Rothblum, and Kimberly F. Balsam, "Pioneers in partnership: Lesbian and gay male couples in civil unions compared with those not in civil unions and married heterosexual siblings," *Journal of Family Psychology* 18 (June 2004): 275–286; Christopher Carrington, *No Place Like Home: Relationships and Family Life Among Lesbians and Gay Men* (Chicago: University of Chicago Press, 1999).

10. These statistics were calculated from data provided by the Organization of Economic Cooperation and Development labor market statistics databank, www.oecd.org (accessed May 5, 2006).

11. See, e.g., Warner, *The Trouble With Normal*.

12. See Eskridge, *The Case for Same-Sex Marriage*: 10, 82; Andrew Sullivan, *Virtually Normal* (New York: Vintage, 1996), 105–107; Rauch, *Gay Marriage,*

138–158; Richard Posner, *Sex and Reason* (Cambridge, MA: Harvard University Press, 1992).

13. See, e.g., Allen, "An economic assessment of same-sex marriage laws"; Maggie Gallagher, "(How) will gay marriage weaken marriage as a social institution: A reply to Andrew Koppelman," *University of St. Thomas Law Review* 2 (2004): 33–70.

14. Eskridge and Spedale, *Gay Marriage*, 146–147.

15. Thomas S. Dee, "Forsaking all others? The effects of 'gay marriage' on risky sex," *Economic Journal* 118 (July 2008): 1055–1078.

16. Eskridge and Spedale, *Gay Marriage*: 164–165.

17. Sondra E. Solomon, Esther D. Rothblum, and Kimberly F. Balsam, "Money, housework, sex, and conflict: Same-sex couples in civil unions, those not in civil unions, and heterosexual married siblings," *Sex Roles* 52 (May 2005): 561–575.

18. The European Values Survey is part of the World Values Survey project. The exact question wording: "Here is a list of things which some people think make for a successful marriage. Please tell me, for each one, whether you think it is very important, rather important or not very important for a successful marriage?"

19. Gilbert Herdt and Robert Kertzner, "I do, but I can't: The impact of marriage denial on the mental health and sexual citizenship of lesbians and gay me in the United States," *Sexuality Research & Social Policy* 3 (March 2006): 39.

20. Naomi Quinn, "An anthropological perspective on marriage," paper prepared for the "Unions" volume, explaining family change and variation project.

21. Ibid., 19.

22. The differences between GLB people and heterosexual people of the same sex are statistically significant at the 5% level for about half of the questions; exceptions are statements 2 (divorce), 5 (rewards), 6 (warm), and 8 (family) for women and statements 2 (divorce), 6 (warm), and 8 (family) for men. However, while the average response may differ significantly in a statistical sense, there is obviously much more agreement than disagreement between GLB and heterosexual people.

23. EOS Gallup Europe, "Homosexual marriage, child adoption by homosexual couples: Is the public ready?" (2003), http://www.ilga-europe.org/content/download/3434/20938/file/Gallup%20Europe%202003%20report.pdf.

24. Overall, 80% of marriages among Turkish and Moroccan Dutch residents are to someone from the same group. R. P. W. Jennissen and J. Oudhof, eds., "Ontwikkelingen in de maatschappelijke participatie van allochtonen," Central Bureau of Statistics (2007), http://www.cbs.nl/NR/rdonlyres/7DCAG41A4-ED04-4511-8O23-B1BFFDB6E960/0/2007jaarrapportintegratiepub.pdf.

25. "Dutch migrants-to-be must watch gay kiss" (March 13, 2006), www.gay.com/news/article.html?2006/03/12/3.

26. Few Danish couples report feeling pressure, according to Eskridge and Spedale, *Gay Marriage*, 104, perhaps because registered partnership is viewed by heterosexuals as different from marriage or because of a more low-key cultural expectation about marriage.

27. For instance, see Oswald's discussion of the exclusion of partners from "family" photos at weddings; Ramona Faith Oswald, "A member of the wedding? Heterosexism and family ritual," *Journal of Social and Personal Relationships* 17 (June 1, 2000): 349–368.

28. Quinn, An anthropological perspective on marriage, 5.

29. Eskridge and Spedale report a similar finding for Danish couples; Eskridge and Spedale, *Gay Marriage*, 155.

30. Gallagher, "(How) will gay marriage weaken marriage as a social institution," 53.

31. Posner, Sex and Reason.

32. Ibid., 312.

33. Statistics Netherlands reports that about 7 million people were married in 2005. Only about 10,000 same-sex couples have married since 2001, representing 0.3% of married individuals. That means that 99.7% of married Dutch people have a different-sex partner.

34. For the United States, see Judith Stacey and Timothy J. Biblarz, "(How) does the sexual orientation of parents matter?" *American Sociological Review* 66 (2001): 159–183. For the Netherlands, see Henny Bos, *Parenting in Lesbian Families* (Amsterdam: University of Amsterdam Press, 2005).

NOTES TO CHAPTER 6

1. Cherlin, "The deinstitutionalization of American marriage," 848.

2. Ibid., 851.

3. Ibid.

4. Katherine M. Franke, "The politics of same-sex marriage politics," *Columbia Journal of Gender and Law* 15 (January 2006): 236–248; Auchmuty, "Same-sex marriage revived," 101–126; Ruthann Robson, "Resisting the family: Repositioning lesbians in legal theory," *Signs* 19 (Summer 1994): 975–995.

5. Bumpass et al., "The role of cohabitation in declining rates of marriage," 913–927; Clarkberg et al., "Attitudes, values, and entrance into cohabitational versus marital unions," 609-32.

6. Coontz, *Marriage: A History*.

7. Milton C. Regan, Jr., "Law, marriage, and intimate commitment," *Virginia Journal of Social Policy & the Law* 9 (Fall 2001): 116–152.

8. Chai R. Feldblum, "Gay is good: The moral case for marriage equality and more," *Yale Journal of Law and Feminism* 17 (Spring 2005): 178.

9. Some debate remains about whether both men and women benefit from

being in a heterosexual marriage. My reading of the evidence is that both gain, although not necessarily by the same amount in each outcome measure.

10. For general reviews, see Catherine E. Ross, John Mirowsky, and Karen Goldsteen, "The impact of the family on health: The decade in review," *Journal of Marriage and the Family* 52 (1990): 1059–1078; Linda J. Waite and Maggie Gallagher, *The case for marriage* (New York: Broadway Books, 2000). For studies showing that married people live longer, see Lee A. Lillard and Constantijn W. A. Panis, "Marital status and mortality: The role of health," *Marital Status and Mortality: The Role of Health* 33 (1996): 313–127; John E. Murray, "Marital protection and marital selection: Evidence from a historical-prospective sample of American men," *Demography* 37 (2000): 511–521. For studies showing that married people smoke less, see Debra Umberson, "Gender, marital status, and the social control of behavior," *Social Science and Medicine* 34 (1992): 907–917; Tarani Chandola, Jenny Head, and Mel Bartley, "Socio-demographic predictors of quitting smoking: How important are household factors?" *Addiction* 99 (2004): 770-777; Ulla Broms, Karri Silventoinen, Eero Lahelma, Markku Koskenvuo, and Jaakko Kaprio, "Smoking cessation by socioeconomic status and marital status: The contribution of smoking behavior and family background," *Nicotine Tobacco Research* 6 (2004): 447-455; S. Lee, E. Cho, F. Grodstein, I. Kawachi, F. B. Hu, and G. A. Colditz, "Effects of marital transitions on changes in dietary and other health behaviours in U.S. women," *International Journal of Epidemiology* 34 (2005): 69–78; C. A. Schoenborn, "Marital status and health: United States, 1999–2002," *Division of Health Interview Statistics, National Center for Health Statistics* (2004): 351. For studies showing that married men earn more, see C. Cornwell, and P. Rupert, "Unobservable individual effects, marriage and the earnings of young men," *Economic Inquiry* 35 (1997): 285–294; S. Korenman and D. Neumark, :Does marriage really make men more productive?" *The Journal of Human Resources* 26 (1991): 282–307; K S. Korenman and D. Neumark, "Marriage, motherhood, and wages," *Journal of Human Resources* 27 (1992): 233–255; E. S. Loh, "Productivity differences and the marriage wage premium for white males," *Journal of Human Resources* 31 (1996): 566-589; J. Waldfogel, "Understanding the 'family gap' in pay for women with children," *Journal of Economic Perspectives* 12 (1198): 137–156; J. Hersch and L. S. Stratton, "Household specialization and the male marriage premium," *Industrial and Labor Relations Review* 54 (2000): 78–94; H. Chun and I. Lee, "Why do married men earn more: Productivity or marriage selection?" *Economic Inquiry* 39 (2001): 307–319; Donna Gunther and Madeline Zavodny, "Is the male marriage premium due to selection? The effect of shotgun weddings on the return to marriage," *Journal of Population Economics* 14 (2001): 313-328; L. S. Stratton, "Examining the wage differential for married and cohabiting men," *Economic Inquiry* 40 (2002): 199–212; P. N. Cohen, "Cohabitation and the declining marriage premium for men," *Work and Occupations* 29 (2002): 346–363. For studies finding

that married people are less depressed, see Kathleen A. Lamb, Gary R. Lee, and Alfred DeMaris, "Union formation and depression: Selection and relationship effects," *Journal of Marriage and Family* 65 (November 2003): 953–962; R. W. Simon, "Revisiting the relationships among gender, marital status, and mental health," *American Journal of Sociology* 107 (2002): 1065–1096; S. L. Brown, "The effect of union type on psychological well-being: Depression among cohabitors versus marrieds," *Journal of Health and Social Behavior* 41 (2002): 241–255; A. V. Horwitz, H. R. White, and S. Howell-White, "Becoming married and mental health: A longitudinal study of a cohort of young adults," *Journal of Marriage and Family* 58 (1996): 895–907.

11. Umberson, "Gender, marital status, and the social control of behavior," 907-17; Debra Umberson, "Family status and health behaviors: Social control as a dimension of social integration," *Journal of Health and Social Behavior* 28 (1987): 306–319; Linda J. Waite, "Does marriage matter?" *Demography* 32 (1995): 483–507.

12. Herdt and Kertzner, "I do, but I can't," 33–49.

13. Ash and Badgett, "Separate and unequal," 582–99.

14. The common experience of discrimination and exclusion has shaped the development of the LGB community and sense of identity (e.g., John D'Emilio, *Sexual Politics, Sexual Communities: The Making of a Homosexual Minority in the United States, 1940-1970* (Chicago and London: University of Chicago Press, 1984), and the end of exclusion will likely have cultural effects such as those that I discuss in the next chapter. Here I consider the impact of exclusion on individuals, though.

15. See reviews in Susan D. Cochran, "Emerging issues in research on lesbians' and gay men's mental health: Does sexual orientation really matter?" *American Psychologist* 56 (2001): 932–947; Ilan Meyer, "Prejudice, social stress, and mental health in lesbian, gay, and bisexual populations: Conceptual issues and research evidence," *Psychological Bulletin* 129 (2003): 674–697.

16. See review in Vickie M. Mays, Susan D. Cochran and Namdi W. Barnes, "Race, race-based discrimination, and health outcomes among african Americans," *Annual Review of Psychology* 58 (2007): 201–225. For effect of minority stress on gay people, see Ilan Meyer, "Minority stress and mental health in gay men," *Journal of Health and Social Behavior* 36 (March 1995): 38–56; Vickie M. Mays and Susan D. Cochran, "Mental health correlates of perceived discrimination among lesbian, gay, and bisexual adults in the United States," *American Journal of Public Health* 91 (2001): 1869–1876.

17. See Glenda Russell, *Voted Out: The Psychological Consequences of Anti-Gay Politics* (New York: New York University Press, 2000); Glenda. Russell, "The dangers of a same-sex marriage referendum for community and individual well-being: A summary of research findings," *Angles* 7 (June 2004). See also Ellen D.

B. Riggle, Jerry D. Thomas, and Sharon S. Rostosky, "The marriage debate and minority stress," *PS: Political Science and Politics* (April 205): 221–224 on the connection of minority stress to the marriage debate.

18. Jonathan J. Mohr and Ruth E. Fassinger, "Sexual orientation identity and romantic relationship quality in same-sex couples," *Personality and Social Psychology Bulletin* 32 (2006): 1085-1099; Porche and Purvin, "Never in our lifetime," 144-159.

19. Many studies in different contexts find that GLB people learn to live with the background feelings of difference. Meyer, "Prejudice, social stress, and mental health in lesbian, gay, and bisexual populations," 674–697.

20. Lewin, *Recognizing Ourselves*. See also Hull, *Same-Sex Marriage*.

21. Danish couples who had registered as partners also expressed a greater sense of commitment; see Eskridge and Spedale, *Gay Marriage,* 139–145.

22. Robert-Jay Green, "Risk and resilience in lesbian and gay couples: Comment on Solomon, Rothblum, and Balsam," *Journal of Family Psychology* 18 (2004): 290–292.

23. Solomon et al., "Money, housework, sex, and conflict," 561–575; Lawrence A. Kurdek, "Are gay and lesbian cohabiting couples really different from heterosexual married couples?" *Journal of Marriage and Family* 66 (November 2004): 880–900.

24. Solomon et al., "Money, housework, sex, and conflict," 561–575.

25. However, it is difficult to separate out the selection effect in which couples whose marriages would have been short decide not to marry to begin with. See Lee A. Lillard, Michael J. Brien, and Linda J. Waite, "Premarital cohabitation and subsequent marital dissolution: A matter of self-selection?" *Demography* 32 (August 1995): 437–457.

26. Kimberly F. Balsam, Theodore P. Beauchaine, Esther D. Rothblum, and Sondra E. Solomon, "Three-year follow-up of same-sex couples who had civil unions in Vermont, same-sex couples not in civil unions, and heterosexual married couples," *Developmental Psychology* 44 (2008): 102–116. In another study of a nonrandom group of American couples, Kurdek found that dissolution rates for childless gay and lesbian couples were higher than rates for heterosexual married couples with children but similar to rates for heterosexual married couples without children; Kurdek, "Are gay and lesbian cohabiting couples really different from heterosexual married couples?" 880-900.

27. Ross von Metzke, "Gay divorce rate in Netherlands equal to heterosexuals," http://amsterdam.gaymonkey.com/article.cfm?section=9&id=5853 (accessed April 6, 2005).

28. Andersson et al., "The demographics of same-sex 'marriages' in Norway and Sweden," 79–98.

29. Eskridge and Spedale, *Gay Marriage*.

30. Rauch, *Gay Marriage*; Brooks, "The power of marriage"; Eskridge, *The Case for Same-Sex Marriage*; Warner, *The Trouble With Normal.*

31. For recent evidence from the United States and Australia, see Michael Bittman, Paula England, Liana Sayer, Nancy Folbre, and George Matheson, "When does gender trump money? Bargaining and time in household work," *American Journal of Sociology* 109 (July 2003): 186–214.

32. Kurdek, "The allocation of household labor in gay, lesbian, and heterosexual married couples"; Kurdek, "Lesbian and gay couples"; Lawrence A. Kurdek, "Differences between partners from heterosexual, gay, and lesbian cohabiting couples," *Journal of Marriage and Family* 68 (May 2006): 509–528; Blumstein and Schwartz, *American Couples*; Carrington, *No Place Like Home.*

33. Chan et al., "Division of labor among lesbian and heterosexual parents," 402–419; Patterson et al., "Division of labor among lesbian and heterosexual parenting couples"; Solomon et al., "Money, housework, sex, and conflict," 561–575.; Mignon R. Moore, "Gendered power relations among women: A study of household decision-making in black, lesbian stepfamilies," *American Sociological Review* 73 (April 2008): 335–356.

34. Jyl Josephson, "Citizenship, same-sex marriage, and feminist critiques of marriage," *Perspectives on Politics* 3 (June 2005): 269–284.

35. George Chauncey, *Why Marriage? The History Shaping Today's Debate Over Gay Equality* (New York: Basic Books 2004), 70.

NOTES TO CHAPTER 7

1. As quoted in Wyatt Buchanan, "Alternative to same-sex union," *San Francisco Chronicle* (July 27, 2006).

2. Robert George, "First things blog: Beyond gay marriage," http://www.firstthings.com/onthesquare/?p=330 (August 2, 2006) (accessed July 29, 2008); Robert George, "First things blog: Same-sex marriage and Jon Rauch," http://www.firstthings.com/onthesquare/?p=373 (August 10, 2006) (accessed July 29, 2008); Stanley Kurtz, "The confession: Have same-sex marriage advocates said too much?," *National Review Online* (October 31, 2006).

3. Jonathan Rauch, "Independent gay forum: Not so fast, Mr. George," http://www.indegayforum.org/blog/show/31025.html (August 2, 2006) (accessed February 15, 2007); Carpenter, "The Volokh Conspiracy: Left, right, and betwixt on gay marriage and polygamy," August 3, 2006, http://volokh.com/archives/archive_2006_07_30_2006_08_05.shtml/#1154616146

4. Gert Hekma, "Queer: The Dutch case," *GLQ: A Journal of Lesbian and Gay Studies* 10 (2004): 276–280.

5. Pamela Lannutti, "The influence of same-sex marriage on the understanding of same-sex relationships."

6. Egan and Sherrill, "Marriage and the shifting priorities of a new generation of lesbians and gays."

7. Schoenberg, "Our love is here to stay"; D'Augelli et al., "Lesbian and gay youths'aspirations for marriage and raising children."

8. See Coontz, *Marriage: A History*, for a discussion of the commonness of polygamy in many parts of the world; see Judith Stacey, "Backward toward the postmodern family: Reflections on gender, kinship and class in the Silicon Valley," in *Rethinking the Family: Some Feminist Questions*, ed. Barrie Thorne and Marilyn Yalom (Boston: Northeastern University Press, 1992), for a discussion of heterosexual-centered families that include these kinds of family relationships.

9. Simmons and O'Connell, *Married Couples and Unmarried Partner Households*.

10. Franke, "The politics of same-sex marriage politics," 244.

11. "Beyond same-sex marriage: A new strategic vision for all our families & relationships" (2006), http://www.beyondmarriage.org/full_statement.html; Kath Weston, "Families in queer states: The rule of law and the politics of recognition," *Radical History Review* 93 (Fall 2005): 122–141.

12. Robson, "Resisting the family: Repositioning lesbians in legal theory"; Richard Kim, "The descent of marriage," *The Nation Online* (February 27, 2004), http://www.thenation.com/doc/20040315/kim; Nancy D. Polikoff, "N.J.'s historic 'civil union' opportunity," *Philadelphia Inquirer* (October 27, 2006).

13. See M. V. Lee Badgett, *Money, Myths, And Change: The Economic Lives of Lesbians and Gay Men* (Chicago: University of Chicago Press, 2001) for a longer discussion.

14. Ash and Badgett, "Separate and unequal"; Badgett, *Money, Myths, and Change*; Nicole Raeburn, *Changing Corporate America From Inside Out* (Minneapolis: University of Minnesota Press, 2004).

15. Blanton cites a survey suggesting that 91% of New England employers offering domestic partner benefits would continue to do so; Kimberly Blanton, "Benefits for domestic partners maintained," *Boston Globe* (August 22, 2004). See also Steve Wasik, "State of the (same-sex) union: The impact of same-sex marriage on HR and employee benefits," presented at Out & Equal Conference (September 22, 2005), http://www.outandequal.org/summit/2005/workshops/documents/StateofSameSexUnion.pdf (accessed February 11, 2007). He reports on a Hewitt Associates survey that found that fewer than 1% of employers that offered domestic partner benefits dropped coverage in Massachusetts.

16. Funders for Lesbian and Gay Issues, *Lesbian, gay, bisexual, transgender and queer grantmaking by U.S. foundations (calendar year 2004)* (2006), http://www.workinggroup.org/files/LGBTQ_funding_20041.pdf..

17. Marci L. Eads and Matthew C. Brown, *An Exploratory Look at the Financial Side of the Lesbian, Gay, Bisexual, and Transgender Rights Movement* (Denver: Gill Foundation, 2005).

18. Funders for Lesbian and Gay Issues, Lesbian, gay, bisexual, transgender and queer grantmaking by U.S. foundations (calendar year 2004).

19. Independent Sector and the Foundation Center, *Highlights of Social Justice Grantmaking: A Report on Foundation Trends* (2005), http://foundationcenter.org/gainknowledge/research/pdf/socialjustice.pdf.

20. Robert Wood Johnson Foundation, http://www.rwjf.org/about/mission.jhtml (accessed November 30, 2006).

21. The "Beyond Same-Sex Marriage" statement makes this point. John D'Emilio, "The marriage fight is setting us back," *Gay & Lesbian Review* (November/December 2006): 10–11, makes a similar argument for change in the U.S. context.

22. See Lisa Duggan and Richard Kim, "Beyond gay marriage," *The Nation* (July 18, 2005).

23. Evan Wolfson, *Why Marriage Matters: America, Equality, and Gay People's Right to Marry* (New York: Simon & Schuster, 2004), 136.

24. Allowing same-sex couples to marry should make it easier for transgender people to marry, since marriage would no longer require a state determination about the legal gender of each individual. In California, for instance, the marriage license forms now require no indication of sex. See Celia Kitzinger and Sue Wilkinson, "Genders, sexualities, and equal marriage rights," *Lesbian and Gay Psychology Review*, 7 (2006): 174–179.

25. See Kath Weston, *Families We Choose: Lesbians, Gays, Kinship* (New York: Columbia University Press, 1991) for discussions of "families we choose"; see also Green, "Risk and resilience in lesbian and gay couples."

26. See, for example, Warner, *The Trouble With Normal*; Judith Levine, "Stop the wedding! Why gay marriage isn't radical enough," *Village Voice* (July 23–29, 2003) (accessed February 15, 2007).

27. Arland Thornton and L. Young-DeMarco, "Four decades of trends in attitudes toward family issues in the United States: The 1960s through the 1990s," *Journal of Marriage and the Family* 63 (2001): 1009–1037.

28. Ibid., p. 1024.

29. On education, see Christine R. Schwartz and Robert D. Mare, "Trends in educational assortative marriage from 1940 to 2003," *Demography* 42 (November 2005): 621–646; on income see Megan M. Sweeney and Maria Cancian, "The changing importance of white women's economic prospects for assortative mating," *Journal of Marriage and the Family* 66 (November 2004): 1015–1028.

30. The economist Gary Burtless shows that the tighter link between husbands' and wives' incomes pushed personal income inequality up by 13% between 1979 and 1996; Gary Burtless, "Effects of growing wage disparities and

changing family composition on the U.S. income distribution," Center on Social and Economic Dynamics Working Paper no. 4 (1999).

31. Lisa K. Jepsen and Christopher A. Jepsen, "An empirical analysis of matching patterns of same-sex and opposite-sex couples," *Demography* 39 (August 2002): 435–453.

32. Burtless, "Effects of growing wage disparities and changing family composition on the U.S. income distribution."

33. Ibid. Other studies confirm that the falling proportion of married people was a major source of increasing family income inequality, even taking into account increases in cohabitation; Mary C. Daly and Robert G. Valletta, "Inequality and poverty in United States: The effects of rising dispersion of men's earnings and changing family behaviour," *Economica* 73 (February 2006): 75–98.

34. Naomi Gerstel and Natalia Sarkisian, "Marriage: The good, the bad, and the greedy," *Contexts* 5 (Fall 2006): 16–21; Naomi Gerstel and Natalia Sarkisian, "Intergenerational care and the greediness of adult children's marriages," in *Interpersonal Relations Across the Life Course*, ed. Timothy J. Owens and J. Jill Suitor (Greenwich, CT: Elsevier/JAI Press, 2007), 153–188.

35. Gerstel and Sarkisian, "Marriage," suggest this possibility.

36. Weston, *Families We Choose*, 209.

37. See Badgett, *Money, Myths, and Change*, for a longer discussion.

38. Coontz, *Marriage: A History*.

39. Lewin, *Recognizing Ourselves*.

40. Cherlin, "The deinstitutionalization of American marriage," 855.

NOTES TO CHAPTER 8

1. Focus on the Family, *"Focus on the family's position statement on same-sex 'marriage' and civil unions,"* (2004) (accessed March 26, 2006), http://www.family.org/cforum/fos.marriage/ssuap/a0029773.cfm.

2. Equal Rights Colorado, *ERC UPDATE: SB06-166 dies in committee* (2006).

3. 365gay.com, "Colorado GOP domestic bill stalls," (February 28, 2006) (accessed March 23, 2006).

4. Steve Jordahl, "Focus on the Family explains endorsement of reciprocal benefits," *Family News in Focus* (February 16, 2006).

5. Denver Post , "A fresh focus on domestic partners," *Denver Post* (editorial) (February 6, 2006), B-07, http://www.denverpost.com/search/ci_3479371 (accessed February 22, 2006).

6. See the discussion on Cameron's Web site, http://www.familyresearchinst.org/Default.aspx?tabid=116 (accessed March 23, 2006).

7. Thomas Coleman, "Reciprocal beneficiary laws mask a larger political

battle," *Column One: Eye on Unmarried America* (March 13, 2006), http://www. unmarriedamerica.org/column-one/3-13-06-reciprocal-beneficiaries.htm (accessed March 23, 2006).

8. Family Research Institute, "Dobson's bill rewards homosexuals," *FRI Press Releases* (February 22, 2006), http://covenantnews.com/familyresearch060224. htm (accessed March 23, 2006). It is important to note that this is not Cameron's main objection to the bill, however.

9. Warner, *The Trouble With Normal*; Nancy Polikoff, "Ending marriage as we know it," *Hofstra Law Review* 32 (2003): 201–232; Polikoff, *Beyond (Straight and Gay) Marriage* (Boston: Beacon Press, 2008).

10. Eskridge and Spedale argue that the compromise of a new status that is not called marriage will hasten the development of alternatives to marriage for heterosexuals and, consequently, the continued decline of marriage's attractiveness for heterosexual couples; Eskridge and Spedale, *Gay Marriage*.

11. Equity is not the only basis for making policy related to marriage, of course, although the rules for access to marriage have often been rooted in concerns about fair treatment in the United States. The 1967 U.S. Supreme Court decision in *Loving v. Virginia* ruled that states could not bar interracial couples from marrying. Subsequent decisions found that neither unpaid child support (*Zablocki v. Redhail*) nor incarceration (*Turner v. Safley*) was a legitimate reason to deny the right to marry to individuals who want to marry a different-sex partner. However, it is also important to note that equity is not sufficient for determining rules of access. All states set a minimum age for marriage, forbid marriages by close relatives, and prohibit someone who is already married from marrying someone else. In those cases, alternative (nonequity-based) justifications for those policies might be offered. As noted earlier, though, I want to focus on equity claims because they lie behind the alternatives to marriage raised in the course of public debate.

12. Of course, because of the Defense of Marriage Act, the U.S. government also does not currently recognize same-sex marriages, even from Massachusetts. Also, some states that allow civil unions respect same-sex marriages contracted in other states.

13. Yuval Merin, *Equality for Same-Sex Couples: The Legal Recognition of Gay Partnerships in Europe and the United States* (Chicago: University of Chicago Press, 2002), 281.

14. Avi Salzman, "Tying the half knot," *New York Times* (April 17, 2005).

15. See, for example, the statement on civil unions by Love Makes a Family of Connecticut, the group that had been lobbying for opening up marriage to same-sex couples:

> Civil unions will provide needed rights and protections for couples and families in our state. But although this law is a step in the right direction, it must not remain the end product. The struggle for marriage

equality has always been about more than rights and protections; it is also about dignity and respect and equal treatment under the law. Civil unions create a separate status for one class of people and as long as there remain two lines at the Town Hall—one for same-sex couples and one for everyone else—Love Makes a Family will continue to be here, working towards a day when the final discriminatory barriers to marriage are finally struck down. (http://www.lmfct.org/site/PageServer?pagename=whoislmf) (accessed October 20, 2005).

16. Wolfson, *Why Marriage Matters,* 136.

17. Mary Lyndon Shanley, *Just Marriage* (Oxford: Oxford University Press, 2004); Michael Lerner, "The right way to fight for gay marriage," *New York Daily News* (June 8, 2006).

18. Carl F. Stychin, "Civil solidarity or fragmented identities? The politics of sexuality and citizenship in France," *Social & Legal Studies* 10 (September 2001): 347–375; Wendy Michallat, "Marions-nous! gay rites: The campaign for gay marriage in France," *Modern and Contemporary France* 14.0 (August 2006): 305–316.

19. Paula Ettelbrick, "Since when is marriage a path to liberation?" *OUT/LOOK National Gay and Lesbian Quarterly* 6 (Fall 1989): 14–17; Warner, *The Trouble With Normal.* However, research in the United States and elsewhere suggests that cohabiting different-sex couples are a heterogeneous lot, reducing their ability to agree or to organize for political change. For instance, some cohabiting couples are in long-term relationships, but a large proportion of cohabiting couples dissolve within a short period of time. Kiernan, "Unmarried cohabitation and parenthood," 24; L. L. Bumpass and J. Sweet, "National estimates of cohabitation," *Demography* 26 (1989): 615–625.

20. James Alm, M. V. Lee Badgett, and Leslie Whittington, "Wedding bell blues: The income tax consequences of legalizing same-sex marriage," *National Tax Journal* 53 (January 2000): 201–214.

21. Ash and Badgett, "Separate and unequal," 582–599.

22. Waaldijk, *More or Less Together.* These figures relate to different-sex couples. Some, but not all, countries recognize both different-sex and same-sex cohabiting couples in granting these cohabitation benefits and obligations. Cohabiting same-sex couples usually gain a smaller number of benefits, typically because parenting rights differ dramatically for same-sex couples.

23. Grace Ganz Blumberg, "Unmarried partners and the legacies of *Marvin v. Marvin*: The regularization of nonmarital cohabitation: Rights and responsibilities in the American welfare state," *Notre Dame Law Review* 76 (October 2001): 1265-1310.

24. Thanks to Canadian court rulings, same-sex couples were treated the same as different-sex couples several years before court rulings began to open up marriage in several provinces; Radbord, "Lesbian love stories."

25. See, e.g. Fineman or Cossman in Shanley, *Just Marriage.*

26. Olivier De Schutter and Kees Waaldijk, "Major legal consequences of marriage, cohabitation and registered partnership for different-sex and same-sex partners in Belgium," in Waaldijk, *More or Less Together*, 50.

27. Law Commission of Canada, *Beyond Conjugality: Recognizing and Supporting Close Personal Adult Relationships* (2001), http://www.cga.ct.gov/2002/rpt/-002-R-0172.htm.

28. Deborah Stone, *Policy Paradox* (rev. ed.) (New York: Norton, 2001).

29. See Alliance Defense Fund Web site, http://www.alliancedefensefund.org/about/history/founders.aspx (accessed March 28, 2006).

30. As quoted in Pete Winn, "Focus explains support for Colorado benefits bill," *CitizenLink: A Website of Focus on the Family* (February 15, 2006) (accessed February 22, 2006).

31. In 1998, Hawaiian voters passed an amendment to the state constitution (Article I, Section 23) that gave the legislature the power to limit marriage to different-sex couples, thus ending the lawsuit.

32. Winn, "Focus explains support for Colorado benefits bill."

33. David Moats, *Civil Wars: A Battle for Gay Marriage* (Orlando, FL: Harcourt, 2004).

34. Badgett, Sears, and Ho, "Supporting families, saving funds," 8–93.

35. Merin, *Equality for Same-Sex Couples*.

36. Daniel Borillo, "The "pacte civil de solidarité" in France: Midway between marriage and cohabition," in *The Legal Recognition of Same-Sex Partnerships: A Study of National, European and International Law*, ed. Robert Wintemute and Mads Andenaes (Oxford: Hart, 2001): 478-479; Martin and Théry, "The PACS and marriage and cohabitation in France."

37. Daniel Borillo and Eric Fassin, "The PACS, four years later: A beginning or an end?" paper presented at the conference "Same-sex couples, same-sex partnerships, and homosexual marriages: A focus on cross-country differentials," Stockholm, Sweden (2003); Martin and Théry, "The PACS and marriage and cohabitation in France."

38. Borillo, "The "pacte civil de solidarité"; Eric Fassin, "Same sex, different politics: "Gay marriage" debates in France and the United States," *Public Culture* 13 (Spring 2001): 215–232; Stychin, "Civil solidarity or fragmented identities?," 347–375.; Martin and Théry, "The PACS and marriage and cohabitation in France."

39. Waaldijk, "Major legal consequences of marriage, cohabitation and registered partnership for different-sex and same-sex partners in the Netherlands"; Nancy G. Maxwell, "Opening civil marriage to same-gender couples: A Netherlands-United States comparison," *Arizona Journal of International and Comparative Law* 18 (Spring 2001): 150.

40. Waaldijk, "Major legal consequences of marriage, cohabitation and registered partnership for different-sex and same-sex partners in the Netherlands."

41. Eskridge, *Equality Practice*.

42. Waaldijk, "Major legal consequences of marriage, cohabitation and registered partnership for different-sex and same-sex partners in the Netherlands," 450–451.

43. Ingrid Lund-Andersen, "The Danish registered partnership act," in *Legal Recognition of Same-Sex Couples in Europe*, ed. Katharina Boele-Woelki and Angelika Fuchs (Antwerp, Belgium: Intersentia, 2003), 13–23.

44. Guðný Björk Eydal and Kolbeinn Stefánsson, "Restrained reform: Securing equality for same-sex couples in Iceland," paper presented at the conference "Same-sex couples, same-sex partnerships, and homosexual marriages: A focus on cross-country differentials," Stockholm, Sweden (2003).

45. Matti Savolainen, "The Finnish and Swedish partnership acts–similarities and differences," in *Legal Recognition of Same-Sex Couples in Europe*, ed. Katharina Boele-Woelki and Angelika Fuchs (Antwerp, Belgium: Intersentia, 2003): 24–40.

46. Karin M. Linhart, "Decriminalization of homosexuality and its effects on family rights: A German-U.S.-American comparison," *German Law Journal* 6 (June 1, 2005): 943–966.

47. Badgett, Sears, and Ho, "Supporting families, saving funds," 8–93.

48. New Jersey Permanent Statutes, Title 26, Section 8:A-4.1.

49. De Schutter and Waaldijk, "Major legal consequences of marriage, cohabitation and registered partnership for different-sex and same-sex partners in Belgium."

50. See, e.g., Linda Nielsen, *National Report: Denmark*, "Study on matrimonial property regimes and the property of unmarried couples in private international law and internal law." The Hague and Louvain-la-Neuve, April 30, 2003, http://ec.europa.eu/justice_home/doc_centre/civil/studies/doc/regimes/denmark_report_en.pdf; see Elena Urso, "De facto families and the law: Dealing with rules and freedom of choice," *International Society of Family Law* (Bristol: Jordan, 2001): 187–222, on Italy; Turid Noack, "Cohabitation in Norway: An accepted and gradually more regulated way of living," *International Journal of Law, Policy & the Family* 15.0 (April 2001): 102-117, on Norway; Waaldijk, "Major legal consequences of marriage, cohabitation and registered partnership for different-sex and same-sex partners in the Netherlands."

51. See generally Waaldijk, *More or Less Together*, 52. Noack, "Cohabitation in Norway," 108.

53. Urso, "De facto families and the law," 187–222; Walter Rechberger, *National Report: Austria* (The Hague and Louvain-la-Neuve: European Commission, 2001); Law Commission of Canada, *Beyond Conjugality*.

54. Noack, "Cohabitation in Norway," 102-117.

55. Richard McCoy, Vermont Department of Public Health, personal communication, March 19, 2007.

56. Office of Legislative Counsel, *Report of the Vermont Civil Union Review Commission* (Montpelier, VT: Office of Legislative Counsel, 2002).

57. McCoy, 2007.

58. See Nancy Polikoff, *Beyond (Straight and Gay) Marriage* (Boston: Beacon Press, 2008), for a similar analysis of coercion and choice in marriage.

NOTES TO CHAPTER 9

1. Lerner, "The right way to fight for gay marriage."
2. Etzioni, "A communitarian position for civil unions," p. 66.
3. This phrase is part of the title of the final legislation.
4. Van Velde, *No Gay Marriage in the Netherlands*.
5. Waaldijk, "Small change."
6. Ibid., 440.
7. Merin, *Equality for Same-Sex Couples*, 309.
8. This debate about why change occurs relates to more than just laws. Social scientists and historians have long debated why all social institutions—those "rules that structure social interactions in particular ways"—exist in the first place; Jack Knight, *Institutions and Social Conflict* (Cambridge: Cambridge University Press, 1992), 2.
9. Gary S. Becker, *A Treatise on the Family* (Cambridge, MA: Harvard University Press, 1991).
10. Robert Pollak, "A transaction cost approach to families and households," *Journal of Economic Literature* 23.0 (June 1985): 581–608.
11. See a related argument for allowing same-sex couples to marry in Badgett, *Money, Myths, and Change*.
12. Eskridge, *The Case for Same-Sex Marriage*.
13. Julie A. Nelson, "Household economies of scale in consumption: Theory and evidence," *Econometrica* 56 (November 1988): 1301–1314.
14. Nancy Folbre, "'Holding hands at midnight': The paradox of caring labor," *Feminist Economics* 1 (Spring 1995): 73–92.
15. One possible source of competitive pressure is suggested by the work of Florida and Gates, who find a positive correlation between the proportion of same-sex couples in a metropolitan area and that area's concentration and growth of high-technology industries in the United States. They interpret the finding as evidence that social diversity and tolerance attract talented workers and that talented workers in a diverse environment attract economic development. If partnership recognition laws both create and reflect national values promoting sexual or family diversity, then having those laws might disproportionately attract more highly educated migrants who value diversity. Richard Florida and Gary Gates, "Technology and Tolerance: The Importance of Diversity to High-Technology Growth," *The Brookings Institution Survey Series*, Center on Urban and Metropolitan Policy, June 2001. We have no direct evidence in support of this hypothesis, however. When Florida and Tinagli extend this argument to the international

context, they do not appear to find a correlation between their "Euro-Tolerance Index" and the size of the crucial economic growth factor in their model, the "creative class." Richard Florida and Irene Tinagli, *Europe in the Creative Age* (London: Demos, 2004). Allen makes the argument from an oppositional position: letting same-sex couples marry will inevitably lead to changes in a form of marriage that has evolved to its current ideal form. Allen, "An economic assessment of same-sex marriage laws." As previous chapters suggest, though, I believe he is wrong about same-sex couples changing marriage.

16. The legal historian Mary Ann Glendon offers a view of change consistent with my increasing visibility hypothesis: "Second, as we examine the effect of rapidly changing mores upon older legal norms, we will notice that as the discrepancy widens between legal rules and actual marriage behavior in society, the outline of a shadow institution of marriage within the set of de facto unions often becomes increasingly discernible. As the shadow of the formal institution of marriage grows in extent and importance to the point where the legal system one way or another must take it into account, the relationship among law, behavior, and ideas shift again." Mary Ann Glendon, *Abortion and Divorce in Western Law* (Cambridge, MA: Harvard University Press, 1989), 15. Ironically, Glendon has been a vocal critic of letting same-sex couples marry, but the social-legal dynamic that she outlines could lead to the inclusion of same-sex couples within the realm of marriage. Glendon, "For better or for worse?"

17. As quoted in Tobin Coleman, "Senate backs civil unions," *Stamford Advocate* (April 7, 2005).

18. Gosta Esping-Andersen, *Social Foundations of Postindustrial Economics* (Oxford: Oxford University Press, 1999); see also Francesca Bettio and Janneke Plantenga, "Comparing care regimes in Europe," *Feminist Economics* 10 (2004): 85–113.

19. See, e.g., Knight, *Institutions and Social Conflict*; Daron Acemoglu, "Root causes: A historical approach to assessing the role of institutions in economic development," *Finance & Development* 40 (June 2003): 27–30; Daron Acemoglu and James A. Robinson, "Political losers as a barrier to economic development," *American Economic Review Papers & Proceedings* 90 (May 2000): 126–130; Daron Acemoglu, Simon Johnson, and James Robinson, "Reversal of fortune: Geography and institutions in the making of the modern world income distribution," *Quarterly Journal of Economics* 117 (November 2002): 1231–1294; Nancy Folbre, *Who Pays for the Kids? Gender and the Structures of Constraint* (London: Routledge, 1994); Bina Agarwal, "'Bargaining' and gender relations: Within and beyond the household," *Feminist Economics* 3 (March 1997): 1–51.

20. Scott Barclay and Shauna Fisher, "The states and the differing impetus for divergent paths on same-sex marriage, 1990-2001," *Policy Studies Journal* 31 (August 2003): 331-352; Donald P. Haider-Markel and Kenneth J. Meier, "The politics of gay and lesbian rights: Expanding the scope of the conflict," *Journal of*

Politics 58 (May 1996): 332–349; Donald P. Haider-Markel, Mark R. Joslyn, and Chad J. Kniss, "Minority group interests and political representation: Gay elected officials in the policy process," *Journal of Politics* 62 (May 2000): 568–577; Gregory B. Lewis, "Contentious and consensus gay rights issues: Public opinion and state laws on discrimination and same-sex marriage," Association for Public Policy Analysis and Management meeting, Washington, DC, November 2003; Kenneth D. Wald, James W. Button, and Barbara A. Rienzo, "The politics of gay rights in American communities: Explaining antidiscrimination ordinances and policies," *American Journal of Political Science* 40 (November 1996): 1152–1178.

21. This Pareto efficiency argument focuses on the possible material gains or losses. Some observers, such as Posner, point out that utility, if not resources, might be lessened by the revulsion that some people may feel toward the idea of allowing gay couples to marry; Posner, *Sex and Reason*.

22. See Congressional Budget Office, "The potential budgetary impact of recognizing same-sex marriages" (2004), http://www.cbo.gov/doc.cfm?index=5559; accessed May 26, 2008); M. V. Lee Badgett and R. Bradley Sears, "Putting a price on equality? The impact of allowing same-sex couples to marry on California's budget," *Stanford Law & Policy Review* 16 (2005): 197–232.

23. Some selections from the Vatican document on same-sex marriage and partnership laws:

> Those who would move from tolerance to the legitimization of specific rights for cohabiting homosexual persons need to be reminded that the approval or legalization of evil is something far different from the toleration of evil. In those situations where homosexual unions have been legally recognized or have been given the legal status and rights belonging to marriage, clear and emphatic opposition is a duty. . . .
> When legislation in favour of the recognition of homosexual unions is proposed for the first time in a legislative assembly, the Catholic lawmaker has a moral duty to express his opposition clearly and publicly and to vote against it.

Vatican, Offices of the Congregation for the Doctrine of Faith, Considerations Regarding Proposals to Give Legal Recognition to Unions Between Homosexual Persons (2003), http:www.vatican.va/roman_curia/congregations/cfaith/documents/re_con_cfaith_doc.20030731_homosexual-unions-en.html.

24. See, e.g., David Kirkpatrick, "Conservatives use gay union as rallying cry," *New York Times* (February 8, 2004).

25. Eskridge, *Equality Practice*.

26. Social scientists have long debated the most appropriate empirical methods for inferring the factors that cause certain social phenomena or changes; e.g., Arend Lijphart, "Comparative politics and the comparative method," *American*

Political Science Review 65 (September 1971): 682–693. Comparative research uses either qualitative or quantitative research methods, or sometimes a combination of both. The scale of studies ranges from case studies of individual countries to comparisons across countries. For a good overview of the debate over comparative research, see Charles C. Ragin, *The Comparative Method: Moving Beyond Qualitative and Quantitative Strategies* (Berkeley and Los Angeles: University of California Press, 1987).

27. For example, see Eskridge and Spedale, *Gay Marriage,* for an account of Denmark's pioneering choice.

28. For purposes of this chapter, I have relied almost exclusively on English-language publications, although they are usually written by observers from the country in question and include translations of important documents or debates.

29. Henning Bech, "Report from a rotten state: 'marriage' and 'homosexuality' in "Denmark," in *Modern Homosexualities: fragments of lesbian and gay experience,* ed. Ken Plummer (London: Routledge, 1992), 134–147.

30. Fassin, "Same sex, different politics."

31. Karsten Thorn, "The German law on same-sex partnerships," in *Legal Recognition of Same-Sex Couples in Europe,* ed. Katharina Boele-Woelki and Angelika Fuchs (Antwerp, Belgium: Intersentia, 2003), 84–98.

32. International Gay Association, IGA Pink Book 1985: A Global View of Lesbian and Gay Oppression and Liberation (Amsterdam: IGA, 1985).

33. Judith Schuyf and Andre Krouwel, "The Dutch lesbian and gay movement: The politics of accommodation," in *The Global Emergence of Gay and Lesbian Politics: National Imprints of a Worldwide Movement,* ed. Barry D. Adam, Jan Willem Duyvendak, and Andre Krouwel (Philadelphia: Temple University Press, 1999), 158–183.

34. Ingrid Lund-Andersen, "The Danish registered partnership act," in *Legal Recognition of Same-Sex Couples in Europe,* ed. Katharina Boele-Woelki and Angelika Fuchs (Antwerp, Belgium: Intersentia, 2003), 13–23.

35. Van Velde, *No Gay Marriage in the Netherlands.*

36. Rune Halvorsen, "The ambiguity of lesbian and gay marriages: Change and continuity in the symbolic order," *Journal of Homosexuality* 35 (Autumn/ Winter 1998): 207–231; Karin Lützen, "Gay and lesbian politics: Assimilation or subversion: A Danish perspective," *Journal of Homosexuality* 35 (Autumn/Winter 1998): 233–243.

37. Kees Waaldijk, "Towards the recognition of same-sex partners in european union law: Expectations based on trends in national law," in *The Legal Recognition of Same-Sex Partnerships: A Study of National, European and International Law,* ed. Robert Wintemute and Mads Andenaes (Oxford: Hart, 2001): 637–638.

38. David Chambers analyzes the role of the AIDS epidemic in shaping the spread of domestic partnership laws in the United States; David Chambers, "Tales of two cities: AIDS and the legal recognition of domestic partnerships in

San Francisco and New York," *Law & Sexuality* 2 (1992): 181–208; Borillo, "The 'pacte civil de solidarité' in France"; Steven Ross Levitt, "New legislation in Germany concerning same-sex unions," *ILSA Journal of International & Comparative Law* 7 (Spring 2001): 469–473; Stychin, "Civil solidarity or fragmented identities?"; Eskridge and Spedale, *Gay Marriage*.

39. Ingrid Lund-Andersen, "The Danish Registered Partnership Act, 1989: Has the Act meant a change in attitudes?" in *The Legal Recognition of Same-Sex Partnerships: A Study of National, European and International Law*, ed. Robert Wintemute and Mads Andenaes (Oxford: Hart, 2001), 417–426.

40. Hans Ytterberg, "'From society's point of view, cohabitation between two persons of the same sex is a perfectly acceptable form of family life': A Swedish story of love and legislation," in *The Legal Recognition of Same-Sex Partnerships: A Study of National, European and International Law*, ed. Robert Wintemute and Mads Andenaes (Oxford: Hart, 2001.

41. Savolainen, "The Finnish and Swedish partnership acts."

42. Waaldijk, "Small change."

43. Borillo, "The 'pacte civil de solidarité' in France."

44. Eskridge and Spedale, *Gay Marriage*; Knut Heidar, "Norway," *European Journal of Political Research* 26 (December 1994): 389–395.

45. Fassin, "Same sex, different politics"; Borillo, "The 'pacte civil de solidarité' in France."

46. See also Stychin, "Civil solidarity or fragmented identities?"

47. Waaldijk, "Small change."

48. Boris Dittrich, "Going Dutch," Speech to Williams Institute Annual Update, UCLA School of Law (February 23, 2007).

49. Ronald Schimmel and Stefanie Heun, "The legal situation of same-sex partnerships in Germany: An overview," in *The Legal Recognition of Same-Sex Partnerships: A Study of National, European and International Law*, ed. Robert Wintemute and Mads Andenaes (Oxford: Hart, 2001), 575–590; Thorn, "The German law on same-sex partnerships."

50. Erik Albaek, "Political ethics and public policy: Homosexuals between moral dilemmas and political considerations in Danish parliamentary debates," *Scandinavian Political Studies* 26 (September 2003): 245–267; Eskridge and Spedale, *Gay Marriage*.

51. Albaek, "Political ethics and public policy."

52. Kolbeinn Stefansson and Gudny Bjork Eydal, "Restrained reform: Securing equality for same-sex couples in Iceland," paper presented at the conference "Same-sex couples, same-sex partnerships, and homosexual marriages: A focus on cross-national differentials," Institut National d'Etudes Demographiques, Paris (2004).

53. Eskridge and Spedale, *Gay Marriage*; Borillo, "The 'pacte civil de solidarité' in France."

54. Eskridge and Spedale, *Gay Marriage*.

55. Borillo, "The 'pacte civil de solidarité' in France."

56. Alessandra Rizzo, "Same-sex union protest planned in Rome," http://www.gay.com/news/article.html?2007/05/11/2 (accessed May 11, 2007).

57. Bech, "Report from a rotten state," p. 143.

58. Ibid.; Eskridge and Spedale, *Gay Marriage*.

59. Schuyf and Krouwel, "The Dutch lesbian and gay movement."

60. Rydström, "From outlaw to in-law," p. 1.

61. Borillo, "The 'pacte civil de solidarité' in France"; Stychin, "Civil solidarity or fragmented identities?"; Camille Robcis, "How the symbolic became French: Kinship and republicanism in the PACS debates," *Discourse* 26.0 (Fall 2004): 110–135.

62. Fassin, "Same sex, different politics"; Stychin, "Civil solidarity or fragmented identities?"

63. As noted later, Hungary and Portugal (among other countries) treat same-sex couples the same way they treat unmarried heterosexual couples, who are treated similarly to married couples in some areas of law. Since gay couples have no way to clearly establish and publicly register their relationship in a way that is at least somewhat parallel to marriage, I count these two as countries "without" partnership recognition. In 2009, Hungary will establish registered partnerships for same-sex and different-sex couples. For more details, see Rosa Martins, "Same-sex partnerships in Portugal: From de facto to de jure?" *Utrecht Law Review* 4 (June 2008): 222–235; and Orsolya Szeibert-Erdős, "Same-sex partners in Hungary: Cohabitation and registered partnership," *Utrecht Law Review* 4 (June 2008): 212–221.

64. Several states and territories have developed registries so that same-sex couples can gain the rights received by de facto couples, or different-sex unmarried but cohabiting couples.

65. 365gay.com Newscenter Staff, "Australia offers small olive branch to gays," (April 29, 2008).

66. Merin, *Equality for Same-Sex Couples*.

67. Human Rights Campaign, undated. For Connecticut, see Daniela Altimari, "A gay rights milestone: Rell signs civil unions bill; opponents call it a sad day," *Hartford Courant* (April 21, 2005).

68. Domestic Partnership Equality Amendment Act of 2006, D.C. Law 16-79, effective April 4, 2006.

69. For more details, see M. V. Lee Badgett, "Predicting partnership rights: Applying the european experience to the United States," *Yale Journal of Law and Feminism* 17 (Spring 2005): 71–88.

70. Simmons and O'Connell, *Married Couples and Unmarried Partner Households*, 4.

71. Lewis, "Contentious and consensus gay rights issues."

72. The survey data were collected by Dale E. Jones, Sherri Doty, Clifford Grammich, James E. Horsch, Richard Houseal, Mac Lynn, John P. Marcum, Kenneth M. Sanchagrin, and Richard H. Taylor, *Evangelical Denominations--Total Adherents* (2000), http://www.glenmary.org/grc/RCMS_2000/method.htm (accessed April 18, 2005).

73. These data omit figures for several large African American churches and for the National Baptist Convention. Since some of these groups might be considered evangelical, the measure used in this book underestimates the proportion of a state's population that adheres to an evangelical religion. However, to the extent that these missing evangelicals would be more likely to live in the states that have high proportions of reported evangelicals, the comparison used here is not very sensitive to the omissions. That is, the focus here is on states with low proportions of evangelicals relative to the average, so the relative position of those states is not likely to change. See Jones et al., *Evangelical Denominations—Total Adherents*.

74. Senate Bill 597, "Recordation and Transfer Taxes—Exemptions—Domestic Partners," http://mlis.state.md.us/2008rs/bills/sb/sb0597e.pdf (accessed May 5, 2008), and Senate Bill 566, "Health Care Facility Visitation and Medical Decisions—Domestic Partners," http://mlis.state.md.us/2008rs/bills/sb/sb0566t.pdf (accessed May 5, 2008).

75. See www.eqnm.org/legislation.html (accessed May 15, 2007).

NOTES TO CHAPTER 10

1. Geert Mak, *Amsterdam* (Cambridge, MA: Harvard University Press, 2000).

2. Coontz, *Marriage: A History*; Glendon, *Abortion and Divorce in Western Law*.

3. See, e.g. Chauncey, *Why Marriage?*; Coontz, *Marriage: A History*; Merin, *Equality for Same-Sex Couples*; Graff, *What Is Marriage For?*

NOTES TO APPENDIX 1

1. Ronald Inglehart et al., *World Values Surveys and European Values Surveys, 1981–1984, 1990–1993, 1995–1997* (computer file and codebook) (Ann Arbor, MI: ICPSR, 2000).

2. Inglehart et al., *World Values Surveys and European Values Surveys, 1997*.

3. International Gay Association, *IGA Pink Book 1985*; International Lesbian and Gay Association, *Second ILGA Pink Book: A Global View of Lesbian and Gay Liberation and Oppression*, Vol. 12 (Utrecht: Interfacultaire Werkgroep Homostudies, Rijksuniversiteit Utrecht, 1988); Rob Tielman and Hans Hammelburg, "World survey on the social and legal position of gays and lesbians," in *The Third Pink Book: A Global View of Lesbian and Gay Liberation and Oppression*, ed.

Aart Hendriks, Rob Tielman and Evert van der Veen (Buffalo, NY: Prometheus Books, 1993): 249–342.

4. Some variables in Table A.2, such as the divorce rate, Catholic background, and national gay organization, were never statistically significant, so they are left out of the regressions reported in Table A.2.

5. Cohabitation is positively correlated with positive attitudes about homosexuality.

6. This question was not asked in Switzerland and Poland, so, in Table A.4, I substituted the value derived from the question about whether homosexuality is ever justified.

7. Note that there was one contradictory term in 1990, that is, a combination of values has both countries with and without SSPR laws. See text for further discussion.

NOTES TO APPENDIX 2

1. Boele-Woelki et al., *Huwelijk of Geregistreerd Partnerschap?*

2. Statistics Netherlands, "Population: Age, sex, and nationality, January 1," http://statline.cbs.nl/StatWeb/table.asp?LYR=G2:0&LA=en&DM=SLE N&PA=03743eng&D1=a&D2=0-7,60&D4=0,4,9,l&HDR=G3,T&STB=G1(accessed 2/13/08). "Population by origin and generation, January 1," http:// statline.cbs.nl/StatWeb/Table.asp?STB=G1&LA=en&DM=SLEN&PA=373 25eng&D1=a&D2=0-2,127,133,198,216&D3=0&D4=0&D5=0&D6=a,!0- 5&HDR=T&LYR=G4:0,G3:0,G2:0,G5:5 (accessed 2/13/08).

3. Statistics Netherlands, "More than 850 thousand Muslims in the Netherlands," *Web Magazine* (October 25, 2007), http://www.cbs.nl/en-GB/menu/ themas/bevolking/publicaties/artikelen/archief/2007/2007-2278-wm.htm (accessed 2/13/08).

4. Anselm L. Strauss, *Qualitative Analysis for Social Scientists* (Cambridge and New York: Cambridge University Press, 1987).

5. Ibid., p. 28.

6. Ibid., p. 58.

Index

activist judges. *See* judicial activism
AIDS epidemic, 185
Alabama, 196t
Alaska, 196t, 197t
Alliance Defense Fund, 165
alternatives to marriage, 151–174;
    access to benefits, 156–157; American experience with, 63, 155, 166; ascription (government-assigned rights and responsibilities for unmarried cohabiting couples), 161; blurring of political lines, 154; civil partnerships in United Kingdom, 9t; civil unions (*see* civil unions); closeness of the alternative to marriage, 167–169; cohabitation (*see* cohabitation); cohabitation agreements, 19, 35–36, 61, 161; commitment ceremonies in United States, 43, 123–124, 147; common-law marriage in United States, 161–162; as compromises to avoid opening marriage to same-sex couples, 162, 165–166, 173, 210; convergence dynamics, 167–169; demands for, 171–173, 209–210; disentangling legal status from a religious ritual, 158–159; domestic partnerships (*see* domestic partnerships); equity as a goal in recognizing relationships, 164, 170, 171, 210, 252n11; equity-based comparisons of different family structures, summary

of, 155t; "equity frames," 164–165; European experience with, 63, 155, 166, 173; fairness, 164; interdependency and caretaking as markers of recognizable relationships, 163; "law of small change," 168; legal cohabitants, 62, 163; "life partnership" *(Lebenspartnerschaft)* in Germany, 168, 183; marriage as solely religious, 158–159; married couples compared to nonromantic relationships, 162–165; married couples compared to same-sex couples who can't marry, 156–159; married couples compared to unmarried couples, 159–162; opt-in/opt-out dilemma, 171; PACS *(Pacte Civil de Solidarité)* in France *(see* PACS); political equity trap, 165–171; political power, 164–165, 181–182, 189; preference for marriage compared to, 56–63, 93–94, 153, 172–173, 203–204; proposed alternatives, list of, 153–154; reciprocal beneficiary status *(see* reciprocal beneficiary status); registered cohabitation, 9t, 161; registered partnerships *(see* registered partnerships); same-sex marriage *(see* same-sex marriage); slippery equity slope, 154, 155–162, 210; unmarried heterosexual couples, legal status of, 152

policy changes on, 85; marriage equality for same-sex couples, 141–142; as people age, 135; practical value, 46–47; to same-sex couples, 204–205, 213; same-sex marriage's impact on, 108–113; today *vs.* fifty or more years ago, 116, 150

Merin, Yuval, 177, 184

Mexico, 83t

Michigan, 196t, 197t

"migrant marriages," 101, 243n24

Minnesota, 196t

Mississippi, 196t

Missouri, 196t

Mitchell, Shawn, 151–152

monogamy, 94–97, 118, 126, 143–144

Montana, 196t

Movement Advancement Project, 139

Muslims in Netherlands, 25, 42, 101–102, 225

National Association of Evangelicals, 151

National Baptist Convention, 262n73

National Gay and Lesbian Task Force, 11

National Review Online, 12

National Survey of Family Growth, 99

Nebraska, 196t

Netherlands: "allochtone" population, 225; binational couples, 110; children, families with, 73, 78; children born having unmarried parents, 91; church weddings, 32; cohabitation, informal, 161; cohabitation agreements, 19, 35–36, 61; couples studied, 229; different-sex couples, 61; divorce rate, 70, 71, 125; employment rate of men and women, 94; equivalence of gay and straight relationships, 31–32; factors making for successful marriages, view of, 96–99; feminism, feminists in, 2–3, 4, 18, 34; flash annulments, 61; gay culture, 132–133; gay people's interest in marriage, 202; heterosexual marriage, children born before, 91; heterosexual marriage, divorce rate, 125; heterosexual marriages, number of, 87; immigration of foreign spouses, 93; intermarriage between immigrants and Dutch natives, 93; "law of small change" in, 168, 177; lesbians' view of marriage, 2–3; marriage, abolition of, 18; marriage as outdated, belief in, 53, 83t; marriage equality movement, 176–177, 187, 193; marriage in, 113–114, 158; marriage rate, 65–67, 68, 69, 70; marriage rights and responsibilities, 19, 234n14; methods in author's Dutch couples study, 223–229; "migrant marriages" in, 101, 243n24; mother's marital status as marker of strength of children's families, 78–79; Muslims in, 25, 42, 101–102, 225; nonmarital birth rate, 64, 72, 75–76, 77, 78; from nonrecognition of same-sex couples to full marriage rights, 168; open curtains and big windows, 200; percent of parent couples that are married, 80; practical and political variables data, 217t, 221t, 222t; registered partnerships (*see* registered partnerships in Netherlands); relationship options to choose from, 17, 19, 46–47, 58, 60–61; same-sex marriage (*see* same-sex marriage in Netherlands); tolerance, history of, 25, 184, 187; unmarried, people who remain, 41; unmarried cohabiting couples, 37, 47, 70; women's labor force participation rates, 205; women's role, 126

About the Author

M. V. LEE BADGETT is Professor of Economics and the director of the Center for Public Policy and Administration at the University of Massachusetts Amherst; research director of the Williams Institute at UCLA; and author of *Money, Myths, and Change: The Economic Lives of of Lesbians and Gay Men.*